Note to the reader

We want express our sincere hope that this book will enrich your spiritual journey. In these turbulent times, developing a personal connection with Christ is more important than ever.

We also want to let you know that we've designed this book to make it easier for you to find references within each paragraph. The two-column layout was specifically chosen to make the book more compact and easier to read.

We genuinely appreciate your decision to acquire this book and we hope that it exceeds your expectations. Thank you so much for choosing us!

Design by SaintilWay Productions LLC

You are free to

Distribute, remix, adapt, and build upon the material in any medium or format, so long as attribution is given to the creator. If you remix, adapt, or build upon the material, you must license the modified material under identical terms.

Table of Contents

The Great Controversy

Chapter 1—Weeping Over Jerusalem

Chapter 2—Cleansing the Temple

Chapter 3—Jesus and the Pharisees

Chapter 4—Denouncing the Pharisees

Chapter 5—In the Outer Court

Chapter 6—The Passover Supper

Chapter 7—In the Garden

Chapter 8—In the Judgment Hall

Chapter 9—Condemnation of Jesus

Chapter 10—Calvary

Chapter 11—At the Sepulcher

Chapter 12—The Conflict Ended

Chapter 13—The Resurrection

Chapter 14—The Women at the Tomb

Chapter 15—Jesus at Emmaus

Chapter 16—In the Upper Chamber

Chapter 17—Jesus at Galilee

Chapter 18—Meeting of the Brethren

Chapter 19—Ascension of Christ

Chapter 20—The Pentecost

Chapter 21—The Cripple Healed

Chapter 22—The Seven Deacons

Chapter 23—Conversion of Saul

Chapter 24—Paul Commences His Ministry

Chapter 25—The Ministry of Peter

Chapter 26—Deliverance of Peter

Chapter 27—Ordination of Paul and Barnabas

Chapter 28—Preaching Among the Heathen

Chapter 29—Jew and Gentile

Chapter 30—Imprisonment of Paul and Silas

Chapter 31—Opposition at Thessalonica

Chapter 32—Paul at Berea and Athens

Chapter 33—Paul at Corinth

Chapter 34—Paul at Ephesus

Chapter 35—Trials and Victories of Paul

Chapter 36—Martyrdom of Paul and Peter

The Great Controversy

Chapter 1
Weeping Over Jerusalem

The triumphal ride of Christ into Jerusalem, just prior to his crucifixion, was the dim foreshadowing of his coming in the clouds of heaven with power and glory amid the triumph of angels and rejoicing of the saints. Then will be fulfilled the words of Christ: "Ye shall not see me henceforth, till ye shall say, Blessed is He that cometh in the name of the Lord." Zechariah, in prophetic vision, was shown the day of final triumph, when Christ shall come in glory; and also the condition of the Jews who rejected him at his first advent: "And they shall look upon me whom they have pierced, and they shall mourn for him, as one mourneth for his only son, and shall be in bitterness for him, as one that is in bitterness for his firstborn." (3SP 9.1)

The tears of Christ as he wept over Jerusalem were for the sins of all time. The Jewish nation was a symbol of the people of all ages who scorn the pleadings of Infinite love. Those who profess to be the representatives of Christ upon earth, yet whose lives are a continual denial of him, may read their own condemnation in Christ's denunciation of the self-righteous Jews. The Saviour came to the world bringing the light of truth; but his counsel has ever been rejected and his mercies despised by those who have allowed selfishness and the love of mammon and worldly honor to possess the temple of the heart. (3SP 9.2)

The sin of Jerusalem was in the rejection of her then present mercies and warnings. As a tender father pities a loved but erring and rebellious son, so had Jesus compassion upon Jerusalem. He had sent prophets and wise men with counsel, entreaties, and warnings of threatened judgments if she refused to forsake her sins. Sacrificial blood had flowed continuously for centuries, symbolizing the great atonement of the Son of God, to be offered for the salvation of man. But though the sacrifices of beasts had been abundant, they could not supply the place of true sorrow for sin and obedience to God. A broken heart and contrite spirit would have been of far more value in the sight of God than multitudes of offerings without true repentance. (3SP 10.1)

Jerusalem had not improved her privileges; she had rejected the warnings of the prophets, and slain the holy representatives of God. But the generation that Jesus denounced was not responsible for the sins of their fathers, only so far as they followed their evil practices, and thus made themselves accountable for their course of hatred and revenge in persecuting the ancient messengers of God. It was the present mercies and warnings which that generation were rejecting that fastened upon them guilt which the blood of bulls and goats could not wash away. Proud, self-righteous, and independent, they had separated farther and farther from Heaven until they had become willing subjects of Satan. The Jewish nation for centuries had been forging the fetters which that generation were irrevocably fastening upon themselves. (3SP 10.2)

The tears of Christ expressed his anguish at seeing his people bringing sure destruction upon themselves. Gladly would he have broken from their necks the yoke of bondage to a heathen nation. But, while the Pharisees bitterly complained of their humiliation and oppression, they refused with hatred the only help that could relieve them from captivity, and make them a free and happy people. The voice of the Saviour had been heard for three years inviting the weary and heavy-laden to come unto him and he would give them rest. He had scattered blessings wherever his feet had trod. But, instead of returning his love with gratitude, they thrust Christ from them, and were now about to seal their own doom by putting him to death. (3SP 11.1)

The earthly Jerusalem represents a large majority of the professed Christians of this age of the world. The Saviour has dispensed his blessings to us at the infinite sacrifice of his own life. This is our day of mercies and privileges. In every age of the world there is given to men their day of light and privileges, a probationary time in which they may become reconciled with God. But there is a limit to this grace. Mercy may plead for years and be rejected and slighted; but there comes a time when mercy makes her last plea. The sweet, winning voice entreats the sinner no longer, and reproofs and warnings cease. (3SP 11.2)

That day had now come to Jerusalem. Jesus, from the summit of Olivet, in a voice broken by irrepressible sobs and tears, makes his last appeal to the nation of his choice: "If thou hadst known, even thou, at least in this thy day, the things which belong unto thy peace-" A little remnant of the day still remained, in which Jerusalem might see and repent of her fatal error, and turn to Christ. While the fast westering sun yet lingered in the heavens there was time for her to be saved. The angel of mercy had long pleaded for the impenitent city; but now she prepared to step down from the golden throne, while the words of irrevocable justice were spoken: "But now they are hid from thine eyes." (3SP 11.3)

The words of Christ, spoken upon the mount, reach to our time. His tears were for our impenitence. He has sent great light to us, as he did to the Jews. There have been given to us reproofs, entreaties, warnings, and the Saviour's yearning love. As the temple courts were desecrated by unholy traffic in the days of Christ, so the temple of the heart where Christ should be enshrined is defiled by selfishness, love of the world, malice, envy, and unholy passions. The Saviour sends messages to warn the sinner of danger and rouse his heart to repentance, but they are too often received as idle tales. Many of those who profess godliness are as unsanctified by the Spirit of God today as were the Pharisees in the days of Jesus. The light of truth is rejected by thousands because it involves a cross; it does not harmonize with their practices, and the natural inclinations of their hearts. (3SP 12.1)

The prophets of God did not find favor with apostate Israel because through them their hidden sins were brought to light. Ahab regarded Elijah as his enemy, because the prophet was faithful to unfold the monarch's secret iniquities. So, today, the servant of Christ, the reprover of sin, meets with scorn and rebuffs. Bible truth, the religion of Christ, struggles against a strong current of moral impurity. (3SP 12.2)

Prejudice is even stronger now in the hearts of men than it was in Christ's day. Men, prompted by Satan, raise doubts as to the truth of God's Word, and exercise their independent judgment. They choose darkness rather than light at the peril of their souls; for God does not propose to remove every objection against his truth which the carnal heart can offer. The mysteries of the Word of God remain such forever to those who refuse to accept the precious rays of light which would illuminate their darkness. Divine love sheds tears of anguish over men formed in the likeness of their Maker who will not accept his love and receive the impress of his divine image. (3SP 13.1)

Christ overlooked the world and all ages from the height of Olivet; and his words are applicable to every individual who slights the pleadings of his divine mercy. Scorner of his love, he addresses you today. It is " thou, even thou," who shouldst know the things which belong to thy peace. The retribution of the sinner will be proportionate to the light which he has received. (3SP 13.2)

The most responsible period for the Jews was when Jesus was in their midst. And yet even the disciples appreciated but lightly the presence of God's Son until it was removed from them, when Christ ascended to Heaven. The Redeemer was unwilling to sever his connection with the Jewish nation. He had borne with its impenitence and abuse for years. He regarded them with the same unselfish devotion which a mother feels toward the child of her care. For centuries he had stayed the bolts of God's wrath from falling on Jerusalem. But now she had filled up the cup of her iniquity by persecution of the Son of God, and divine vengeance was to fall upon her. Jesus gazed with inexpressible anguish upon the city and the temple he had loved. "O Jerusalem, Jerusalem, thou that killest the prophets, and stonest them that are sent unto thee, how often would I have gathered thy children together, even as a hen gathereth her chickens under her wings, and ye would not!" (3SP 13.3)

If the Jewish people would have thrown off their bigotry and blind unbelief long enough to have looked into the depths of the loving, compassionate heart of Jesus, they could never have crucified the Lord of glory. But they were perverse and self-righteous; and when the priests and rulers heard the prophetic voice of the past sounded in trumpet tones by the multitude, in answer to the question, "Who is this?" they did not accept it as the voice of inspiration. The long list of ancient authorities pointing forward to Jesus as the Messiah, and which were quoted by

Chapter 1 - Weeping Over Jerusalem (3SP 14.1)

the disciples, brought no proof to their hearts. But they were too much amazed and angered to express their indignation in words. Just as they were secretly and artfully laying their plans to put Jesus to death, behold! the humble Galilean is suddenly invested with honor that he had never before claimed, and receives homage which he had hitherto refused. (3SP 14.1)

The dignitaries of the temple are dumb with astonishment. Where now is the boasted power of priests and rulers over the people! The authorities had announced that whoever should acknowledge Jesus to be the Christ was to be put out of the synagogue and deprived of its sacred privileges. Yet here are the enthusiastic multitude shouting loud hosannas to the Son of David, and recounting the titles given him by the prophets. As well might the priests and rulers attempt to deprive the earth of the shining face of the sun, as to shut from the world the beams of glory from the Sun of Righteousness. In spite of all opposition, the kingdom of Christ was confessed by the people. (3SP 14.2)

When the priests and rulers recovered their voices, they murmured among themselves, "Perceive ye how ye prevail nothing? Behold, the world is gone after him." But they soon shook off the paralyzing effect of the strange exhibition which they had witnessed, and tried to intimidate the crowd by threatening to complain of them to the civil authorities as raising an insurrection. Some of the Pharisees carried out their threats, and angrily denounced Jesus to the Roman officers present as the leader of a rebellion. Others joined them, accusing the Saviour of setting himself up as king in defiance of the Roman power. Annas the priest urged that he was about to take possession of the temple, and reign as king in Jerusalem. (3SP 15.1)

But the calm voice of Jesus hushed for a moment the clamorous throng as he proclaimed that his kingdom was not of this world; that he had not come to establish a temporal rule; that he should soon ascend to his Father, and his accusers should see him no more until he should come again in glory; and then, too late for their salvation, they should acknowledge him, saying, "Blessed is He that cometh in the name of the Lord." (3SP 15.2)

Jesus spoke these words with sadness and with singular power. The Roman officers were silenced and subdued. Their hearts, though strangers to divine influence, were moved as they had never been moved before; and a sudden hush fell upon the multitude. He who could command the elements, whose voice had stilled the angry waters of the deep, could also quell the excitement and apprehension of heathen men who had not rejected his light nor steeled their hearts against him by prejudice. The Roman officers read love, benevolence, and quiet dignity in the calm and solemn face of Jesus. They were stirred by a sympathy they could not understand. Before them was a man of humble mien, but of Godlike bearing. They were more inclined to pay him homage than to arrest him for insurrection. (3SP 16.1)

They perceived that the priests and rulers were the only persons who were angry and creating a disturbance. They therefore turned upon them, and charged them with being the occasion of all the confusion. The priests and Pharisees, chagrined and defeated by this, turned to the people with their complaints, and wrangled among themselves with loud and angry disputation. There was a division of opinion among the priesthood regarding Jesus. Annas vehemently accused him of being an impostor. Caiaphas had publicly acknowledged him to be a prophet, but considered that his death was necessary to the fulfillment of prophecy. These two leaders gathered parties to their opinions. The majority of the common people were in favor of Jesus, declaring that no man could do the works which he had done. (3SP 16.2)

While these angry contentions were going on, Jesus, the subject of all this disputation, passed unnoticed to the temple and looked about it with sorrowful eyes. All was quiet there, for the scene that had transpired upon Olivet had called all the people away from the temple. After looking upon it for a short time with solemn countenance, Jesus withdrew from the temple with his disciples, and passed on to Bethany. And when the people would have placed him upon the throne as king of Israel, he was nowhere to be found. (3SP 17.1)

Jesus spent the entire night in prayer, and in the morning, while returning again from Bethany, he passed a fig-orchard. He was hungry, "And seeing a fig-tree afar off having leaves, he came, if haply he might find any thing thereon; and when he came to it, he found nothing but leaves; for the time of figs was not yet. And Jesus answered and said unto it, No man eat fruit of thee hereafter forever. And his disciples heard it." (3SP 17.2)

It was not the season for ripe figs, except in

certain localities; and on the elevated height of Olivet it might truly be said, "the time of figs was not yet." It is the nature of the fig-tree that before the leaves open the growing fruit appears; so it would follow that upon a tree covered with leaves one would expect to find well matured figs. The tree which Jesus saw was beautiful to look upon, but upon a thorough searching of its branches, he found that its appearance was deceitful, for it bore "nothing but leaves." In order to teach his disciples an impressive lesson, he used the fig-tree as a symbol, and invested it with moral qualities and made it the medium by which to teach a divine truth. (3SP 17.3)

The Jews stood forth distinct from all other nations, professing perfect allegiance to the God of Heaven. They had been specially favored by him, and they claimed a greater piety than any other people, while in reality they were sinful, corrupted by the love of the world and the greed of gain. Boasting of their goodness and knowledge, yet full of hypocrisy and cruelty, and ignorant of the requirements of God, they were like the barren fig-tree that spread its pretentious branches aloft, luxuriant in appearance, and beautiful to the eye, but upon which Jesus found "nothing but leaves." (3SP 18.1)

The Jewish religion with its magnificent display of temple, sacred altars, sacrificial pomp, mitred priests and impressive ceremonies, was but a superficial covering under which pride, oppression and iniquity held sway. The leaves were abundant and beautiful, but the tree bore no goodly fruit. The next morning as they passed by the same orchard, the disciples saw that the fig-tree which Jesus cursed was withered and blasted from root to branch. Jesus presented to his disciples the true condition of the Jews in this striking figure of the barren fig-tree; and, as the tree withered beneath the Saviour's blighting curse, and stood forth sere and blasted, dried up by the roots, so should all pretentious hypocrites be brought low. (3SP 18.2)

The other trees in the fig-orchard were also destitute of fruit; but their boughs were leafless, therefore they raised no expectations and caused no disappointment. These leafless trees represented the Gentiles, who made no boasts of superior piety. In them the words of the scripture finds an application, "the time of figs was not yet." But while the Jews in proud self-confidence stood forth assuming superiority to all others, the Gentiles were in a measure feeling their want and weakness, and longing for a better day, a clearer and more certain light to guide their wandering footsteps. (3SP 18.3)

The Jewish nation were outwardly religious, priding themselves upon their sacred temple, the pomp of priests and the imposing ceremonies of the morning and evening services, gorgeous synagogues and sacrificial offerings. Here were abundant leaves, beautiful and bright, to cover the hollow hypocrisy, malice, and oppression at the heart of all this vain display. The Jews were privileged with the presence of Christ manifested in the flesh. This inestimable blessing which God bestowed upon them should have called forth their devout acknowledgments. But in blind prejudice they refused the mercies offered them by Jesus. His love was lavished upon them in vain, and they regarded not his wondrous works. Sorrow fled at his approach; infirmity and deformity were healed; injustice and oppression shrunk ashamed from his rebuke; while death and the grave humbled themselves in his presence and obeyed his commands. Yet the people of his choice rejected him and his mighty miracles with scorn. The Majesty of Heaven came unto his own, and his own received him not. (3SP 19.1)

The judgment pronounced upon the barren fig-tree not only symbolizes the sentence passed upon the Jews, but is also applicable to the professed Christians of our time, who have become formal, selfish, boasting and hypocritical. Many who profess godliness stand before the world like the barren fig-tree, displaying pretentious leaves but utterly devoid of fruit. They go through the form of worship, yet have not repentance and faith. In the doom of the fig-tree Christ demonstrated how hateful in his eyes are hypocrisy and hollow pretense. Ever pitiful to the truly penitent, ever ready to receive them and to heal their maladies, he thus evidenced that the open sinner is in a more favorable condition before God than the Christian who bears no fruit to his glory. (3SP 19.2)

Important events clustered around the close of Christ's ministry. His triumphal entrance into Jerusalem, his cleansing of the desecrated temple and the blighting of the barren fig-tree, all pointed to the doom of Jerusalem. The tears of Jesus upon the mount, when he overlooked the city of his love and care, while in the midst of the rejoicing and hosannas of thousands, were the last pleadings of rejected love and compassion. (3SP 20.1)

*****

Chapter 2
Cleansing the Temple

As Jesus entered the outer court of the temple it was like entering a vast cattle-yard. Mingled with the lowing of the oxen, the bleating of the sheep and the cooing of the doves, were the sharp clinking of coin and the sound of angry altercation between traffickers, some of whom were ministers of sacred rites. The holy precincts of the temple presented a most unsanctified and painful spectacle to those conscientious Jews who, while deploring the desecration of God's holy place, were unable to prevent it; for the dignitaries of the temple themselves engaged in buying and selling, and the exchange of money. They were artful and avaricious, and the greed of gain overbore all religious scruples, and they carried their traffic to such extremes that they were no better than thieves in the sight of God. (3SP 20.2)

Three years before at the commencement of his ministry, Jesus had driven from the temple those who defiled it by their unholy traffic; and by his stern and God-like demeanor had struck awe to the hearts of the scheming traders. Now, at the close of his earthly mission, he came again to the temple of God and found it still desecrated by the same abominable practices and the same defilers. Little did the priests and rulers realize the solemn, sacred work which it was their office to perform. At every passover and Feast of Tabernacles thousands of cattle were slain, and their blood caught by the priests and poured upon the altar. The Jews had become familiar with blood as a purifier from guilt, and they had almost lost sight of the fact that sin made necessary all this shedding of the blood of beasts, and that it prefigured the blood of God's dear Son which was to be shed for the life of the world, and that by the offering of sacrifices men were to be directed toward a crucified Redeemer. (3SP 21.1)

Jesus looked upon the innocent victims of sacrifice, symbolizing himself, and saw how the Jews had made these great convocations scenes of bloodshed and cruelty, thus in a great measure destroying the solemnity of the institution of sacrifices. The bringing together of such a vast number of cattle and sheep made a noisy market of the temple court, and gave scope to that spirit of avarice and sharp trading which characterized the leaders of the people, who endeavored to keep the business in their own hands. These persons realized immense profits by their exorbitant prices and false dealing. The indignation of Jesus was stirred; he knew that his blood, soon to be shed for the sins of the world, would be as little appreciated by the priests and elders as the blood of beasts which they kept incessantly flowing. (3SP 21.2)

In place of humble repentance of sin the sacrifice of beasts was multiplied, as if God could be conciliated by such heartless service. Samuel said: "Hath the Lord as great delight in burnt offerings and sacrifices, as in obeying the voice of the Lord? Behold, to obey is better than sacrifice." And Isaiah, seeing through prophetic vision the apostasy of the Jews, addressed them as rulers of Sodom and Gomorrah: "Hear the word of the Lord, ye rulers of Sodom; give ear unto the law of our God, ye people of Gomorrah. To what purpose is the multitude of your sacrifices unto me? saith the Lord. I am full of the burnt offerings of rams, and the fat of fed beasts; and I delight not in the blood of bullocks, or of lambs, or of he goats. When ye come to appear before me, who hath required this at your hand, to tread my courts?" "Wash you, make you clean; put away the evil of your doings from before mine eyes; cease to do evil; learn to do well; seek judgment, relieve the oppressed, judge the fatherless, plead for the widow." (3SP 22.1)

The Saviour witnessed the fulfillment of this prophecy. Three years before he had cleansed the temple, but all that defiled its courts at that time existed now in a much greater degree. In fulfillment of ancient prophecy the people had proclaimed Jesus to be the King of Israel; he had accepted their homage and the office of king and priest. He knew that his efforts to reform a corrupted priesthood would be in vain; but nevertheless, his work must be done, the

Chapter 2 - Cleansing the Temple (3SP 22.2)

evidence of his divine mission must be given to an unbelieving people. (3SP 22.2)

As the piercing look of Jesus swept the desecrated court of the temple, all eyes were instinctively turned toward him. The voices of the people and the noise of the cattle were hushed. Priest, ruler, Pharisee and Gentile all looked with mute astonishment and indefinable awe upon the Son of God, who stood before them with the majesty of Heaven's King, divinity flashing through humanity and investing him with a dignity and glory he had never before displayed. A strange fear fell upon the people. Those nearest Jesus instinctively drew as far from him as the crowd would permit. With the exception of a few of his disciples the Saviour stood alone. All sound was hushed; the deep silence seemed unbearable, and when the firm, compressed lips of Jesus parted, and his voice rang out in clarion tones, there was an involuntary groan or sigh of relief from all present. (3SP 23.1)

He spoke in clear accents and with a power that caused the people to sway as if moved by a mighty tempest: "It is written, My house is the house of prayer; but ye have made it a den of thieves." He descended the steps, and, with greater authority than he had there manifested three years before, with indignation that quenched all opposition, in tones that rang like a trumpet through the whole temple, commanded, "Take these things hence." The displeasure of his countenance seemed like a consuming fire; there was no questioning his authority; all fled in the greatest haste from his presence, taking with them, and driving before them, the cattle and merchandise that had desecrated the temple of the Most High. Here Christ evidenced to the world that, with all his infinite love and mercy, he could execute stern justice. (3SP 23.2)

Three years before the dignitaries of the temple had been ashamed of their precipitous flight before the command of the youthful Jesus, and had since wondered at their own fears and unquestioning obedience of a single humble man. They had felt that it was impossible for such an undignified surrender on their part to be repeated. Yet a second time they were more terrified and in greater haste than before to obey his command. After the buyers and sellers had been expelled, Jesus looked upon the flying crowd with the most profound pity. Many remained anxiously hoping that this man, who assumed such power and authority, was the longed for Messiah. (3SP 24.1)

The crowd, rushing from the temple courts, driving their cattle before them, met a throng that came, bearing with them the sick and dying, and inquiring for the great Healer. The flying people gave the most exaggerated report of the act of Christ in cleansing the temple. Upon hearing this some of those who were hastening to find Jesus turned back, fearing to meet one so powerful, whose very glance had driven the priests and rulers from his presence. But a large number pressed their passage through the hurrying throng, eager to reach Him who was their only hope, and feeling that should he fail to relieve them of their sorrows and maladies they might as well die at once, as his power was greater than that of all others. (3SP 24.2)

A wonderful spectacle is now presented before the disciples; the court of the temple, cleansed from its defilers, is filled with the sick and suffering, some of whom are brought in a dying condition before Jesus. These afflicted ones feel their distressing need; they realize that they must perish unless the great Physician takes pity upon them. They fix their eyes imploringly upon the face of Christ, expecting to see there that severity of which they had heard from those whom they met leaving the temple; but they read in that dear face only love and tender pity. (3SP 25.1)

Jesus kindly received the sick, and disease and approaching death fled at a touch of his hand. He gave hope to the sorrowing and despondent, and lifted the burdens from the hearts of those who sought him. The dumb, blind and paralytic went from his presence rejoicing in perfect soundness. He gathered little children in his arms as tenderly as would a loving mother, soothed their fretful cries, banished the fever and pain from their little forms, and handed them back, smiling and healthful, to their grateful parents. (3SP 25.2)

That morning the court had been a scene of trade and traffic, full of the noisy clamor of men and of beasts; now, all was calm within that sacred enclosure; and the eager multitude heard the words of eternal life from the lips of the Saviour. Nothing interrupted his discourse save new applications for mercy and freedom from disease, and the glad shouts of praise to the Healer as he relieved them from their suffering. (3SP 25.3)

The priests and rulers were involuntarily

drawn back to the temple. After the first panic of terror had abated they were seized with an anxiety to know what would be the next movement of Jesus. They expected him to take the throne of David. Quietly returning to the temple, they heard the voices of men, women and children praising God. Upon entering, they stood transfixed before the strange scene being enacted before them. They saw the sick healed, the blind restored to sight, the deaf receive their hearing and the cripple leap for joy. The children were foremost in rejoicing. They repeated the hosannas that were shouted the day before, and waved palm-branches triumphantly before the Saviour. The temple echoed and re-echoed with acclamations of "Blessed is he who cometh in the name of the Lord!" "Behold, thy King cometh unto thee. He is just and having salvation!" "Hosanna to the son of David!" (3SP 25.4)

As the dignitaries of the temple beheld all this commotion, and heard the happy unrestrained voices of the children, their old intolerance returned and they set about putting a stop to such demonstrations. They represented to the people that the holy temple was polluted by the feet of the children and by their noisy shouts and rejoicing. They who had permitted and even engaged in angry altercations, and buying and selling within those sacred walls, who had heard unmoved the distracting noise of the various animals allowed within the precincts, were apparently overwhelmed with indignation that the innocent rejoicing of glad children should be tolerated within the temple court. (3SP 26.1)

The priests and rulers, finding that they made no impression upon the people who had felt and witnessed the power of the divine Teacher, ventured to appeal to Christ himself, "And said unto him, Hearest thou what these say? And Jesus saith unto them, Yea; have ye never read, Out of the mouth of babes and sucklings thou hast perfected praise?" Had the voices of those happy children been silenced, the very pillars of the temple would have sounded the Saviour's praise. Jesus was ever a lover of children; he accepted their childish sympathy and their open, unaffected love. The grateful praise from their pure lips was music in his ears, and refreshed his spirits which were depressed by the hypocrisy of the Jews. On this occasion he had healed the maladies of the children, clasped them in his arms, received their kisses of grateful affection, and they had fallen asleep upon his breast while he was teaching the people.

Wherever the Saviour went the benignity of his countenance, and his gentle, kindly manner won the love and confidence of children. (3SP 26.2)

The Pharisees were utterly perplexed and disconcerted at the turn things had taken and the failure of their attempt to quell the enthusiasm of the people. One was in command whom they could not intimidate with their assumption of authority. Jesus had taken his position as guardian of the temple. Never before had he assumed such kingly authority; never before had his words and acts possessed so great power. He had done great and marvelous works throughout Jerusalem, but never in such a solemn and impressive manner. (3SP 27.1)

Jesus, in taking charge of the temple court, had wrought there a wonderful change. He had banished the buyers and sellers, the money-changers and the cattle; "and would not suffer that any man should carry any vessel through the temple." So sacred did the world's Redeemer regard the building dedicated to the worship of God. The priests and rulers dared not show open hostility to Jesus in presence of the people who had witnessed his wonderful works. Though enraged and confounded by his answer they were unable to accomplish anything farther that day. (3SP 27.2)

On the following morning the Sanhedrim was assembled for the purpose of deciding what should be done with Jesus. His singular invasion of the temple was so presumptuous and surpassingly strange in their eyes, that they urged the propriety of calling him to account for the boldness of his conduct in interfering with the authorized keepers of the temple. Three years before they had challenged him to give them a sign of his Messiahship. Since that time he had wrought mighty works in their midst. He had healed the sick, miraculously fed thousands of people, walked upon the boisterous waves, and spoken peace unto the troubled sea. He had repeatedly read the secrets of their hearts like an open book; he had cast out demons, and raised the dead to life; yet they still refused to see and acknowledge the evidences of his Messiahship. (3SP 28.1)

They now decided to demand no sign of his authority for his bold action regarding the temple, but to confront him with questions and charges calculated to draw out some admissions or declarations by which they might condemn him. After carefully arranging their plan they repaired to the temple where Jesus was preaching

Chapter 2 - Cleansing the Temple (3SP 28.2)

the gospel to the people, and proceeded to question him as to what authority he had for his acts in the temple. They expected him to reply that God had invested him with the authority which he had there manifested. This assertion they were prepared to deny. But instead of this Jesus met them with a question apparently pertaining to another subject: "The baptism of John, was it from Heaven, or of men?" His questioners were at a loss how to reply. If they should deny the mission of John and his baptism unto repentance, they would lose influence with the people–for John was acknowledged by them to be a prophet of God. But if they should acknowledge that John's mission was divine, then they would be obliged to acknowledge Jesus as the Messiah; for John had repeatedly pointed him out to the people as the Christ, saying, "Behold the Lamb of God that taketh away the sins of the world." John had spoken of Jesus as one whose shoe-latchet he was not worthy to unloose. (3SP 28.2)

Jesus laid the burden of decision upon them as to the true character of John's mission. "And they reasoned with themselves, saying, If we shall say from Heaven, he will say, Why believed ye him not? But and if we say, Of men, all the people will stone us; for they be persuaded that John was a prophet." In their hearts they did not accept the teachings of John. If they had done so they could not have rejected Jesus, of whom John prophesied. But they had deceived the people by assuming to believe in the ministry of John; and now they dared not, in answer to the Saviour's question, declare that John's mission was divine lest Jesus should demand their reason for not receiving the prophet's testimony concerning him. He might have said, If John was from Heaven, so am I; my ministry and work is so closely connected with his that they cannot be separated. (3SP 29.1)

The people were listening with bated breath to hear what answer the priests and rulers would make to the direct question of Jesus, as to the baptism of John, whether it was from Heaven or of men. They expected them to acknowledge that John was sent of God; but, after conferring secretly among themselves, the priests decided to be as wary as possible; "and they answered, that they could not tell whence it was. And Jesus said unto them, Neither tell I you by what authority I do these things." Scribes, priests and rulers stood confused and disappointed before the people, whose respect they had lost in a great degree by their cowardice and indecision. (3SP 30.1)

All these sayings and doings of Christ were important, and their influence was to be felt in an ever increasing degree after the crucifixion, the resurrection and the ascension. Many of those who had anxiously awaited the result of the questioning of Jesus, were finally to become his disciples, first drawn towards him by his words on that eventful day. The scene in the temple court was never to fade from their minds. The contrast between the appearance of Jesus and the high priest, as they talked together, was very marked. The mighty dignitary of the temple was clothed in rich and gorgeous garments, with a glittering tiara upon his head. His majestic bearing, and his hair and long flowing beard silvered by age, gave him a strikingly venerable appearance, calculated to inspire the people with profound awe. (3SP 30.2)

The Majesty of Heaven stood before this august personage without ornament or display. His garments were travel-stained; his face was pale and expressed a touching sadness; yet there was a dignity and benevolence written there which contrasted strangely with the proud, self-confident and angry air of the high priest. Many of those who were witnesses of the marvelous words and deeds of Jesus in the temple, enshrined him in their hearts from that time as the prophet of God. But the hatred of the priests toward Jesus increased as the popular feeling turned in his favor. The wisdom by which he escaped the nets set for his feet, added fresh fuel to their hatred, being a new evidence of his divinity. (3SP 30.3)

As they stood mortified and silent before the Saviour, humiliated in presence of the great multitude, he improved his opportunity of presenting before them their true characters, and the retribution sure to follow their evil deeds. He arranged the lesson in such a manner that the priests and elders should pronounce their own condemnation: "But what think ye? A certain man had two sons; and he came to the first, and said, Son, go work today in my vineyard. He answered and said, I will not; but afterward he repented, and went. And he came to the second, and said likewise. And he answered and said, I go, sir; and went not. Whether of them twain did the will of his father?" (3SP 31.1)

This abrupt question threw them off their guard; they had followed the parable closely and now immediately answered, "The first." Fixing his steady eye upon them, Jesus responded in stern and solemn accents: "Verily I say unto you, That the publicans and the harlots go into the kingdom of God before you. For John came unto you in the way of righteousness, and ye believed him not; but the publicans and the harlots believed him; and ye, when ye had seen it, repented not afterward, that ye might believe him." (3SP 31.2)

These terrible truths struck home to the hearts of the hypocritical priests and rulers. The first son in the parable represented the publicans and harlots who at first refused obedience to the teachings of John, but afterwards repented and were converted. The second son represented the Jews who professed obedience and superior virtue, but insulted God by rejecting the gift of his Son. By their wicked works they forfeited the favor of Heaven. They despised the mercies of God. The most thoughtless and abandoned are represented by Jesus as occupying a more favorable position before God than the haughty and self-righteous priests and rulers. (3SP 32.1)

They were unwilling to bear these searching truths, but remained silent, hoping that Jesus would say something which they could turn against him; but they had still more to bear. Jesus looked back upon the past, when his ministers, the prophets of God, were rejected and their messages trampled upon by the ancestors of the very men who stood before him. He saw that the sons were following in the footsteps of their fathers, and would fill up the cup of their iniquity by putting to death the Lord of Life. He drew from the past, present and future to compose his parable:– (3SP 32.2)

"Hear another parable: There was a certain householder, which planted a vineyard, and hedged it round about, and digged a winepress in it, and built a tower, and let it out to husbandmen, and went into a far country. And when the time of the fruit drew near, he sent his servants to the husbandmen, that they might receive the fruits of it. And the husbandmen took his servants, and beat one, and killed another, and stoned another. Again, he sent other servants more than the first; and they did unto them likewise. But last of all he sent unto them his son, saying, They will reverence my son. But when the husbandmen saw the son, they said among themselves, This is the heir; come, let us kill him, and let us seize on his inheritance. And they caught him, and cast him out of the vineyard, and slew him. When the Lord therefore of the vineyard cometh, what will he do unto those husbandmen?" (3SP 32.3)

Jesus addressed all the people present; but the priests and rulers, not anticipating that the parable was to be applied to them, answered at once, "He will miserably destroy those wicked men, and will let out his vineyard unto other husbandmen, which shall render him the fruits in their seasons." Again they perceived that they had pronounced their own condemnation in presence of the people who were listening, with rapt interest to Jesus. The Saviour referred to messenger after messenger that had been sent in vain to Israel with reproofs, warnings and entreaties. These faithful bearers of truth had been slain by those to whom they were sent, even as the faithful servants were slain by the wicked husbandmen. In the beloved son whom the Lord of the vineyard finally sent to his disobedient servants, and whom they seized and slew, the priests and rulers suddenly saw unfolded before them, a distinct picture of Jesus and his impending fate. Already they were planning to slay Him whom the Father had sent to them as a last and only appeal. In the retribution visited upon the ungrateful husbandmen was portrayed the doom of those who should slay Christ. (3SP 33.1)

In the parable of the vineyard Jesus brought before the Jews their real condition. The householder represented God, the vineyard the Jewish nation hedged in by divine law which was calculated to preserve them as a people separate and distinct from all other nations of the earth. The tower built in the vineyard represented their temple. The Lord of the vineyard had done all that was necessary for its prosperity. So God had provided for Israel in such a manner that it was in their power to secure the highest degree of prosperity. The Lord of the vineyard required of his husbandmen a due proportion of the fruit; so God required of the Jews a life corresponding with the sacred privileges he had given them. But as the servants who demanded fruit in their master's name were put to death by the unfaithful husbandmen, so had the Jews slain the prophets who had come to them with messages from God. Not only were these rejected, but when he sent his only Son to them, the destined Heir to the vineyard, thinking to preserve the vineyard to themselves, and to secure the honor and profit accruing therefrom, the haughty Jews, the unfaithful servants, reasoned among themselves, saying, "This is the heir; come, let us kill him." Thus Jesus revealed in his parable the

Chapter 2 - Cleansing the Temple (3SP 34.1)

dark purposes of the Jews against himself. (3SP 34.1)

After Jesus had heard them pronounce sentence upon themselves in their condemnation of the wicked husbandmen, he looked pityingly upon them and continued: "Did ye never read in the scriptures, The stone which the builders rejected the same has become the head of the corner; this is the Lord's doing, and it is marvelous in our eyes? Therefore say I unto you, The kingdom of God shall be taken from you, and given to a nation bringing forth the fruits thereof. And whosoever shall fall on this stone shall be broken; but on whomsoever it shall fall, it will grind him to powder." (3SP 34.2)

The Jews had often repeated the words of this prophecy while teaching the people in the synagogues, applying it to the coming Messiah. But Jesus connected the heir so cruelly slain with the stone which the builders rejected, but which eventually became the principal stone of the whole building. Christ himself was the originator of the Jewish system, the very foundation of the costly temple, the antitype to whom all the sacrificial services pointed. The Jews had watched with apparent anxiety for the coming of Christ. The scribes, who were learned in the law and acquainted with the declarations of the prophets regarding his coming, knew from prophetic history that the time of looking and waiting for his advent to the world had expired. Through the parables which Jesus spoke to the Jews, he brought their minds to prophecies which had foretold the very things which were then being enacted. He sought by every means within his power to awaken their consciences and to enlighten their understanding, that they might consider well the steps they were meditating. (3SP 35.1)

In these parables he laid the purposes of the Pharisees before them, together with the fearful consequences resulting. A solemn warning was thus given to them. And to leave the matter without a shadow of doubt, Jesus then dropped all figures and stated plainly that the kingdom of God should be taken from them and given to a nation bringing forth fruit. At this the chief priests and scribes were so enraged they could scarcely restrain themselves from using violence against him; but perceiving the love and reverence with which the people regarded him they dared not follow out the malice of their hearts. (3SP 35.2)

*****

Chapter 3
Jesus and the Pharisees

In building the temple of Solomon the stones were entirely prepared at the quarry, so that when they were brought to the place of building the workmen had only to place them in position; the hewing, squaring and polishing had all been done. "And the king commanded, and they brought great stones, costly stones, and hewed stones, to lay the foundation of the house. And Solomon's builders and Hiram's builders did hew them, and the stone-squarers. So they prepared timber and stones to build the house." "And the house, when it was in building, was built of stone made ready before it was brought thither; so that there was neither hammer nor ax nor any tool of iron heard in the house, while it was in building." (3SP 36.1)

Not an instrument was to be used upon the stone when it was brought to the place of building. One stone of irregular shape was brought from the quarry to be used in the foundation of the temple. But the workmen could find no place for it and would not accept it. There it lay unused, and the laborers passed around it or stumbled over it, greatly annoyed by its presence. Long it remained a rejected stone. But when the builders came to the laying of the corner-stone, for a long time they searched in vain for a stone of sufficient size and strength, and of the proper shape, to take that particular place and bear the great weight which would rest upon it. Should they make an unwise selection of a stone for this important place, the safety of the entire building would be endangered; they must find a stone capable of resisting the influence of the sun, frost and tempest. Several stones had been chosen at different times; but when subjected to the pressure of immense weights they had crumbled to pieces. Others would not bear the test of sudden atmospheric changes, and were therefore pronounced unfit for the place. (3SP 36.2)

But there lay the stone so long rejected by the builders; it had endured exposure to the air and to the scorching rays of the sun without revealing a seam or the slightest crack. Storms had beaten upon it, yet it remained the same. The attention of the builders was finally attracted to this large stone, and they examined it closely. It had already borne every test but one. If it could bear the test of severe pressure they decided to accept if for the corner-stone. The trial was made to the satisfaction of all. The stone was accepted, brought to its assigned position and found to be an exact fit. (3SP 37.1)

In prophetic vision Isaiah was shown that this stone was a symbol of the Saviour of the world. He says: "Sanctify the Lord of hosts himself; and let him be your fear, and let him be your dread. And he shall be for a sanctuary; but for a stone of stumbling and for a rock of offense to both the houses of Israel, for a gin and for a snare to the inhabitants of Jerusalem. And many among them shall stumble, and fall, and be broken, and be snared, and be taken." Carried down in prophetic vision to the first advent, the prophet is shown that Christ is to bear trials and tests of which the treatment of the chief corner-stone in the temple of Solomon is a symbol: "Therefore thus saith the Lord God, Behold, I lay in Zion for a foundation a stone, a tried stone, a precious corner-stone, a sure foundation; he that believeth shall not make haste." (3SP 37.2)

God in infinite wisdom chose the foundation stone and laid it himself. He called it a "sure stone;" the entire world may lay upon it their burdens and griefs, yet it can endure them all. They may build upon this stone with perfect safety. Christ is a "tried stone," and never disappoints those who trust in him. He has borne every test imposed upon him. He failed not in the wilderness of temptation when he endured the pressure of Adam's guilt and that of his posterity. He came off more than conqueror of the powers of evil. He has borne the burdens cast upon him by those who, falling upon this rock, have been broken. In Christ their guilty hearts have found relief. Those who make Him their foundation rest in perfect security. (3SP 38.1)

Chapter 3 - Jesus and the Pharisees (3SP 38.2)

Christ is represented by the chief corner-stone. Jew and Gentile must build upon this foundation, and their connection with Christ, this "precious stone" makes them living stones. Peter in the following figure clearly shows to whom Christ is a foundation stone and to whom a stone of stumbling:– (3SP 38.2)

"If so be ye have tasted that the Lord is gracious. To whom coming, as unto a living stone, disallowed indeed of men, but chosen of God, and precious, ye also, as lively stones, are built up a spiritual house, an holy priesthood, to offer up spiritual sacrifices, acceptable to God by Jesus Christ. Wherefore also it is contained in the scripture, Behold, I lay in Sion a chief corner-stone, elect, precious; and he that believeth on him shall not be confounded. Unto you therefore which believe, he is precious; but unto them which be disobedient, the stone which the builders disallowed, the same is made the head of the corner, and a stone of stumbling, and a rock of offense, even to them which stumble at the word, being disobedient; whereunto also they were appointed." (3SP 39.1)

In revealing to the Jews their doom for rejecting the Son of God and making of him a stumbling-block, Jesus also addresses all those who are impenitent and do not accept him as their Redeemer. The fate of the unbelieving Jews will be theirs. The only safety is to build upon the right foundation. Millions are today building their hopes and prospects upon foundations that have not been tested and proven; they will soon totter and fall, bearing with them the flimsy structures built upon them. (3SP 39.2)

Jesus had passively borne the abuse of sinners, just as the rejected stone had borne the abuse of the workmen who stumbled over it. But the time was to come when they would see him exalted, even as the despised and rejected stone was made the head of the corner. Then the rejectors of Christ were to be punished for their iniquity. The city and temple of the Jews were to be destroyed. The stone was to fall upon them by which all their glory would be broken and scattered as the dust which the wind driveth away. (3SP 39.3)

Jesus has set before us the only true foundation upon which we may securely build. It is broad enough for all and strong enough to sustain the weight and burden of the whole world. To fall upon this stone and be broken is to give up our self-righteousness and to go to Christ with the humility of a child, repenting of our transgressions and believing in his forgiving love. All who build upon this foundation, which is Christ, become living stones by connection with Him, the chief corner-stone. Many persons are hewn, polished and beautified by their own endeavors, but they never will become "living stones" because they are not connected with Christ. When the rain falls, and the tempest rages, and the floods come they will fall in ruin because they are not riveted to the eternal rock, the chief corner-stone, Christ Jesus. (3SP 40.1)

The stones were not prepared for their respective places just as they were about to be laid in the wall of the temple; all the fitting and planning was done previous to their being brought to the place of building. So it is that all the hewing, fitting and polishing of character must be done during man's probation. When Christ shall come again to earth it will not be to purify and refine the characters of men, and to fit them for Heaven. His work then will only be to change their corruptible bodies and fashion them like unto Christ's most glorious body. Only a symmetrical and perfect character will in that day entitle men to the finishing touch of immortality. (3SP 40.2)

Earth is the quarry and the work-shop where men are to be fitted and refined for the courts of Heaven. As the stones composing Solomon's temple came together in the wall a perfect fit, without the touch of ax or hammer or any other instrument, so will the resurrected saints, and those who are alive at the time of his coming be caught up together to meet the Lord in the air, each one fitted for the great change and taking his proper place in the temple of God's love. (3SP 41.1)

But when Christ shall visit the wicked, his judgments will fall not only upon the Jews but upon all who have refused the heavenly benefits of the grace of God. The stone that was passive, bearing humbly all the abuse heaped upon it, will then lift itself in life and power above those who despised and rejected it. They will see in this their rock of offense, an avenging mountain falling upon and crushing them. (3SP 41.2)

Hoping to entrap him in his words, the chief priests and rulers sent the most malicious enemies of Jesus to him, who pretended to be interested in his teachings and desiring to be profited by his divine wisdom. They expected Jesus would be deceived by their pious pretensions, thrown off his guard and led to speak that which they could take advantage of to condemn him. They were mortified and angry that they had been compelled to endure the penetrating address of Jesus, laying bare their true condition and condemning their wickedness, yet were utterly unable to refute his words. (3SP 41.3)

They privately arranged with the Herodians to accompany them and hear the words of Jesus, that they might be witnesses against him when he should be arraigned on trial for his life. The Pharisees had ever fretted and chafed under the exaction of taxes or tribute by the Romans. They took the position that it was contrary to the law of God. They now laid a snare by which they thought Jesus would surely become entangled and offend either the Jewish laws or the Roman authority. The spies came to him in a most courteous manner and expressed great confidence in his teachings. After plying him with flattery as to his straightforward course, irrespective of the favor or frowns of men, they, with an assumed candor, asked as if for information, "Is it lawful to give tribute unto Caesar, or not?" (3SP 41.4)

But their wicked device was plain to the Saviour, and turning upon them he answered them, "Why tempt ye me, ye hypocrites? Show me the tribute money." Thrown off their guard by the unexpected manner in which Jesus met their advances, and which plainly showed that he was not deceived for a moment by their specious flattery, his questioners immediately brought him a coin bearing the image and superscription of the Roman ruler. "And he saith unto them, Whose is this image and superscription? They say unto him, Caesar's. Then saith he unto them, Render therefore unto Caesar the things which are Caesar's, and unto God the things that are God's." (3SP 42.1)

The wily spies felt themselves baffled and defeated. The summary way in which their question had been settled left nothing farther for them to say. Their plans were all disarranged. They had expected Jesus to answer their question directly in one way or the other. If he should say, It is unlawful to give tribute unto Caesar, there were those present whose task it was to immediately bear the report to the Roman authorities, and have Jesus arrested at once as one who was creating rebellion among the Jews. This they hoped would insure his condemnation. But in case he should say, It is lawful to give tribute unto Caesar, they designed to call the attention of the Jewish people to his decision, and accuse him as one opposed to the divine law. (3SP 42.2)

Jesus read their motives, and, holding in his hand the Roman coin, upon which was stamped the name and image of Caesar, declared that, as they were living under the protection of the Roman power, they should render to that power the support it claimed, so long as it did not conflict with their duty to God. But that they should at all times render obedience to God, answering his claims, yet peaceably subject to the laws of the land. His interrogators, unprepared for this response of Jesus, "marveled and left him, and went their way." Although the wrath of the priests and rulers knew no bounds, and they longed to seize Jesus and slay him with their own hands to avenge themselves for the mortification he had caused them, yet they dared not attack him before the crowd. With a masterly effort they maintained a fair exterior while they went about laying plans to destroy him. (3SP 43.1)

The Saviour knew just what answer would meet the exigencies of the case. He gave no advantage to either the Roman or Jewish power. His answer to the intriguing Jews, "Render unto God the things which are God's," was a severe rebuke to them. Had they answered the claims of God and faithfully fulfilled their obligations to him, they would not have become a broken nation, subject to a foreign power. No Roman ensign would have waved over Jerusalem, no Roman sentinel would have stood at her gates, no Roman governor ruled within her walls. The Jewish nation was then paying the penalty of its apostasy from God. (3SP 43.2)

But no sooner were the Pharisees silenced than the Sadducees came with their artful questions, seeking to entrap the Saviour. The Sadducees were a sect of the Jews that differed materially in faith from the Pharisees. The only bond of union between the two seemed their mutual opposition to the Saviour and his teachings, and their desire to put him to death. The Pharisees placed their traditions on a level with the law of God, and frequently made them take the place of the law. Jesus had declared that they made void the law of God by their traditions, external ceremonies, divers washings, fastings and long prayers, ostentatious alms-giving and rigorous seclusion from the Gentiles. These constituted the main features of their religion. In superstition and formality they resembled the Roman Catholic church of the present time. But among them were some of

Chapter 3 - Jesus and the Pharisees (3SP 44.1)

genuine piety who received the teachings of Christ. (3SP 44.1)

The Sadducees had no respect for the traditions of the Pharisees. They professedly believed the greater portion of the Scriptures and regarded them as their rule of action; yet they denied the existence of angels, and also the resurrection of the body, in which the Pharisees firmly believed. The Sadducees rejected the doctrine of a future life, with its rewards and punishments. (3SP 44.2)

They believed in God as the only being superior to man; but they claimed that, having created man, God left him to pursue his own course. They argued that an overruling Providence sustaining the machinery of the universe, and a foreknowledge of events would deprive man of free moral agency, and lower him to the position of a slave. They therefore disconnected the Creator from the creature, maintaining that man was independent of a higher influence; that his destiny was in his own hands. Denying as they did that the Spirit of God worked through human efforts, or natural means, they still held that man, through the proper employment of his own natural powers, could become elevated and enlightened, and that his life could be purified by rigorous and austere exactions. (3SP 44.3)

There was but little union among them; a people who refused to acknowledge the influence of the Spirit of God upon the actions of men, would have but little respect for the opinions and feelings of one another. They lived for themselves; their natural sympathies were brought within a narrow compass; their hearts were not touched by the sorrow and want of others; for in their belief it was possible for all to secure the comforts and blessings of life. (3SP 45.1)

In common with the rest of the Jews, the Sadducees boasted much upon their birthright as children of Abraham after the flesh, and upon the strictness with which they observed the outward requirements of the law; but their views were inconsistent and heterogeneous. They entirely rejected the doctrine of the resurrection of the dead, and reasoned that if the same particles of matter which constituted the mortal body must also compose the future immortal being, then that body must have flesh and blood, and resume in the eternal world the carnal life interrupted on earth, all the frailties and passions of this life being perpetuated in the life beyond. (3SP 45.2)

In the days of Christ the Sadducees loved controversy, and vehemently urged their objections to the resurrection of the dead. In their discussions with the Pharisees, the latter became confused in their faith concerning the future state of the dead. Death became to them a dark and unexplainable mystery. They learned to look upon it as the most dreaded calamity which could come upon man. (3SP 46.1)

But life and immortality were brought to light through Jesus Christ. Those who accepted him as the world's Redeemer saw more clearly than before the future life of the resurrected dead. Christ passing through death, coming forth from the grave, and appearing again to man in his own person, and as such ascending to the Father, forever settles the sacred facts of the resurrection and the future, immortal life of the just, in the the minds of all who believe in Christ. (3SP 46.2)

The Sadducees were very annoying to the Pharisees, because the latter could not prevail over them in argument. The discussions between the two parties usually resulted in angry disputation, and left them further apart than before. But many of the Sadducees, living only for this life, were wealthy and influential; they were therefore eligible to the office of high priest with the express stipulation that their infidel views should not be made prominent. As the Pharisees were far more numerous, the Sadducees were to concede to their doctrines outwardly when holding any priestly office. But the very fact of their being eligible to such office gave influence to their erratic views. Had the Pharisees been pure in life they might have been able to enlighten the Sadducees; but as it was they had little influence over them. (3SP 46.3)

The teachings of Jesus were utterly refused by the Sadducees, as he was animated by a spirit which they refused to acknowledge as manifesting itself thus. They conceived of God as a Supreme Being, exalted above man, and unapproachable by him. Having created man, he left him to control his own life, and shape the events of the world. The doctrine of Christ directly opposed the belief of the Sadducees. The word and works of Christ testified to a divine power which accomplishes miraculous results, of a future, eternal life exalted above the finite life, of God as a Father to the children of men, watchful of their true interests, and guarding them. He taught that God was a rewarder of the righteous, and a punisher of the transgressor. He was not an intangible spirit, but a living ruler of the universe. This gracious Father was constantly working for the good of man, and mindful of all that concerns him. The very hairs of his head are numbered. Not even a sparrow falls to the ground without the notice of the Heavenly Father, and man is more valuable than many sparrows. Jesus presented before them their ignorance of the Scriptures in assigning to human power that which could be wrought only through the power of the Spirit of God. He declared that their confusion of faith and darkness of mind resulted mainly from this cause, and that spiritual things must be spiritually discerned. (3SP 47.1)

All that blessed the life of man was given by his Heavenly Father. He gave the bright sunshine to warm the earth. He sent the showers which caused vegetation to flourish. Angels of God were continually ministering to the children of men, keeping up the connection between Heaven and earth, uniting finite man with the Infinite God. Yet, while God had a care over the temporal interests of man, Jesus expressly taught that he had much greater care for his eternal interests. (3SP 48.1)

The Sadducees had arranged their questions so that they felt confident of bringing Jesus into disrepute by answering them, if they were not the direct means of condemning him. Should he agree with them in regard to the resurrection of the dead, he would be entirely cut off from any fellowship with the Pharisees. Should he differ from them, they designed to present his faith to the people in a ridiculous light, and turn their influence against him by showing the apparent absurdity of the doctrine of the resurrection of the body. They were accustomed to dispute upon this point, and their arguments were greatly dreaded by those who believed in the literal resurrection of the identical body which had moldered away in the grave. (3SP 48.2)

The Sadducees reasoned that if the dead were raised with bodies formed of the same particles of matter of which they had formerly been composed, and were actuated by the same propensities, then the relationships of the earthly life would be resumed, husband and wife would be united, marriage would be consummated, and all the affairs of life would go on the same as before death. From this belief they shrank with repugnance, and, in their efforts to grasp a higher ideal, groped in thick darkness. (3SP 48.3)

But, in answer to their questions on this point, Jesus lifted the veil from the future life and said to them, "In the resurrection they neither marry nor are given in marriage, but are as the angels of God in Heaven." He unhesitatingly showed that the Sadducees were wrong in their belief. He proved their premises to be false and the structure of their faith to be built upon a false foundation. "Ye do err," said he, "not knowing the Scriptures nor the power of God." He did not charge them with hypocrisy as he had charged the Pharisees, but with error of belief. (3SP 49.1)

The Sadducees had flattered themselves that, of all men living, they were strictly adherent to the Scriptures; but Jesus declared that they had not known their true interpretation. That knowledge must be brought home to the heart by the enlightening power of the grace of God. The Sadducees were seeking to bring the mysteries of God to a level with their finite reasoning instead of opening their minds to the reception of those sacred truths by which their understanding would have been expanded. Thousands become infidels because their finite minds cannot fathom the hidden mysteries of God. They cannot explain the wonderful exhibition of divine power, as manifested in the providences of God, and they therefore reject the evidences of such power, and attribute all to some natural agency which they can comprehend still less. Man should accept God as the Creator of the universe, One who commands and executes all things. He should get broad views of the character of God and the mysteries of his agencies. (3SP 49.2)

Christ would teach his questioners that if there be no resurrection of the dead, the Scriptures which they profess to believe would be of no avail. Said he, "But as touching the resurrection of the dead, have ye not read that which was spoken unto you by God, saying, I am the God of Abraham, and the God of Isaac, and the God of Jacob? God is not the God of the dead, but of the living." The precious dead, from Abel down to the last saint who dies, will hear the voice of the Son of God, and will come forth from their graves and live again. God will be their God and they shall be his people. There will be a close and tender relationship between God and his resurrected saints. This is in accordance with the divine plan. (3SP 50.1)

The dignity and power with which Jesus opened to the darkened minds of his hearers the truths of the Scriptures concerning the resurrection of the dead, and the divine power exercised in the temporal affairs of life, astonished his audience and put the Sadducees to silence. They had not a word to answer him. "But when the Pharisees had heard that he had put the Sadducees to silence, they were gathered together." They thought it would not do for Jesus to take the field of contest in so victorious a manner. In the dispute with the Sadducees they had prevailed nothing against him, but were themselves put to confusion, and their ignorance made manifest by the wisdom of his answers. Not a word had been spoken of which the least advantage could be taken to use in the condemnation of Jesus. His adversaries had gained nothing but the contempt of the people. (3SP 50.2)

But the Pharisees did not yet despair of driving him to speak that which they could use against him. They prevailed upon a certain learned scribe to question Jesus, as to which of the ten precepts was of the greatest importance. (3SP 51.1)

The Pharisees had exalted the first four commandments, which point out the duty of man to his Maker, as of far greater importance than the other six, which point out the duty of man to his fellow-man. In consequence they greatly failed of practical godliness, and in the relations and duties of life. Jesus had been charged with exalting the last six commandments above the first four, because he showed the people their great deficiency, and taught the necessity of good works, deeds of mercy and benevolence, and that a tree is known by its fruits. (3SP 51.2)

The learned lawyer approached Jesus with a direct question: "Master, which is the great commandment in the law?" The answer of Jesus is as direct and forcible: "Thou shalt love the Lord thy God with all thy heart, and with all thy soul, and with all thy mind. This is the first and great commandment. And the second is like unto it, Thou shalt love thy neighbor as thyself. On these two commandments hang all the law and the prophets." (3SP 51.3)

He here explicitly shows the questioner the two great principles of the law: Love to God and love to man. Upon these two principles of God's moral government hang all the law and the prophets. The first four commandments indicate the duty of man to his Creator; and the first and great commandment is, Thou shalt love the Lord thy God with all thy heart. This love is not a passion, nor a fruitless faith in the existence and power of God, a cold acknowledgment of his boundless love; but it is a living, active principle, manifested in willing obedience of all his requirements. (3SP 51.4)

Jesus taught his hearers that not one of the precepts of Jehovah could be broken without violating one or both of the great principles upon which rested the whole law and the prophets: Love to God and love to man. Every precept is so connected with the others in meaning and obligation that in breaking one, the whole is broken; for they are all united in one symmetrical body. It is impossible for man to love God with all his heart and yet to have other gods before the Lord. This supreme love to God does not consist in a mere acknowledgment of his universal power, and the offering of a prescribed form of worship to him, while the heart finds delight in serving idols. Self-love, love of the world, or an undue affection for any created thing, is idolatry in the sight of God, and separates the affections from him. God requires the heart's best and holiest affections, and he will accept nothing less. He must reign supreme in the mind and heart. (3SP 52.1)

If the first commandments are loyally observed, the other six, which define the duty of man to his fellow-man, will be as faithfully observed. When God has his rightful place on the throne of the heart the duties assigned in the last six commandments will be performed as there directed. Love to God comprehends love for those who are formed in his own image. "If a man say, I love God, and hateth his brother, he is a liar. For he that loveth not his brother, whom he hath seen, how can he love God, whom he hath not seen?" Thus Christ taught that the last six commandments are like unto the first. The two commandments which he indicated are two great principles springing from one root. The first cannot be kept and the second broken, nor the second kept while the first is broken. (3SP 52.2)

The scribe was well read in the law, and he was astonished at the answer of Jesus; for he had not expected to find him possessed of so deep and thorough a knowledge of the Scriptures as was indicated by his answer. The learned lawyer was much impressed by the wisdom of the youthful Galilean; and before the assembled priests and rulers he honestly acknowledged that Jesus had given the right interpretation of the law. This scribe had received a deeper and broader view of the principles underlying the sacred precepts than he had ever before possessed, and he responded to the words of Jesus with unfeigned earnestness:– (3SP 53.1)

"Well, Master, thou hast said the truth; for there is one God; and there is none other but he. And to love him with all the heart, and with all the understanding, and with all the soul, and with all the strength, and to love his neighbor as himself, is more than all whole burnt-offerings and sacrifices." Here was a Pharisee who had some idea of what constitutes true religion; that it is not in outward ceremonies and vain display, but in humble obedience and love to God, and unselfish regard for others. The readiness of the scribe to acknowledge the reasoning of Jesus as correct, the decided and prompt response to that reasoning which he made before the people, manifested an entirely different spirit from that shown by the priests and rulers in their questioning. (3SP 53.2)

The wisdom of the Saviour's answers convicted the scribe. He knew that the Jewish religion consisted more in outward acts than inward piety. He had some sense of the unworthiness of merely ceremonial offerings, and the continual flowing of blood in expiation of sin, while the object of the offering was foreign from the mind. The principles of love and true goodness of heart appeared to him of more value in the sight of God than all these rites. The heart of Jesus went out in pity to the honest scribe who dared to face the frowns of the priests and threats of the rulers, and speak the honest convictions of his heart. "And when Jesus saw that he answered discreetly, he said unto him, Thou art not far from the kingdom of God. And no man after that durst ask him any question." (3SP 54.1)

What the scribe needed was the touch of divine enlightenment which would enable him to feel the need of repentance for sin and faith in the Saviour; that no man can be saved through the law but through repentance and faith toward Christ, the sinner's Advocate with the Father. The scribe was near to the kingdom of God, in that he recognized deeds of righteousness to be more acceptable to God than burnt-offerings and sacrifices. Yet he still needed to acknowledge Jesus as the Son of God. All the religious service of the Jews was of no value whatever unless connected with living faith in Christ Jesus, who was the substance of which that service was the shadow. Christ had repeatedly shown that his Father's law contained something deeper than mere authoritative commands. The moral law contains the gospel in principle. (3SP 54.2)

The Pharisees had gathered close about Jesus as he answered the questions of the scribe. He now turned to them and put them a question: "What think ye of Christ? Whose son is he?" Jesus was evidently testing the faith of the Pharisees in his divinity, whether they regarded him simply as a man, or the divine Son of God. A chorus of voices answered simultaneously, "The son of David." This was the title which prophecy had given to the Messiah. When Jesus had revealed his divinity by his mighty miracles, when the sick were healed and the dead restored to life, the people had marveled and inquired among themselves, "Is not this the son of David?" The Syrophenician woman, blind Bartimeus, and many others had cried aloud to him for help, "Thou son of David, have mercy on me!" Only a few hours before, while riding into Jerusalem, he had been hailed with joyful "Hosannas to the son of David, Blessed is He who cometh in the name of the Lord," and the little children in the temple had that day echoed the same glad shouts. (3SP 55.1)

In reply to the answer of the people, that Christ was the son of David, Jesus said: "David in Spirit [the Spirit of inspiration from God,] called him Lord, saying, The Lord said unto my Lord, Sit thou on my right hand, till I make thine enemies thy footstool. If David then called him Lord, how is he his son? And no man was able to answer him a word, neither durst any man from that day forth ask him any more questions." (3SP 55.2)

Chapter 4
Denouncing the Pharisees

The common people heard Jesus gladly and gathered about him in the temple to receive his teachings. Never before had such a scene been enacted. There stood the young Galilean, bearing no earthly honor nor royal badge. His dress was coarse and travel-stained. Surrounding him were priests in their gorgeous apparel, rulers with robes and badges significant of their exalted position, and scribes with scrolls in their hands to which they made repeated reference. Yet Jesus stood calmly with the dignity of a king invested with the authority of Heaven looking unflinchingly upon his adversaries, who had rejected and despised his teachings and had long thirsted for his life. On this occasion they had assailed him in great numbers with a determination to provoke him to utter words which would ensnare him and serve as means by which they might condemn him. But their questions only opened the way for him to set before them their real condition, and the fearful retribution that awaited them if they continued to provoke God by their many and grievous sins. (3SP 56.1)

The interest of the people steadily increased as Jesus boldly met challenge after challenge of the Pharisees and presented the pure, bright truth in contrast with their darkness and error. They were charmed with the doctrine he taught, but were sadly perplexed. They had respected their acknowledged teachers for their intelligence and apparent piety. They had ever yielded implicit obedience to their authority in all religious matters. Yet they now saw these very men trying to bring Jesus into disrepute, a teacher whose virtue and knowledge shone forth brighter than before from every assault of his adversaries. They looked upon the lowering countenances of the priests and elders, and there saw discomfiture and confusion. They marveled that the rulers would not believe on Jesus, when his teachings were so plain and simple. They themselves knew not what course to take, and watched with eager anxiety the movements of those whose counsel they had always followed. (3SP 56.2)

The parables of Jesus were spoken to warn and condemn the rulers, and also to instruct the inquiring minds of those present. But, in order to break the chain which bound the people to customs and traditions, and unquestioning faith in a corrupt priesthood, he exposed more fully than ever before the character of the rulers and elders. It was his last day of teaching in the temple, and his words were not only to reach the audience before him, but were to go down through ages to the close of time, in every tongue and unto every people. (3SP 57.1)

The gems of truth that fell from his lips on that eventful day were hidden in the hearts of many who were present. For them a new history commenced, new thoughts started into life, and new aspirations were awakened. After the crucifixion and resurrection of Christ these persons came to the front, and fulfilled their divine commission with a wisdom and zeal corresponding with the greatness of the work. They bore a message that appealed to the hearts and minds of men, and weakened old superstitions that had long dwarfed the lives of thousands. Theories, philosophies, and human reasonings before their testimonies became as idle fables. Mighty were the results springing from the words of the humble Galilean to that wondering, awe-struck crowd, in the great temple of Jerusalem. (3SP 57.2)

Reading the conflicting emotions of the people, and the anxiety with which they regarded their leaders and teachers, Jesus proceeded to further enlighten their minds, saying, "The scribes and the Pharisees sit in Moses' seat. All therefore whatsoever they bid you observe, that observe and do; but do not ye after their works; for they say, and do not." The scribes and Pharisees claimed to be invested with divine authority similar to that of Moses. They assumed to take his place as expounders of the law and judges of the people. As such they claimed all deference and obedience from the people. But

Jesus admonished his hearers to do that which the priests taught according to the law; but not to follow their example; for they neglected the duties which they taught others to observe. (3SP 58.1)

Said he, "They bind heavy burdens and grievous to be borne, and lay them on men's shoulders; but they themselves will not move them with one of their fingers." The Pharisees enjoined a multitude of minute regulations having their foundation in tradition, and unreasonably restraining personal liberty of action. They strictly expounded certain portions of the law, exacting from the people rigorous observances and ceremonies, which they themselves secretly ignored, and actually claimed exemption from if detected in their omission. (3SP 58.2)

The severest denunciations that ever fell from the Saviour's lips were directed against those who, while making high pretensions to piety, secretly practiced iniquity. The religion of the priests, scribes, and rulers, like that of the modern Roman Church, consisted mainly in outward ceremonies, and was destitute of spiritual and practical godliness. God said unto Moses, Thou shalt bind these commandments of the Lord for a sign upon thy hand; and they shall be as frontlets between thine eyes. The Jews construed these words into a command that the precepts of scripture should be worn upon the person. They were accordingly lettered on cloth in a very conspicuous manner and bound about their heads and wrists. But wearing these precepts thus did not cause the law of God to take firmer hold of their minds and hearts, as God had designed. The precepts which should have purified their lives, and prompted them to righteous deeds, and acts of kindness and mercy, were worn as badges to attract observation, and give the wearers an air of piety and devotion which would excite the veneration of all beholders. Jesus struck a heavy blow at all this vain show of religion in these words:– (3SP 58.3)

"But all their works they do for to be seen of men; they make broad their phylacteries, and enlarge the borders of their garments, and love the uppermost rooms at feasts, and the chief seats in the synagogues, and greetings in the markets, and to be called of men, Rabbi, Rabbi. But be not ye called Rabbi; for one is your Master, even Christ; and all ye are brethren. And call no man your father upon the earth; for one is your Father, which is in Heaven. Neither be ye called masters; for one is your Master, even Christ." In such plain words the Saviour revealed the selfish ambition of the Pharisees, ever reaching for power and place, displaying a mock humility, while their hearts were filled with envy and avarice. When persons were invited to a feast the guests were seated according to their rank and station; and those who were given the most honorable places received the first attention, and most special favors. The Pharisees were ever eager and scheming to receive these honors. (3SP 59.1)

Jesus also revealed their vanity in loving to be called of men Rabbi, meaning master. He declared that such a title did not belong to men, but only to Christ. Priests, scribes and rulers, expounders of the law and administrators of it, were all brethren, children of one God. Jesus would impress upon the minds of the people that they were to give no man a title of honor, indicating that he had any control of their conscience or faith. (3SP 60.1)

If Christ were on earth today, surrounded by the religious teachers of the age who bear the titles of Reverend and Right Reverend, would he not repeat his saying to the Pharisees: "Neither be ye called master; for one is your Master, even Christ"? Many who assume these honorary titles are utterly devoid of the wisdom and true righteousness which they indicate. Too many hide worldly ambition, despotism, and the basest sins beneath the broidered garment of a high and holy office. The Saviour continued:– (3SP 60.2)

"But he that is greatest among you shall be your servant. And whosoever shall exalt himself shall be abased; and he that shall humble himself shall be exalted." True greatness is measured by moral worth. Greatness of character in the estimation of Heaven consists in living for the welfare of our fellow-men, in doing works of love and benevolence. Christ was a servant to fallen man; yet he was the King of Glory. He still continued his denunciations of the rich and powerful men before him:– (3SP 60.3)

"But woe unto you, scribes and Pharisees, hypocrites! for ye shut up the kingdom of Heaven against men; for ye neither go in yourselves, neither suffer ye them that are entering to go in." By perverting the meaning of the Scriptures the priests blinded the understanding of those who would otherwise have seen the nature of Christ's kingdom, and that inward, divine life which is essential to true holiness. By their endless round of forms they

Chapter 4 - Denouncing the Pharisees (3SP 61.1)

fastened the minds of the people upon external services to the neglect of true religion. (3SP 61.1)

They not only rejected Christ themselves but took the most unfair means to prejudice the people against him, deceiving them by false reports and gross misrepresentations. In all ages of the world truth has been unpopular; its doctrines are not congenial to the natural mind; for it searches the heart, and reproves its hidden sin. Those who persecute the advocates of God's truth have ever, like the Pharisees, misrepresented their words and motives. Jesus resumed:– (3SP 61.2)

"Woe unto you, scribes and Pharisees, hypocrites! for ye devour widows' houses, and for a pretense make long prayer; therefore ye shall receive the greater damnation." The Pharisees so wrought upon the minds of many conscientious widows that they believed it a duty to devote their entire property to religious purposes. These deluded women would trust the appropriation of their money to the scribes and priests, in whom they placed implicit confidence; and those wily men would use it for their own benefit. To cover their dishonesty they made long prayers in public, and a great show of piety. Jesus declared that this hypocrisy would bring them the greater damnation. Many professors of exalted piety in our day come under the same ban. Selfishness and avarice stain their lives; yet they throw over all this a garment of seeming purity, and deceive honest souls; but they cannot deceive God; he reads every purpose of the heart and will mete out to every person according to his works. The Saviour continued his denunciations:– (3SP 61.3)

"Woe unto you, ye blind guides, who say, Whosoever shall swear by the temple, it is nothing; but whosoever shall swear by the gold of the temple, he is a debtor! Ye fools and blind; for whether is greater, the gold, or the temple that sanctifieth the gold? And, Whosoever shall swear by the altar, it is nothing; but whosoever sweareth by the gift that is upon it, he is guilty. Ye fools and blind; for whether is greater, the gift, or the altar that sanctifieth the gift?" The priests interpreted the requirements of God to meet their false and narrow standard. They presumed to make nice distinctions between the comparative guilt of various sins, passing over some lightly, and treating others of perhaps less consequence as unpardonable. They accepted money from persons in return for excusing them from their vows; and in some cases crimes of an aggravated character were passed over in consideration of large sums of money paid to the authorities by the transgressor. At the same time these priests and rulers would pronounce severe judgment against others for trivial offenses. (3SP 62.1)

"Woe unto you, scribes and Pharisees, hypocrites! for ye pay tithe of mint and anise and cummin, and have omitted the weightier matters of the law, judgment, mercy, and faith; these ought ye to have done, and not to leave the other undone." According to the requirements of God the tithing system was obligatory upon the Jews. But the priests did not leave the people to carry out their convictions of duty in giving to the Lord one-tenth of all the increase of the marketable products of the land. They carried the requirements of the tithing system to extremes, making them embrace such trifling things as anise, mint and other small herbs which were cultivated to a limited extent. This caused the tithing plan to be attended with such care and perplexity that it was a wearisome burden. While they were so exact in things which God had never required of them, and were confusing their judgment and lessening the dignity of the divine system of benevolence by their narrow views, they were making clean the outside of the platter while the inside was corrupt. Exact in matters of little consequence, Jesus accuses them of having "omitted the weightier matters of the law, judgment, mercy, and faith." No outward service, even in that which is required by God, can be a substitute for an obedient life. The Creator desires heart service of his creatures. (3SP 63.1)

The Jews read in the requirements given to Moses that nothing unclean should be eaten. God specified the beasts that were unfit for food, and forbade the use of swine's flesh and the flesh of certain other animals, as likely to fill the blood with impurities and shorten life. But the Pharisees did not leave these restrictions where God had left them. They carried them to unwarranted extremes; among other things the people were required to strain all the water used, lest it might contain the smallest insect, undiscernible to the eye, which might be classed with the unclean animals. Jesus, in contrasting these trivial exactions of external cleanliness with the magnitude of their actual sins, said to the Pharisees: "Ye blind guides, who strain at a gnat and swallow a camel." (3SP 63.2)

"Woe unto you, scribes and Pharisees, hypocrites! for ye are like unto whited

Chapter 4 - Denouncing the Pharisees (3SP 66.1)

sepulchers, which indeed appear beautiful outward, but are within full of dead men's bones, and of all uncleanness." All the pomp and ceremony of the priests and rulers were but a cloak to conceal their iniquity, as the white and beautifully decorated tomb covers the putrefying remains within it. Jesus also compared the Pharisees to hidden graves which, under a fair exterior, conceal the corruption of dead bodies: "Even so ye also outwardly appear righteous unto men, but within ye are full of hypocrisy and iniquity." All the high pretensions of those who claimed to have the law of God written in their hearts as well as borne upon their persons, were thus shown to be vain pretense. Jesus continued:– (3SP 64.1)

"Woe unto you, scribes and Pharisees, hypocrites! because ye build the tombs of the prophets, and garnish the sepulchers of the righteous, and say, If we had been in the days of our fathers, we would not have been partakers with them in the blood of the prophets. Wherefore ye be witnesses unto yourselves, that ye are the children of them who killed the prophets." The Jews were very particular to beautify the tombs of the dead prophets as evidence of their esteem for them; yet they did not profit by their teachings, nor regard their reproofs and warnings. (3SP 64.2)

In the days of Christ a superstitious regard was cherished for the tombs of the dead. This was frequently carried to the verge of idolatry, and vast sums of money were lavished upon their decoration. The same species of idolatry is carried to great lengths today, and especially by the Roman Church. But the Christian world at large are guilty of neglecting the widow and the fatherless, the poor and afflicted, to erect expensive monuments in honor of the dead. Time, money, and labor are not stinted for this purpose, while duties to the living are neglected. The Pharisees built the tombs of the prophets and garnished their sepulchers, and said one to another, If we had lived in those days we should not have been partakers with those who shed the blood of God's servants. Yet at the same time they were planning to destroy the Son of God, and would not have hesitated to imbrue their hands in his blood if they had not feared the people. (3SP 65.1)

This condition of the Pharisees should be a lesson to the Christian world of the present day; it should open their eyes to the power of Satan to deceive human minds when they once turn from the precious light of truth, and yield to the control of the enemy. Many follow in the track of the Pharisees. They revere the martyrs who died for their faith; and declare that, had they lived in the days when Christ was upon earth, they would have gladly received his teachings and obeyed them; they would never have been partakers of the guilt of those who rejected the Saviour. But these very persons stifle their honest convictions at any cost rather than yield obedience to God when it involves self-denial and humiliation. In our day the light shines clearer than in the time of the Pharisees. Then the people were to accept Christ as revealed in prophecy, and to believe on him through the evidences which attended his mission. The Jews saw in Jesus a young Galilean without worldly honor, and, though he came as prophecy foretold he would come, they refused to accept their Messiah in poverty and humiliation, and crucified him, as prophecy foretold they would do. (3SP 65.2)

The Christian world now has a Saviour who has fulfilled all the specifications of prophecy in regard to his life and death; yet many reject his teachings, they do not follow his precepts, they crucify the Saviour every day. Should they be tested as were the Jews at the first advent of Christ, they would not accept him in his humiliation and poverty. (3SP 66.1)

From the time that the first innocent blood was shed, when righteous Abel fell by the hand of his brother, iniquity had increased upon the earth. From generation to generation the priests and rulers had slighted the warnings of the prophets whom God had raised up and qualified to reprove the sins of the people. There had been great need of these men, who, in every age, had lifted their voices against the sins of kings, rulers, and subjects, speaking the words God gave them to utter, and obeying the divine will at the peril of their lives. From generation to generation there had been heaping up a terrible punishment, which the enemies of Christ were now drawing down upon their own heads by their abuse and rejection of the Son of God, whose voice was raised in condemnation of the sin existing among the priests and rulers to a greater degree than at any previous time. They were filling to overflowing their cup of iniquity, which was to be emptied upon their own heads in retributive justice, making their generation responsible for the blood of all the righteous men slain from Abel to Christ. Of this, Jesus warned them:–

Chapter 4 - Denouncing the Pharisees (3SP 66.2)

(3SP 66.2)

"That upon you may come all the righteous blood shed upon the earth, from the blood of righteous Abel unto the blood of Zacharias, son of Barachias, whom ye slew between the temple and the altar. Verily I say unto you, all these things shall come upon this generation." The Saviour, with hand uplifted toward Heaven and a divine light enshrouding his person, spoke in the character of a judge of those before him. The listening crowd shuddered as his denunciations were spoken. The impression made upon their minds by his words and looks was never to be effaced in after years. (3SP 67.1)

Israel had little heeded the commands of God. While the words of warning which God had given him to speak were upon the lips of Zacharias, a satanic fury seized the apostate king, and the command was given to slay the prophet of God. The scribes and Pharisees who listened to the words of Jesus knew that they were true, and that the blood of the slain prophet imprinted itself on the very stones of the temple court and could not be erased, but remained to bear its testimony to God, in witness against apostate Israel. As long as the temple should stand, there would remain the stain of that righteous blood, crying to God to be avenged. As Jesus referred to these fearful crimes a thrill of horror ran through the hearts of the multitude. (3SP 67.2)

His voice had been heard upon earth in gentleness, entreaty, and affection; but now that the occasion required it, he spoke as judge, and condemned the guilt of the Jews. The Saviour, looking forward, foretold that their future impenitence, and intolerance of God's servants, would be the same as it had been in the past:- (3SP 68.1)

"Wherefore, behold, I send unto you prophets, and wise men, and scribes. And some of them ye shall kill and crucify; and some of them shall ye scourge in your synagogues, and persecute them from city to city." (3SP 68.2)

Prophets and wise men full of faith and the Holy Ghost, represented by Stephen, James, Paul, and many others, scribes, men of learning, who understood the Scriptures and could present them in all their bearings as revealed by God, would be scorned and persecuted, condemned and put to death. (3SP 68.3)

The Saviour spoke no words of retaliation for the abuse he had received at the hands of his enemies. No unholy passion stirred that divine soul; but his indignation was directed against the hypocrites whose gross sins were an abomination in the sight of God. The conduct of Christ upon this occasion reveals the fact that the Christian can dwell in perfect harmony with God, possess all the sweet attributes of love and mercy, yet feel a righteous indignation against aggravating sin. (3SP 68.4)

Divine pity marked the pale and mournful countenance of the Son of God as he cast one long, lingering look upon the temple and then upon his hearers, and with a voice choked by deep anguish of heart and bitter tears exclaimed: "O Jerusalem, Jerusalem, thou that killest the prophets, and stonest them which are sent unto thee, how often would I have gathered thy children together, even as a hen gathereth her chickens under her wings, and ye would not!" (3SP 69.1)

Pharisees and Sadducees were alike silenced. Jesus called his disciples and prepared to leave the temple, not as one defeated and forced from the presence of his adversaries, but as one whose work was accomplished. He retired a victor from the contest with his bigoted and hypocritical opponents. Looking around upon the interior of the temple for the last time, he said with mournful pathos, "Behold, your house is left unto you desolate. For I say unto you, Ye shall no more see me henceforth till ye shall say, Blessed is he that cometh in the name of the Lord." Hitherto he had called it his Father's house, but now, as the Son of God passed out from those walls, God's presence was withdrawn forever from the temple built to his glory. Henceforth its services were to be a mockery, and its ceremonies meaningless; for Jerusalem's day of probation was at an end. (3SP 69.2)

Jesus had spoken clear and pointed words that day, which cut his hearers to the heart. Their effect might not be seen at once, but the seed of truth sown in the minds of the people was to spring up and bear fruit to the glory of God, and be the means of saving many souls. After the crucifixion and resurrection of the Saviour, the lessons he had given that day would be revived in the hearts of many attentive listeners, who would in turn repeat the instruction which they had heard, for the benefit of future generations to the close of time. The disciples were astonished at the bold and authoritative manner in which their Master had denounced the hypocritical Pharisees. And the priests, scribes, and rulers were never to forget the last words Jesus addressed to them in the temple: "Behold, your house is left unto you desolate." The words fell solemnly upon their ears, and struck a nameless terror to their hearts. They affected indifference; but the question kept rising in their minds as to what was the import of those words. An unseen danger seemed to be threatening them. Could it be possible that the magnificent temple, which was the nation's glory, was soon to be a heap of ruins? (3SP 69.3)

The disciples shared in the general foreboding of evil, and anxiously waited for Jesus to make a more definite statement in regard to the subject. As they passed out of the temple with their Master, they called his attention to its strength and beauty and the durability of the material of which it was composed, saying, "Master, see what manner of stones and what buildings are here." Jesus, to make his words as impressive as possible, also called attention to the lofty structure: "See ye not all these things? Verily, I say unto you, There shall not be left here one stone upon another that shall not be thrown down." (3SP 70.1)

This was a startling statement to the disciples. The matter was now made plain: The glorious edifice, built at immense cost, which had been the pride of the Jewish nation, was to be destroyed from its very foundation. Not one of those massive stones–some of which had borne the devastation of Nebuchadnezzar's army, and stood firmly through the storm and tempest of centuries–was to be left upon another. They did not clearly comprehend the purpose of all this ruin. They did not discern that in a few days their Saviour was to be offered up as a victim for the sins of the world. The temple and its services would then be of no more use. The blood of beasts would be of no virtue to expiate sin, for type would then have met antitype, in the Lamb of God who would have voluntarily offered his life to take away the sins of the world. Later, when all had been accomplished, the disciples understood fully the words of Jesus, and the reason of the calamity which he foretold. (3SP 71.1)

Jesus lingered near the court where the women were depositing their offerings in the treasury. He observed the large donations of many of the rich, but made no comment upon their liberal offerings. He looked sadly at the comers and goers, many of whom presented large gifts in an ostentatious and self-satisfied manner. Presently his countenance lighted as he saw a poor widow approach hesitatingly, as though fearful of being observed. As the rich and haughty swept past her to deposit their offerings, she shrank back as if scarcely daring to venture farther. And yet her heart yearned to do something, little though it might be, for the cause she loved. She looked at the mite in her hand; it was very small in comparison with the gifts of those around her, yet it was her all. Watching her opportunity, she hurriedly threw in her two mites and turned to beat a hasty retreat. But in doing so she caught the eye of Jesus which was fastened earnestly upon her. (3SP 71.2)

The Saviour called his disciples to him and bade them mark the widow's poverty; and as they stood looking at her, words of commendation from the Master's lips fell unexpectedly upon her ear: "Verily, verily, I say unto you, that this poor widow hath cast in more than they all." Tears of joy filled the poor woman's eyes as she felt that her act was understood and appreciated by Jesus. Many would have advised her to appropriate her small pittance to her own use rather than to give it into the hands of well-fed priests, to be lost among the many and costly gifts donated to the temple; but Jesus understood the motives of her heart. She believed in the service of the temple as appointed by God, and she was anxious to do her utmost to sustain it. She did what she could, and her act was destined to be as a monument to her memory through all time, and her joy in eternity. Her heart went with her gift, the amount of which was estimated, not by its intrinsic value, but by the love to God and interest in his work which had prompted the deed. (3SP 72.1)

It is the motive which gives true value to our acts, and stamps them with high moral worth or with ignominy. It is not the great things which every eye can see and which every tongue praises that count to our eternal credit, but the little duties cheerfully done, the little gifts which make no show, and which human eyes regard as worthless. A heart of love and genuine faith in a worthy object is more acceptable to God than the most costly gift. The poor widow gave her living to do the little that she did. She deprived herself of food to give those two mites to the cause she loved; and she did it in faith, believing that her Heavenly Father would not overlook her great necessity. It was this unselfish spirit and unwavering faith that won the commendation of Jesus. (3SP 72.2)

Many humble souls feel under so great

Chapter 4 - Denouncing the Pharisees (3SP 73.1)

obligations for receiving the truth of God that they greatly desire to share with their more prosperous brethren the burdens imposed by the service of God. Let them lay up their mites in the bank of Heaven. The slender offerings of the poor should not be rejected; for if given from a heart burdened with love to God, those trifles in value become consecrated gifts, priceless offerings, which God smiles upon and blesses. (3SP 73.1)

Jesus said of the poor widow, "She hath given more than they all." The rich had bestowed from their abundance, many of them merely to be seen of others and to be honored of them for their large donations. They denied themselves none of the comforts or luxuries of life in order to make their gift, and therefore it was no sacrifice and could not be compared in true value with the widow's mite. (3SP 73.2)

Chapter 5
In the Outer Court

"And there were certain Greeks among them that came up to worship at the feast. The same came therefore to Philip, which was of Bethsaida of Galilee, and desired him, saying, Sir, we would see Jesus. Philip cometh and telleth Andrew, and again Andrew and Philip tell Jesus." (3SP 74.1)

These Gentiles were excluded from the temple court where Jesus was sitting over against the treasury. They had heard much in favor of and against Jesus, and were desirous to see and hear him for themselves. They could not come to him, but were obliged to wait in the court of the Gentiles. As the disciples bore the message of the Greeks to Jesus and awaited his answer, he seemed to be in a deep study, and answered them: "The hour is come that the Son of man should be glorified. Verily, verily, I say unto you, Except a corn of wheat fall into the ground and die, it abideth alone; but if it die, it bringeth forth much fruit." The request of the Greeks to see Jesus brought the future before him. The Jews had rejected the only one who could save them. They were soon to imbrue their hands in his blood, and place him with thieves and robbers. The Saviour, rejected by the house of Israel, was to be received by the Gentiles. He looked forward with joy to the period when the partition wall between Jew and Gentile would be thrown down, and the broad harvest field would be the world. (3SP 74.2)

Jesus regarded these Greeks as representatives of the Gentiles at large. In them he discerned the first-fruits of an abundant harvest, when all nations, tongues, and people upon the face of the earth should hear the glad tidings of salvation through Christ. He saw that the gathering of the Gentiles was to follow his approaching death. He therefore presented to his disciples and to the listening crowd the figure of the wheat, to represent how his death would be productive of a great harvest. If he should draw back from the sacrifice of his life, he would abide alone, like the kernel of wheat that did not die; but if he should give up his life, he would, like the kernel of wheat that fell into the ground, rise again as the first-fruits of the great harvest; and he, the Life-giver, would call the dead that were united with him by faith from the graves, and there would be a glorious harvest of ripe grain for the heavenly garner. In the gospel of the death and resurrection of Christ, and the resurrection of the dead, life and immortality are brought to light, and the kingdom of Heaven is thrown open to all believers. (3SP 74.3)

After Jesus had spoken of his own sufferings and death, he said, "He that loveth his life shall lose it; and he that hateth his life in this world shall keep it unto life eternal. If any man serve me, let him follow me; and where I am, there shall also my servant be. If any man serve me, him will my Father honor." The Saviour does not require his followers to travel in a path which he has not himself passed over. Jesus endured shame, insult, and privation from the manger to Calvary. Yet he looked beyond his agony in the garden, his betrayal, the buffeting and scourging, the ignominy of being ranked with malefactors, and dying in anguish upon the cross, to the glorious object of his mission, and the honor he should receive at his Father's right hand, where his true followers would finally be elevated with him. All who had cherished the cross of Christ, and been sharers of his sufferings, denying self and obeying God, should be partakers with him of his glory. They who had for Christ's sake lost their lives in this world would preserve them unto life eternal. It was the joy of Christ in his humiliation and pain that all his true disciples should be glorified with him in Heaven. (3SP 75.1)

Among the chief rulers were many who were convinced that Christ was indeed the Messiah; but, in face of the angry priests and Pharisees, they dared not confess their faith, lest they should be turned out of the synagogue. They loved the praise of men more than the approval of God; and to save themselves from reproach and shame, denied Christ, and lost their only chance of eternal life. To this class the words of Christ were specially applicable: "He that loveth

Chapter 5 - In the Outer Court (3SP 76.1)

his life shall lose it." (3SP 76.1)

The message of the Greeks, indicating as it did the breaking down of the partition wall between Jew and Gentile, brought before Jesus his entire mission, from the time when it was first decided in Heaven that he should come to earth as man's Redeemer, to the death that he knew awaited him in the immediate future. A mysterious cloud seemed to enshroud the Son of God. It was a gloom that was felt by those who were in close contact with him. He sat wrapped in thought. At last the silence was broken by his mournful voice: "Now is my soul troubled; and what shall I say? Father, save me from this hour; but for this cause came I unto this hour." A foreboding of his coming conflict with the powers of darkness, by reason of the position he had voluntarily taken in regard to bearing the guilt of fallen man and taking upon himself the Father's wrath because of sin, caused the spirit of Jesus to faint, and the pallor of death to overspread his countenance. (3SP 76.2)

He remembered the persistence and malice of Satan, who had boldly contended with the angels in Heaven that his sentence was unjust, maintaining that there was no self-denial with God, and that Satan, in struggling to carry out his purposes and have his own way, was only imitating the example of God. If God followed his own will perfectly and continually, why should not the first sons created in his image do so? By this argument Satan deceived many of the holy angels. He complained continually of God's severity, just as children sometimes complain of their parents' severity in restraining them from carrying out plans destructive to the family government. Rather than submit to the will of God he turned from the light of reason, and set himself in opposition to the divine plans. (3SP 77.1)

In the warfare ensuing, Satan for a time seemed to hold the advantage. He could lie; God could not lie. He could move in a thousand crooked and deceiving ways to gain a desired object; God must pursue the straightforward course of truth and righteousness. For a time Satan triumphed in an apparent victory. But God would unmask the enemy and reveal him in his true character. Christ, in taking the nature of man, was divinity clothed in humanity. He came as the light of the world, to shine upon and scatter the thick darkness of Satan's deceptions and reveal his workings to the children of men. Christ practiced the most rigid self-denial in resisting the manifold temptations of the adversary. He conquered Satan in the long fast of the wilderness, and when he came to him as an angel of light, offering the dominion of the world in exchange for his worship; he made sacrifices that will never be required of man, as man can never attain to his exalted character. His whole earthly life was a demonstration of perfect submission to his Father's will. The course of Christ and that of Satan present the complete contrast of the life of an obedient with that of a disloyal son. (3SP 77.2)

The final triumph of Christ over Satan could only be perfected through the death of the former. He thus opened free salvation to man, taking upon himself the stigma of the curse, and, in laying down his precious life, wrested from Satan's hand the last weapon by which he could gain the kingdoms of the world. Man might then be free from the power of evil through his Saviour Jesus Christ. (3SP 78.1)

As the Son of God meditated upon these things, and the whole burden of his mission passed before his mind's eye, he lifted his head and said, "Father, glorify thy name." He thought it not robbery to be equal with God, and called upon him to glorify himself in his Son. A response came from the cloud which had hovered above the head of Jesus: "I have both glorified it, and will glorify it again." (3SP 78.2)

A light darted from the cloud, as the voice was heard, and encircled Christ, as if the arms of Infinite Power were thrown about him like a wall of fire. The people beheld this scene with terror and amazement. No one ventured to utter a word. With silent lips and bated breath they stood with eyes riveted upon Jesus. The testimony of Almighty God having been given, the cloud lifted and scattered in the heavens. The visible communion between the Father and the Son was ended for that time. (3SP 78.3)

The spectators now began to breathe more freely and exchange opinions upon what they had seen and heard. Some solemnly declared their faith in Jesus as the Son of God, while others tried to explain away the remarkable scene they had just witnessed. "The people, therefore, that stood by, and heard it, said that it thundered; others said, An angel spoke to him." But the inquiring Greeks saw the cloud, heard the voice, comprehended its meaning, and discerned Christ indeed; Jesus was revealed to their understanding as the Messiah. (3SP 79.1)

The voice of God had been heard at the

baptism of Jesus at the commencement of his ministry, and again at his transfiguration on the mount; and now, at the close of his ministry, it was heard for the third time, and on this occasion by a larger number of persons and under peculiar circumstances. He had just uttered the most solemn truths regarding the condition of the Jews. He had made his last appeal, and pronounced their doom. The wall of partition between Jew and Gentile was tottering and ready to fall at the death of Christ. (3SP 79.2)

The thoughts of the Saviour now returned from contemplating the past and future. While the people were endeavoring to explain what they had seen and heard according to the impressions made upon their minds, and according to the light they possessed, "Jesus answered and said, This voice came not because of me, but for your sakes." It was the crowning evidence of his Messiahship, the signal of the Father that Jesus had uttered the truth, and was the Son of God. Would the Jews turn from this testimony of high Heaven? They had once asked the Saviour, What sign showest thou that we may see and believe? Innumerable signs had been given all through the ministry of Christ; yet they had closed their eyes and hardened their hearts lest they should be convinced. The crowning miracle of the resurrection of Lazarus did not remove their unbelief, but filled them with increased malice; and now that the Father had spoken, and they could ask for no further sign, their hearts were not softened and they still refused to believe. (3SP 79.3)

Jesus now resumed his discourse where he had left it: "Now is the judgment of this world; now shall the prince of this world be cast out. And I, if I be lifted up from the earth, will draw all men unto me. This he said, signifying what death he should die." In the act of Christ dying for the salvation of man, Heaven was not only made accessible to man, but God and his Son were justified before all Heaven in dealing with the rebellion of Satan, and in his expulsion. The blot which Satan had placed upon Heaven itself was thus to be washed away; and no sin could ever more enter there to all eternity. (3SP 80.1)

The holy angels, and all created intelligences of the worlds where sin had not entered, responded in hallelujahs to the judicial sentence pronounced upon Satan, applauding the act of Christ which removed the mortgage Satan held upon the souls of men. The holy angels, as well as those who are washed by the blood of Christ, are drawn to him by his crowning act of giving his life for the sins of the world. Christ, in being lifted up upon the cross to die, opened the way of life to both Jews and Gentiles, to all nations, tongues, and people. (3SP 80.2)

Alas for the haughty Jews who knew not the day of their visitation! Slowly and regretfully, Christ, with his disciples, left forever the precincts of the temple. (3SP 81.1)

*****

Chapter 6
The Passover Supper

The scribes and priests now counseled together how they might take Jesus without raising a tumult among the people; for many of those who witnessed his mighty works believed him to be the prophet of the Most High, and would have been greatly incensed at any attempt upon his liberty. So the dignitaries decided that open violence would not be good policy, but that treachery must serve their purpose. (3SP 81.2)

Judas, one of the twelve, proposed secretly to betray Jesus into their hands, by leading them to one of the Saviour's resorts for prayer and retirement. In this quiet place they could make sure of their prey, for there would be no multitude to oppose them. Judas, ever greedy for gain, made a contract with the priests and rulers to betray his Master into their hands for thirty pieces of silver. The Lord of life and glory was sold to ignominy and death by one of his disciples for a paltry sum of money. (3SP 81.3)

The heart of Judas had not suddenly grown thus base and corrupt. His love of mammon, like any vice which is left unchecked, had daily grown stronger, until it overbalanced his love for the Saviour, and he had become an idolater. His mind had become debased by covetousness; and a man who is enslaved by avarice is in danger of going to any lengths in crime. (3SP 82.1)

Judas, with the rest of the twelve, had been privileged to listen to the teachings of Jesus, and to witness his acts of sacrifice for the benefit of men. He had noted his forbearance and patience; that when weary, hungry, and pressed upon by the multitude of poor and afflicted, he had pitied their cries and turned none away unrelieved. Judas had seen him perform miracles in giving health to the dying and joy to the despairing. He himself had felt in his person the evidences of his divine power. But when men reject light, and blindly follow their natural inclinations, they are led into darkness, and the plainest facts are unheeded. Judas was naturally avaricious, and he had fostered this evil propensity until it had become the ruling motive of his life. (3SP 82.2)

We look with horror upon the treachery of Judas; but his case represents a large class who file in under the banner of Christ, yet are really his worst enemies. They worship only self and money, and use the name of Christian as a cloak to hide their evil deeds. They sell their integrity for money, and their Saviour for a little worldly advantage. (3SP 82.3)

After Judas had closed the contract by which he agreed to betray his Master into the hands of those who thirsted for his life, he mingled with the other disciples as though innocent of wrong and interested in the work of preparing for the passover. The betrayer thought that his base purposes were hidden from his Master, although every day furnished fresh evidence that the thoughts and intents of all hearts were open unto him. (3SP 83.1)

Jesus met his disciples in the upper chamber, and they soon perceived that something weighed heavily upon his mind. At length, in a voice of touching sadness, he addressed them thus: "With desire I have desired to eat this passover with you before I suffer." He clearly foresaw the events which were to transpire in the near future. His heart was wrung with grief as he contemplated the ingratitude and cruelty of those he had come to save, and saw pictured before him the terrible fate that awaited them in consequence. (3SP 83.2)

The interviews between Jesus and his disciples were usually seasons of calm joy, highly prized by all of them. The passover suppers had been scenes of special interest; but upon this occasion Jesus was troubled in spirit, and his disciples sympathized with his grief although they knew not its cause. This was virtually the last passover that was ever to be celebrated; for type was to meet antitype in the slaying of the Lamb of God for the sins of the world. Christ was soon to receive his full baptism of suffering; but the few quiet hours between him and Gethsemane were to be spent for the benefit of his disciples. (3SP 83.3)

Chapter 6 - The Passover Supper (3SP 86.1)

"And he said unto them, With desire I have desired to eat this passover with you before I suffer; for I say unto you, I will not any more eat thereof, until it be fulfilled in the kingdom of God. And he took the cup, and gave thanks, and said, Take this, and divide it among yourselves; for I say unto you, I will not drink of the fruit of the vine, until the kingdom of God shall come. And he took bread, and gave thanks, and break it, and gave unto them, saying, This is my body which is given for you; this do in remembrance of me. Likewise also the cup after supper, saying, This cup is the New Testament in my blood, which is shed for you." At this last passover the Lord's supper was instituted. (3SP 84.1)

Jesus, by his example, then gave his disciples a lesson of humility. Having girded himself like a servant, he washed the feet of his disciples, conversing with them the while in solemn tenderness. He, the spotless Son of God, stooped to wash the feet of his followers, as one of the last tokens of his love for them. (3SP 84.2)

When he had completed the task, he said unto them, "Know ye what I have done unto you? Ye call me Master and Lord; and ye say well; for so I am. If I then, your Lord and Master, have washed your feet, ye also ought to wash one another's feet; for I have given you an example, that ye should do as I have done unto you." (3SP 84.3)

A contention had arisen among the disciples of Jesus as to who should be most honored in his kingdom; for notwithstanding the express instruction they had so often received to the contrary, they had clung to the idea that Jesus would establish a temporal kingdom in Jerusalem; and the late demonstrations upon his entering the city, and the manner in which he had received them, revived this belief in their minds. Jesus had checked their aspirations for honor, and now strengthened the lesson by an act of humility and love, calculated to impress them with a sense of their obligations to one another, and that instead of quarreling for place, each should count the others better than himself. (3SP 84.4)

As the disciples sat at the passover with their beloved Master, they observed that he still appeared greatly troubled and depressed. A cloud settled over them all, a premonition of some dreadful calamity, the character of which they did not understand. As they ate in silence, Jesus said, "Verily, I say unto you that one of you shall betray me." Amazement and consternation seized them at these words. They could not comprehend how any one of them could deal treacherously by their divine Teacher. For what cause could they betray him, and to whom? Whose heart could give birth to such a design! Surely not one of the favored twelve who had been privileged above all others to hear his teachings and who had experienced his marvelous love, and for whom he had shown such great respect by bringing them into close communion with himself! (3SP 85.1)

As they realized the full import of his words, and remembered how true his sayings were, a sudden fear and self-distrust seized them. They began to examine their own hearts to ascertain if one thought against the Master found lodgment there. With the most painful feelings, one after another inquired, "Lord, is it I?" But Judas sat silent. John, in deep distress, inquired at last, Who is it, Lord? and Jesus answered, "He that dippeth his hand with me in the dish, the same shall betray me. The Son of man goeth as it is written of him, but woe unto that man by whom the Son of man is betrayed; it had been good for that man if he had not been born." The disciples had searched one another's faces closely as they asked, "Lord, is it I?" and now the silence of Judas drew all eyes to himself. Amid the confusion of questions and the expressions of astonishment, Judas had not heard the words of Jesus in answer to John's question. But now, to escape the searching scrutiny of the disciples, he asked as they had done, "Master, is it I?" Jesus replied with solemn accents, "Thou hast said." Confused and overcome by the unexpected discovery of his crime, Judas hastily rose to leave the room; but as he went out, Jesus said, "What thou doest, do quickly." (3SP 85.2)

There was a touching forbearance manifested in the dealing of Jesus with Judas. It evinced an infinite mercy, giving him one more chance of repentance, by showing him that all his thoughts and purposes were fully known to the Son of God. He deigned to give one final, convincing proof of his divinity to Judas before the consummation of his treachery, that he might turn from his purpose before repentance was too late. But Judas, although surprised and alarmed, was not moved to repentance. He only became more firmly settled in his plan as the discovery of his guilt was made apparent. He went forth and proceeded to carry out the work he had engaged to do. (3SP 86.1)

The purpose of the Saviour in pronouncing

the woe upon Judas was twofold: First, to give the false disciple a last opportunity to save himself from the betrayer's doom; and, secondly, to give the disciples a crowning evidence of his Messiahship, in revealing the hidden purpose of Judas. Said Jesus: "I speak not of you all; I know whom I have chosen; but that the scripture may be fulfilled, He that eateth bread with me hath lifted up his heel against me. Now I tell you before it come, that when it is come to pass, ye may believe that I am he." (3SP 87.1)

Had Jesus remained silent, in apparent ignorance of that which was to come upon him, an impression might have been left on the minds of his disciples that their Master had not divine foresight, and had been deceived, surprised and betrayed into the hands of a murderous mob. A year before, Jesus had told the disciples that he had chosen twelve, but that one was a devil; and now his words to Judas on the occasion of the passover, showing that this treachery was fully known to his Master, would strengthen the faith of his true followers during his humiliation. And when Judas should have come to his dreadful end, they would remember the woe which Jesus had pronounced upon the betrayer. (3SP 87.2)

The withdrawal of Judas was a relief to all present. The Saviour's face lighted immediately, and the oppressive shadow was lifted from the disciples, as they saw the peace of Heaven return to the pale, worn countenance of their Lord. Jesus had much to say to his beloved disciples that he did not wish to say in the presence of the multitude, who could not understand the sacred truths he was about to unfold. Even the disciples could not fully understand them till after the resurrection should have taken place. (3SP 87.3)

Looking upon his faithful followers, Jesus said, "Now is the Son of man glorified, and God is glorified in him. If God be glorified in him, God shall also glorify him in himself, and shall straightway glorify him." He then informed them of his approaching separation from them. The ardent Peter could not rest while the matter remained in uncertainty. He inquired, "Lord, whither goest thou?" Jesus answered, "Whither I go, thou canst not follow me now; but thou shalt follow me afterward." But Peter's interest was intensely roused, and he urged Jesus to explain his full meaning, saying, "Lord, why cannot I follow thee now? I will lay down my life for thy sake." Jesus answered sorrowfully, "Wilt thou lay down thy life for my sake? Verily, verily, I say unto thee, The cock shall not crow till thou hast denied me thrice." Then, looking with pitying love upon his little flock, so soon to be left without a shepherd, he sought to draw their minds from the perplexity into which his statements had thrown them, and said tenderly, "Let not your heart be troubled; ye believe in God, believe also in me. In my Father's house are many mansions; if it were not so I would have told you. I go to prepare a place for you. And if I go and prepare a place for you, I will come again and receive you unto myself; that where I am, there ye may be also. And whither I go ye know, and the way ye know." (3SP 88.1)

With the deepest interest Jesus poured forth the burden of his soul in words of comfort, of counsel and prayer, which would ever remain imprinted on the minds and hearts of his disciples. These words from the lips of the Saviour, traced by the inspired John in chapters fifteen, sixteen, and seventeen, were repeated again and again by the disciples to stay their sinking hearts in their great disappointment and trial. Not until after the resurrection, however, were the words spoken upon this memorable occasion fully understood and appreciated. But the truths uttered by the Redeemer in that upper chamber have spread from the testimony of the disciples over all lands, and will live through all ages to comfort the hearts of the desponding, and give peace and hope to thousands who believe. (3SP 88.2)

Jesus with his disciples now left the upper chamber, and crossed the brook Kedron. Sorrow and anguish again pressed heavily upon his heart. With touching sadness he addressed his companions: "All ye shall be offended because of me this night; for it is written, I will smite the Shepherd, and the sheep shall be scattered. But after that I am risen I will go before you into Galilee." Peter, again anxious to assure his Master of his fidelity, said, "Although all shall be offended, yet will not I." Jesus, reproving his confidence as before, said, "Verily, I say unto thee, that this day, even in this night, before the cock crow twice, thou shalt deny me thrice." But Peter only "spake the more vehemently, If I should die with thee I will not deny thee in any wise. Likewise also said they all." (3SP 89.1)

Jesus now repaired with his disciples to the garden of Gethsemane, at the foot of Mount Olivet, a retired place which he had often visited for seasons of communion with his Father. (3SP 89.2)

It was night; but the moon was shining

Chapter 6 - The Passover Supper (3SP 92.1)

bright and revealed to him a flourishing grapevine. Drawing the attention of the disciples to it, he said, "I am the true vine, and my Father is the husbandman. Every branch in me that beareth not fruit he taketh away; and every branch that beareth fruit, he purgeth it, that it may bring forth more fruit." (3SP 89.3)

The Jewish nation was a fruitless branch, and was therefore to be separated from the living vine, which was Christ Jesus. The Gentiles were to be engrafted upon the stalk, to become a living branch, partaker of the life that nourished the true vine. This branch was to be pruned that it might be fruitful. In view of his separation from his disciples, Jesus now exhorted them to connect themselves firmly to him by faith, that they might become a part of the living vine, and bear a rich harvest of fruit. "Abide in me, and I in you. As the branch cannot bear fruit of itself, except it abide in the vine; no more can ye, except ye abide in me. I am the vine, ye are the branches. He that abideth in me, and I in him, the same bringeth forth much fruit; for without me ye can do nothing." (3SP 90.1)

When the sinner has repented of his sins, and is united with Christ, as the branch is engrafted in the vine, the nature of the man is changed, and he is a partaker of the divine nature. He loves the things that Christ loves, and hates that which he hates. His desires are in harmony with the will of God. He treasures up the words of Christ, and they abide in him. The life-giving principle of the Saviour is communicated to the Christian. Just so the little scion, leafless and apparently lifeless, is engrafted into the living vine, and, fiber by fiber, vein by vein, drinks life and strength from it, till it becomes a flourishing branch of the parent stalk. (3SP 90.2)

He still impressed upon them the importance of carrying forward the work which he had begun, and bearing fruit to the glory of God: "Ye have not chosen me, but I have chosen you, and ordained you, that ye should go and bring forth fruit, and that your fruit should remain; that whatsoever ye shall ask of the Father in my name, he may give it you." The disciples were the chosen depositaries of the truth of God. They were witnesses of the Father's acknowledgement of Jesus as the Son of God. They had beheld his miracles, heard his teachings, and it was theirs to give the message of salvation to the world, that through their evidence men might lay hold of Christ by living faith. Thus would the disciples bring forth fruit to the glory of God. (3SP 91.1)

Jesus assured his disciples that he would in no case forsake them, but would be clothed with power, and would become their Advocate at the right hand of the Father, to present the petitions they might ask in the name of his Son. The disciples did not then fully comprehend the words of their Master, but later in their religious experience they cherished the precious promise, and presented their prayers to the Father in the name of Jesus. (3SP 91.2)

Jesus warned his disciples not to expect the commendation of the world. Said he, "If the world hate you, ye know that it hated me before it hated you. If ye were of the world, the world would love his own; but because ye are not of the world, but I have chosen you out of the world, therefore the world hateth you." Those who are of the same spirit with the world receive its smiles and approbation; but the humble disciples of Jesus were to suffer scorn and persecution. Jesus declared that they should be brought before kings and rulers for his name's sake, and whosoever should destroy their lives would be so deceived by Satan as to think they were doing God service. Every indignity and cruelty that the ingenuity of man could devise would be visited upon the followers of Christ. But in all their trials they were to remember that their Master had endured like reproach and suffering. They were to remember his words: "The servant is not greater than his Lord. If they have persecuted me, they will also persecute you; if they have kept my saying, they will keep yours also. But all these things will they do unto you for my name's sake, because they know not Him that sent me." (3SP 91.3)

The disciples were to go on valiantly in the footsteps of the Saviour, keeping the prize of eternal life in view, and winning souls to Christ. Even the opposition they were to meet would develop staunch elements of character and shining virtues. Faith, patience, and trust in God, are the perfect fruit that blossoms and matures best in the shadow of adversity. (3SP 92.1)

Jesus carefully opened before his disciples the events which would follow his death, that when persecution should overtake them they might be prepared to endure it, and not be tempted to apostatize from their faith to avert suffering and dishonor. He led them gently on to understand the great subjects which they were to deliver to the world. He impressed upon them

Chapter 6 - The Passover Supper (**3SP 92.2**)

the importance of their position as those who had witnessed the wonderful manifestations of God to his Son, who had beheld the miracles of Christ, and received his words of wisdom. Said he, "Ye also shall bear witness, because ye have been with me from the beginning." The history of those disciples, and the evidence which they were to record, were to be the study of thinking minds through all ages. (**3SP 92.2**)

Jesus plainly stated to the disciples that he had left the presence of his Father to come unto the world, and that he was now about to leave the world and return to his Father; but he refrained from crowding their minds and confusing their understanding. Said he, "I have many things to say unto you; but ye cannot bear them now." Jesus knew they were not strong enough to hear all the wonderful truths relative to his humiliation and death. After his resurrection they would be better able to understand and appreciate them. (**3SP 93.1**)

Jesus now had but a short time in which to comfort and instruct his little band of followers. His farewell counsel was rich in sympathy and truth. Exceeding precious to his disciples were those last moments passed with their beloved Master. Like a consecrated high priest he now poured forth the burden of his soul to his Father in a petition for his church such as the angels had never before heard. This prayer was deep and full, broad as the earth, and reaching high Heaven. With his human arm he encircled the children of Adam in a firm embrace; and with his strong divine arm he grasped the throne of the Infinite, thus uniting earth to Heaven, and finite man to the infinite God. (**3SP 93.2**)

Chapter 7
In the Garden

The Redeemer, in company with his disciples, slowly made his way to the garden of Gethsemane. The passover moon, broad and full, shone from a cloudless sky. The city of pilgrim's tents was hushed into silence. (3SP 94.1)

Jesus had been earnestly conversing with and instructing his disciples; but as he neared Gethsemane he became strangely silent. His disciples were perplexed, and anxiously regarded his countenance, hoping there to read an explanation of the change that had come over their Master. They had frequently seen him depressed, but never before so utterly sad and silent. As he proceeded, this strange sadness increased; yet they dared not question him as to the cause. His form swayed as if he was about to fall, His disciples looked anxiously for his usual place of retirement, that their Master might rest. (3SP 94.2)

Upon entering the garden he said to his companions, "Sit ye here, while I go and pray yonder." Selecting Peter, James, and John to accompany him, he proceeded farther into the recesses of the garden. He had been accustomed to brace his spirit for trial and duty by fervent prayer in this retreat, and had frequently spent the entire night thus. On these occasions his disciples, after a little season of watching and prayer, would sleep undisturbed at a little distance from their Master until he awoke them in the morning to go forth and labor anew. So. this act of Jesus called forth no remark from his companions. (3SP 94.3)

Every step that the Saviour now took was with labored effort. He groaned aloud as though suffering under the pressure of a terrible burden; yet he refrained from startling his three chosen disciples by a full explanation of the agony which he was to suffer. Twice his companions prevented him from falling to the ground. Jesus felt that he must be still more alone, and he said to the favored three, "My soul is exceeding sorrowful, even unto death; tarry ye here, and watch with me." His disciples had never before heard him utter such mournful tones. His frame was convulsed with anguish, and his pale countenance expressed a sorrow past all description. (3SP 95.1)

He went a short distance from his disciples–not so far but that they could both see and hear him–and fell prostrate with his face upon the cold ground. He was overpowered by a terrible fear that God was removing his presence from him. He felt himself being separated from his Father by a gulf of sin, so broad, so black and deep that his spirit shuddered before it. He clung convulsively to the cold, unfeeling ground as if to prevent himself from being drawn still farther from God. The chilling dews of night fell upon his prostrate form, but the Redeemer heeded it not. From his pale, convulsed lips wailed the bitter cry, "O my Father, if it be possible, let this cup pass from me; nevertheless not as I will, but as thou wilt." (3SP 95.2)

It was not a dread of the physical suffering he was soon to endure that brought this agony upon the Son of God. He was enduring the penalty of man's transgression, and shuddering beneath the Father's frown. He must not call his divinity to his aid, but, as a man, he must bear the consequences of man's sin and the Creator's displeasure toward his disobedient subjects. As he felt his unity with the Father broken up, he feared that his human nature would be unable to endure the coming conflict with the prince of the power of darkness; and in that case the human race would be irrecoverably lost, Satan would be victor, and the earth would be his kingdom. The sins of the world weighed heavily upon the Saviour and bowed him to the earth; and the Father's anger in consequence of that sin seemed crushing out his life. (3SP 95.3)

In the conflict of Christ with Satan in the wilderness of temptation the destiny of the human race was at stake. But Christ was conqueror, and the tempter left him for a season. He had now returned for the last fearful conflict. Satan had been preparing for this final trial

Chapter 7 - In the Garden (3SP 96.1)

during the three years of Christ's ministry. Everything was at stake with him. If he failed here his hope of mastery was lost; the kingdoms of the earth would finally become Christ's who would "bind the strong man" (Satan), and cast him out. (3SP 96.1)

During this scene of the Saviour's anguish, the disciples were at first much troubled to see their Master, usually so calm and dignified, wrestling with a sorrow that exceeded all utterance; but they were tired, and finally dropped asleep, leaving him to agonize alone. At the end of an hour, Jesus, feeling the need of human sympathy, rose with painful effort and staggered to the place where he had left his companions. But no sympathizing countenance greeted him after his long struggle; the disciples were fast asleep. Ah! if they had realized that this was their last night with their beloved Master while he lived a man upon earth, if they had known what the morrow would bring him, they would hardly have yielded to the power of slumber. (3SP 96.2)

The voice of Jesus partially aroused them. They discerned his form bending over them, his expression and attitude indicating extreme exhaustion. They scarcely recognized in his changed countenance the usually serene face of their Master. Singling out Simon Peter, he addressed him: "Simon, sleepest thou? couldest not thou watch one hour?" Oh! Simon, where is now thy boasted devotion? Thou, who didst but lately declare thou couldst go with thy Lord to prison or to death, hast left him in the hour of his agony and temptation, and sought repose in sleep! (3SP 97.1)

John, the loving disciple who had leaned on the breast of Jesus, was also sleeping. Surely, the love of John for his Master should have kept him awake. His earnest prayers should have mingled with those of his loved Saviour in the time of his supreme sorrow. The self-sacrificing Redeemer had passed entire nights in the cold mountains or in the groves, praying for his disciples, that their faith might not fail them in the hour of their temptation. Should Jesus now put to James and John the question he had once asked them: "Can ye drink of the cup that I drink of? and be baptized with the baptism that I am baptized with?" they would not have ventured to answer, "We are able." (3SP 97.2)

The evidence of the weakness of his disciples excited the pity and sympathy of the Son of God. He questioned their strength to endure the test they must undergo in witnessing his betrayal and death. He did not sternly upbraid them for their weakness, but, in view of their coming trial, exhorted them: "Watch and pray, that ye enter not into temptation." Then, his spirit moving in sympathy with their frailty, he framed an excuse for their failure in duty toward him: "The spirit indeed is willing, but the flesh is weak." (3SP 98.1)

Again the Son of God was seized with superhuman agony, and, fainting and exhausted, staggered back to the place of his former struggle. Again he was prostrated to the earth. His suffering was even greater than before. The cypress and palm trees were the silent witnesses of his anguish. From their leafy branches dropped heavy dew upon his stricken form, as if nature wept over its Author wrestling alone with the powers of darkness. (3SP 98.2)

A few hours before, Jesus had stood like a mighty cedar, withstanding the storm of opposition that spent its fury upon him. Stubborn wills, and hearts filled with malice and subtlety strove in vain to confuse and overpower him. He stood forth in divine majesty as the Son of God. But now he was like a bruised reed beaten and bent by the angry storm. A short time before, he had poured out his soul to his disciples in noble utterances, claiming unity with the Father, and giving his elect church into his arms in the language of one who had divine authority. Now his voice uttered suppressed wails of anguish, and he clung to the cold ground as if for relief. (3SP 98.3)

The words of the Saviour were borne to the ears of the drowsy disciples: "O my Father, if this cup may not pass away from me, except I drink it, thy will be done." The anguish of God's dear Son forced drops of blood from his pores. Again he staggered to his feet, his human heart yearning for the sympathy of his companions, and repaired to where his disciples were sleeping. His presence roused them, and they looked upon his face with fear, for it was stained with blood, and expressed an agony of mind which was to them unaccountable. (3SP 99.1)

He did not again address them, but, turning away, sought again his retreat and fell prostrate, overcome by the horror of a great darkness. The humanity of the Son of God trembled in that trying hour. The awful moment had arrived which was to decide the destiny of the world. The heavenly hosts waited the issue with intense interest. The fate of humanity trembled in the balance. The Son of God might even then refuse to drink the cup apportioned to guilty men. He might wipe the bloody sweat from his brow, and leave men to perish in their iniquity. Will the Son of the Infinite God drink the bitter potion of humiliation and agony? Will the innocent suffer the consequence of God's curse, to save the guilty? The words fall tremblingly from the pale lips of Jesus: "O my Father, if this cup may not pass away from me, except I drink it, thy will be done." (3SP 99.2)

Three times has he uttered that prayer. Three times has humanity shrunk from the last crowning sacrifice. But now the history of the human race comes up before the world's Redeemer. He sees that the transgressors of the law, if left to themselves, must perish under the Father's displeasure. He sees the power of sin, and the utter helplessness of man to save himself. The woes and lamentations of a doomed world arise before him. He beholds its impending fate, and his decision is made. He will save man at any cost to himself. He accepts his baptism of blood, that perishing millions through him may gain everlasting life. He left the courts of Heaven, where all was purity, happiness, and glory, to save the one lost sheep, the one world that had fallen by transgression, and he will not turn from the mission he had chosen. He will reach to the very depths of misery to rescue a lost and ruined race. (3SP 99.3)

Having made the decision and reached the final crisis, he fell in a dying condition to the earth from which he had partially risen. Where now were his disciples, to place their hands tenderly beneath the head of their fainting Master, and bathe that brow, marred indeed more than the sons of men? The Saviour trod the winepress alone, and of all the people there was none with him. And yet he was not alone. He had said, "I and my Father are one." God suffered with his Son. Man cannot comprehend the sacrifice made by the infinite God in giving up his Son to reproach, agony, and death. This is the evidence of the Father's boundless love to man. (3SP 100.1)

The angels who did Christ's will in Heaven were anxious to comfort him; but it was beyond their power to alleviate his sorrow. They had never felt the sins of a ruined world, and they beheld with astonishment the object of their adoration subject to a grief beyond all expression. Though the disciples had failed to sympathize with their Lord in the trying hour of his conflict, all Heaven was full of sympathy and waiting the result with painful interest. When it was finally determined, an angel was sent from the throne of God to minister unto the stricken Redeemer. (3SP 100.2)

The disciples were suddenly aroused from their slumber by a bright light shining upon and around the Son of God. They started up in amazement, and beheld a heavenly being, clothed in garments of light, bending over their prostrate Master. With his right hand he lifted the head of the divine sufferer upon his bosom, and with his left hand he pointed toward Heaven. His voice was like the sweetest music, as he uttered soothing words presenting to the mind of Christ the grand results of the victory he had gained over the strong and wily foe. Christ was victor over Satan; and, as the result of his triumph, millions were to be victors with him in his glorified kingdom. (3SP 101.1)

Well was it for the children of men that the angel's errand was not to notify the Saviour that his thrice-repeated prayer, Let this cup pass from me, had been granted. Then indeed might the disciples have slept on, locked in the slumber of hopeless despair. But the angel was sent from Heaven to support the Redeemer in drinking the cup that was presented him. The language of his prayer was now changed; in the spirit of submission he prayed: "If this cup may not pass away from me, except I drink it, thy will be done." A heavenly serenity now rested upon the Saviour's pale and blood-stained face. (3SP 101.2)

The glorious vision of the angel dazzled the eyes of the disciples. They remembered the mount of transfiguration, the glory that encircled Jesus in the temple, and the voice of God issuing from the cloud. They saw the same glory here revealed, and had no farther fear for their Master, since God had taken him in charge and an angel was present to protect him from his foes. They were weary and heavy with sleep, and again they dropped into unconsciousness. (3SP 101.3)

The Saviour of the world arose and sought his disciples, and, for the third time, found them fast asleep. He looked sorrowfully upon them. His words, however, aroused them: "Sleep on now, and take your rest; behold, the hour is at hand, and the Son of man is betrayed into the hands of sinners." (3SP 102.1)

Even while these words were upon his lips,

Chapter 7 - In the Garden (3SP 102.2)

the footsteps of the mob that was in search of him were heard. Judas took the lead and was closely followed by the high priest. Jesus turned to his disciples, as his enemies approached, and said, "Rise, let us be going; behold, he is at hand that doth betray me." The countenance of the Saviour wore an expression of calm dignity; no traces of his recent agony were visible as he stepped forth to meet his betrayer. (3SP 102.2)

He stood in advance of his disciples, and inquired, "Whom seek ye?" They answered, "Jesus of Nazareth." Jesus replied, "I am he." As these words were uttered, the mob staggered back; and the priests, elders, soldiers, and even Judas, dropped powerless to the ground. This gave Jesus ample opportunity to escape from them if he had chosen to do so. But he stood as one glorified amid that coarse and hardened band. When Jesus answered, "I am he," the angel who had lately ministered unto him moved between him and the murderous mob, who saw a divine light illuminating the Saviour's face, and a dove-like form overshadowing him. Their wicked hearts were filled with terror. They could not for a moment stand upon their feet in the presence of this divine glory, and they fell as dead men to the ground. (3SP 102.3)

The angel withdrew; the light faded away; Jesus was left standing, calm and self-possessed, with the bright beams of the moon upon his pale face, and still surrounded by prostrate, helpless men, while the disciples were too much amazed to utter a word. When the angel departed, the Roman soldiers started to their feet, and, with the priests and Judas, gathered about Christ as though ashamed of their weakness, and fearful that he would yet escape from their hands. Again the question was asked by the Redeemer, "Whom seek ye?" Again they answered, "Jesus of Nazareth." The Saviour then said, "I have told you that I am he. If, therefore, ye seek me, let these go their way"–pointing to the disciples. In this hour of humiliation Christ's thoughts were not for himself, but for his beloved disciples. He wished to save them from any farther trial of their strength. (3SP 103.1)

Judas, the betrayer, did not forget his part, but came close to Jesus, and took his hand as a familiar friend, and bestowed upon him the traitor's kiss. Jesus said to him, "Friend, wherefore art thou come?" His voice trembled with sorrow as he addressed the deluded Judas: "Betrayest thou the Son of man with a kiss?" This most touching appeal should have roused the conscience of the betrayer, and touched his stubborn heart; but honor, fidelity, and human tenderness had utterly forsaken him. He stood bold and defiant, showing no disposition to relent. He had given himself up to the control of Satan, and he had no power to resist him. Jesus did not reject the traitor's kiss. In this he gives us an example of forbearance, love, and pity, that is without a parallel. (3SP 103.2)

Though the murderous throng were surprised and awed by what they had seen and felt, their assurance and hardihood returned as they saw the boldness of Judas in touching the person of Him whom they had so recently seen glorified. They now laid violent hands upon Jesus, and proceeded to bind those precious hands that had ever been employed in doing good. (3SP 104.1)

When the disciples saw that band of strong men lying prostrate and helpless on the ground, they thought surely their Master would not suffer himself to be taken; for the same power that prostrated that hireling mob could cause them to remain in a state of helplessness until Jesus and his companions should pass unharmed beyond their reach. They were disappointed and indignant as they saw the cords brought forward to bind the hands of Him whom they loved. Peter in his vehement anger rashly cut off, with his sword, an ear of the servant of the high priest. (3SP 104.2)

When Jesus saw what Peter had done, he released his hands, though held firmly by the Roman soldiers, and saying, "Suffer ye thus far," he touched the wounded ear, and it was instantly made whole. He then said to Peter, "Put up again thy sword into his place; for all they that take the sword shall perish with the sword. Thinkest thou that I cannot now pray to my Father, and he shall presently give me more than twelve legions of angels? But how then shall the Scriptures be fulfilled, that thus it must be?" "The cup which my Father hath given me, shall I not drink it?" Jesus then turned to the chief priest, and captains of the temple, who helped compose that murderous throng, "and said, are ye come out as against a thief with swords and with staves to take me? I was daily with you in the temple teaching, and ye took me not; but the Scriptures must be fulfilled." (3SP 104.3)

When the disciples saw that Jesus did not deliver himself from his enemies, but permitted himself to be taken and bound, they were offended that he should suffer this humiliation to

Chapter 7 - In the Garden (3SP 106.1)

himself and them. They had just witnessed an exhibition of his power in prostrating to the ground those who came to take him, and in healing the servant's ear, which Peter had cut off, and they knew that if he chose he could deliver himself from the murderous mob. They blamed him for not doing so, and mortified and terror-stricken by his unaccountable conduct they forsook him and fled. Christ had foreseen this desertion, and in the upper chamber had forewarned them of the course which they would take at this time, saying, "Behold, the hour cometh, yea, is now come, that ye shall be scattered every man to his own, and shall leave me alone; and yet I am not alone, because the Father is with me." (3SP 105.1)

Judas was himself surprised that Jesus should deliver himself into the hands of those who sought to destroy him. He had frequently known the Saviour's enemies to lay plans to take him, but Jesus would quietly depart and defeat their murderous designs. Now the betrayer saw with astonishment that his Master suffered himself to be bound and led away. The false disciple flattered himself, however, that Jesus had only permitted himself to be taken that he might manifest his power by delivering himself from his enemies in a miraculous manner. He knew that nothing else could free him from that armed band. For three years the Jews had been secretly planning to take him, and now that they had accomplished this they would not let him escape death, if they could prevent it. (3SP 105.2)

Jesus was hurried off by the hooting mob. He moved painfully, for his hands were tightly bound and he was closely guarded. He was first conducted to the house of Annas, the father-in-law of the high priest, the man whose counsel was sought and carried out by the Jewish people as the voice of God. Annas craved the fearful satisfaction of first seeing Jesus of Nazareth a bound captive. Having once been shown to Annas, he was hurried away; for the priests and rulers had decided that if they once had possession of his person, there should be no delays in his trial and condemnation. This was because they feared that the people, remembering his acts of charity and mercy among them, would rescue him out of their hands. (3SP 106.1)

Chapter 8
In the Judgment Hall

The armed band, with their prisoner, threaded the dark and narrow streets, guided by torches and lanterns, for it was yet early morning and very dark. Amid insult and mockery, the Saviour was hurried to the palace of the officiating high priest, Caiaphas. Here he was coarsely accused by his persecutors, and sneeringly questioned by the priest, and reviled by the whole assembly. But while enduring this mockery of an examination, the Saviour's heart was pierced by a keener pang than it was in the power of his enemies to inflict. It was when he heard his beloved disciple deny him with cursing and swearing. (3SP 107.1)

After deserting their Master in the garden, two of the disciples regained their presence of mind and ventured to follow, at a distance, the mob that had Jesus in charge. These disciples were Peter and John. The priest recognized John as a well-known disciple of Jesus, and admitted him to the hall where the Saviour was being questioned because he hoped that John, while witnessing the humiliation of his leader, would become affected with the same spirit that actuated his enemies, and scorn the idea of one who could be subjected to such indignities, being the Son of God. John, having secured himself an entrance, spoke in behalf of his companion, Peter, and gained the same favor for him. (3SP 107.2)

The coldest hour of the night was that preceding the dawn, and a fire had been lighted in the hall. Around this a company were gathered; and Peter presumptuously took his place with the rest by the fire, and stood warming himself. He did not wish to be recognized as one of the disciples of Jesus, and he thought by mingling carelessly with the people he would be taken for one of those who had brought Jesus to the hall. (3SP 107.3)

But, as the light flashed upon Peter's countenance, the woman who kept the door cast a searching glance upon him; she had noticed that he came in with John, and conjectured that he was one of Christ's followers. She interrogated him in a taunting manner: "Art not thou also one of this man's disciples?" Peter was startled and confused; the eyes of the company instantly fastened upon him. He pretended not to understand her, but she was persistent, and said to those around her that this man was with Jesus. Peter, feeling compelled to answer, said angrily, "Woman, I know him not." This was the first denial, and immediately the cock crew. O Peter! So soon ashamed of thy Master! So soon to cowardly deny thy Lord! The Saviour is dishonored and deserted in his humiliation by one of his most zealous disciples. (3SP 108.1)

In the first place Peter had not designed that his real character should be known; and, in assuming an air of indifference, he placed himself on the enemy's ground, and became an easy subject to Satan's temptation. He appeared to be disinterested in the trial of his Master, while in reality his heart was wrung with sorrow as he heard the cruel taunts and saw the mockery and abuse he was suffering. In addition to this he was surprised and angry that Jesus should humiliate himself and his followers by passively submitting to such treatment. Under these conflicting emotions, it was difficult to preserve his character of indifference. His appearance was unnatural, as he endeavored to join with the persecutors of Jesus in their untimely jests, in order to cover his true feelings. (3SP 108.2)

He was acting a lie, and while trying to talk unconcernedly he could not restrain expressions of indignation at the abuse heaped upon his Master. Accordingly attention was called to him the second time, and he was again charged with being a follower of Jesus. He now denied the accusation with an oath. The cock crew the second time; but Peter heard it not, for he was now thoroughly intent upon carrying out the character which he had assumed. One of the servants of the high priest, being a near kinsman to the man whose ear the disciple had cut off, asked him, "Did not I see thee in the garden with him?" "Surely thou art one of them; for thou art a Galilean, and thy speech agreeth thereto." (3SP 109.1)

At this, Peter flew into a rage, and to fully deceive his questioners, and to justify his assumed character, he denied his Master with cursing and swearing. And immediately the cock crew the third time. Peter heard it then; and while the degrading oaths were fresh upon his lips, and the shrill crowing of the cock was yet ringing in his ears, the Saviour turned his face from the frowning judges, and looked full upon his poor disciple. At the same time Peter's eyes were involuntarily fixed upon his Master. He read in that gentle countenance deep pity and sorrow; but there was no anger there. (3SP 109.2)

Peter was conscience-smitten; his memory was aroused; he recalled to mind his promise of a few short hours before, that he would go to prison or to death for his Lord. He remembered his grief when the Saviour told him in the upper chamber that he would deny his Master thrice that same night. Peter had just declared that he knew not Jesus, but he now realized with bitter grief how well his Lord knew him, and how accurately he had read his heart, the falseness of which was unknown even to himself. He groaned in spirit as he realized that not only was his Master enduring the bitterest humiliation at the hands of his enemies, but he was suffering additional dishonor at the hands of one of his disciples, who had forsaken and refused to acknowledge him in the hour of his trial. (3SP 109.3)

The look of Christ conveyed volumes to the repentant Peter. He read in that glance sorrow, love, and pardon. A tide of memories rushed over him. He remembered the Saviour's tender mercy, his kindness and long-suffering, the patience with which he dealt with his followers. He remembered the caution of Jesus to him: "Simon, behold, Satan hath desired to have you, that he may sift you as wheat. But I have prayed for thee, that thy faith fail not." He reflected with horror upon his base ingratitude, his falsehood and perjury. He looked once more at his Master, and saw a sacrilegious hand raised to smite him in the face. Unable to longer endure the scene, he rushed, heart-broken, from the hall. (3SP 110.1)

He pressed on in solitude and darkness, he knew and cared not whither. At last he found himself in the garden of Gethsemane, where a short time before he had slept while the Saviour wrestled with the powers of darkness. The suffering face of his Lord, stained with bloody sweat and convulsed with anguish, rose before him. He remembered with bitter remorse that Jesus had wept and agonized in prayer alone. While those who should have sustained him in that trying hour were sleeping. He remembered his solemn charge: "Watch and pray, that ye enter not into temptation." The scene of a few short hours before came vividly to his mind. He witnessed again the tears and groans of Jesus. It was torture to his bleeding heart to know that he had added the heaviest burden to the Saviour's humiliation and grief. He fell prostrate upon the very spot where his Lord had sunk beneath his inexpressible weight of woe. (3SP 110.2)

Peter's first mistake was in sleeping when Christ had bidden him to watch and pray. At the most critical moment, when the Son of God was in need of his sympathy and heartfelt prayers, he was incapable of giving them to him. The disciples lost much by sleeping; Jesus designed to fortify them for the severe test of faith to which they were to be subjected. If they had spent that mournful period in the garden in watching with the dear Saviour, and in prayer to God, Peter would not have been left to depend upon his own feeble strength; he would not have denied his Lord. (3SP 111.1)

This important night-watch should have been spent by the disciples in noble mental struggles and prayers, which would have brought them strength to witness the terrible agony of the Son of God. It would have prepared them, as they should behold his sufferings upon the cross, to understand in some degree the nature of the overpowering anguish which he endured. They would then have been better able to recall the words he had spoken to them in reference to his sufferings, death, and resurrection; and amid the gloom of that trying hour some rays of hope would have lighted up the darkness, and sustained their faith. Christ had told them before that these things would take place. He knew the power which the prince of darkness would use to paralyze the senses of his disciples when they should be watching and praying. (3SP 111.2)

The disciple John, upon entering the judgment hall, did not try to conceal the fact that he was one of the followers of Jesus. He did not mingle with the rough company that were insulting and mocking his Master. He was not questioned, for he did not assume a false character and thus lay himself liable to suspicion. He sought a retired corner secure from observation of the mob, but as near Jesus as it was possible for him to be. In this place he could hear and see all that transpired at the trial of his Lord. (3SP 112.1)

If Peter had been called to fight for his Master, he would have proved a bold and courageous soldier; but he became a coward when the finger of scorn was pointed at him. Many who do not hesitate to engage in active warfare for the Lord, are driven to deny their faith through the ridicule of their enemies. They place themselves in the way of temptation by associating with those whom they should avoid. They thus invite the enemy to tempt them, and are led to do and say that which they would never have been guilty of under other circumstances. The disciple of Christ, who, in our day, disguises his faith through dread of suffering or reproach, denies his Lord as virtually as did Peter in the judgment hall. There are always those who boast of their freedom of thought and action, and laugh at the scruples of the conscientious who fear to do wrong. Yet if those righteous persons are persuaded to yield their faith, they are despised by the very ones who were Satan's agents to tempt them to their ruin. (3SP 112.2)

Peter, however, as well as John, witnessed much of the mock trial of Jesus. It was necessary that there should be a pretense of legal trial; but great secrecy was maintained lest the people should obtain information of what was being done, and come forward with their testimony in vindication of Jesus, bringing to light the mighty works which he had done. This would bring the indignation of the people upon the Sanhedrim; their acts would be condemned and brought to naught; and Jesus would be liberated and receive new honor at the hands of the people. (3SP 113.1)

While the members of the Sanhedrim council were being called together, Annas and Caiaphas the priest questioned Jesus, with the purpose of provoking him to make some statement which they could use to his disadvantage. They brought two charges against him, by one or both of which they meant to effect his condemnation. One was that he was a disturber of the peace, the leader of a rebellion. If this charge could be verified he would be condemned by the Roman authorities. The other charge was that he was a blasphemer. This, if proved true, would secure his condemnation among the Jews. (3SP 113.2)

The high priest questioned Jesus concerning his doctrine, and the disciples who believed in him. Jesus answered briefly: "I spake openly to the world; I ever taught in the synagogue, and in the temple, whither the Jews always resort; and in secret have I said nothing. Why askest thou me? ask them which heard me, what I have said unto them; behold, they know what I said." (3SP 113.3)

Jesus was well aware that his questioner designed to draw some statement from him which should awaken the fears of the Roman authorities that he was seeking to establish a secret society with the purpose of finally setting up a new kingdom. He therefore plainly stated to Annas that he had no secrets in regard to his purpose or doctrines. Turning upon his interrogator he said with startling emphasis, "Why askest thou me?" Had not the priests and rulers set spies to watch his movements and report his every word? Had they not been present at every gathering of the people, and carried information of all his sayings and doings on these occasions to the priests? "Ask them that heard me, what I have said," replied Jesus; and his words were a rebuke to Annas, who had hunted him for months, striving to entrap him, and to bring him before a secret tribunal, in which the people could have no voice, that he might obtain by perjury what it was impossible to gain by fair means. (3SP 114.1)

The words of Jesus were so close and pointed that the high priest felt that his very soul was being read by his prisoner. Though Annas was filled with hatred against Jesus at these words, he disguised it until a more fitting opportunity presented itself of giving vent to his malice and jealousy. But one of the servants of the high priest, assuming that his master was not treated with due respect, struck Jesus in the face, saying, "Answerest thou the high priest so?" To this insulting question and blow, Jesus mildly returned, "If I have spoken evil, bear witness of the evil; but if well, why smitest thou me?" (3SP 114.2)

The Majesty of Heaven might have summoned to his aid legions of loyal angels to protect him against the malignity of his enemies; but it was his mission, in the character of humanity, meekly to endure taunts and stripes, leaving an example of patient forbearance to the children of men. Those into whose power Jesus had fallen had no respect for this sublime forbearance. The fact that he was a passive captive in their hands was the signal for them to

Chapter 8 - In the Judgment Hall (3SP 117.2)

wreak upon him the basest insults which their corrupt hearts could invent. (3SP 115.1)

When the council was fully assembled in the judgment hall, Caiaphas took his position as presiding officer. This man had ever regarded Jesus as his rival. The combined simplicity and eloquence of the Saviour had attracted large crowds to listen to his teachings, which contained wisdom such as they had never heard from the lips of priests or scribes. The anxiety of the people to hear Jesus, and their readiness to accept his doctrines, had roused the bitter jealousy, of the high priest. (3SP 115.2)

Jesus stood calm and serene before the high priest, while the eyes of the multitude were upon him, and the wildest excitement prevailed around. For a moment Caiaphas looked upon the captive, struck with a sudden admiration for his dignified bearing. A conviction came over him that this man was akin to God. The next instant he banished the thought, scorning the suggestions of his own mind. Immediately, his voice was heard in sneering, haughty tones, requesting Jesus to work before him one of those mighty miracles which had given him such fame among the people; but his words fell upon the ears of the Saviour as though he heard them not. (3SP 115.3)

The people involuntarily compared the excited and malignant deportment of Annas and Caiaphas with the calm, majestic bearing of Jesus. A holy influence seemed to emanate from the Saviour and pervade the atmosphere surrounding him. The question arose even in the minds of the hardened multitude present, Is this man of Godlike presence to be sentenced as a common criminal? Caiaphas, perceiving the influence that was obtaining, hastened the trial. He took his position on the throne of judgment, while Jesus stood at its foot. On either side were the judges and those specially interested in the trial. The Roman soldiers were ranged on the platform, below the throne. (3SP 116.1)

The high priest arose in his gorgeous robe, with glittering tiara and costly breastplate, upon which, in former days, the light of God's glory had often flashed. In strong contrast with this display were the coarse habiliments of Jesus. And yet he who was clad in homely garb had reigned in the courts of Heaven, crowned, and with garments of brightness, attended by holy angels. Yet there he stood at the foot of an earthly throne to be tried for his life. (3SP 116.2)

The priests and rulers had decided in counsel together that Jesus must be condemned, whether or not they could furnish evidence of his guilt. It was necessary to bring charges against him which would be regarded as criminal by the Roman power or they could legally effect nothing against him. His accusers could find plenty who would testify that he had denounced the priests and scribes; that he had called them hypocrites and murderers; but this would weigh nothing with the Romans, who were themselves disgusted with the pretension of the Pharisees. Such testimony would also weigh nothing with the Sadducees; for in their sharp contentions with the Pharisees, they had used to them language of the same import. His accusers were anxious to avoid raising the opposition of the Sadducees against the Pharisees; for if the two parties fell to contending among themselves, Jesus would be likely to escape from their hands. (3SP 116.3)

They could secure abundant evidence that Jesus had disregarded their traditions, and spoken irreverently of many of their ordinances; but such evidence was of no value, as it would have no weight with either the Romans or Sadducees. They dared not accuse him of Sabbath-breaking for fear an examination would reveal what had been the character of his work upon that day. In that event his miracles wrought to heal the afflicted would be brought to light, and defeat the very object they wished to gain. (3SP 117.1)

Christ had said, concerning the temple of his body, that he could destroy it, and raise it again in three days. These words were understood by his hearers to refer to the Jewish temple. Of all that Jesus had said, the priests could find nothing which they could use against him save this. The Romans had engaged in rebuilding and embellishing the temple. They took great pride in it as a work of science and art; and the priests counted upon their indignation when it was proven that Jesus, a humble man, had declared himself able to build it in three days if it should be destroyed. On this ground, Romans and Jews, Pharisees and Sadducees, could meet; for all held the temple in great veneration. (3SP 117.2)

In addition to this they had bribed false witnesses to testify that Jesus was guilty of inciting rebellion and seeking to establish a separate government. This they hoped would farther excite the apprehensions of the Romans and accomplish the desired object. But when

Chapter 8 - In the Judgment Hall (3SP 118.1)

these witnesses were called, their testimony was so vague and contradictory that it was worthless. Upon cross-questioning, they were led to falsify their own statements. It was becoming apparent to the people that the charges against Jesus could not be maintained. The life of the Saviour had been so faultless, and his doctrine so pure, that envy and malice could find little in either capable of being misrepresented. (3SP 118.1)

Two witnesses were at last found whose evidence was not so contradictory as the others had been, One of them, a corrupt man who had sold his honor for a sum of money, spoke of Christ as on a level with himself. Said he, "This fellow said, I am able to destroy the temple of God, and to build it in three days." In the figurative language of prophecy, Jesus had thus foretold his own death and resurrection, his conflict and victory; but his enemies had misconstrued his words to suit their own purposes. The words of Jesus were truth and verity; the evidence was false and malicious. If the words of Jesus had been reported exactly as he uttered them, there would have been nothing offensive in them. If he had been a mere man, as they assumed him to be, his declaration would only have indicated an unreasonable, boastful spirit, but could not have been construed into blasphemy. (3SP 118.2)

Caiaphas urged Jesus to answer to the charge made against him; but the Saviour, knowing that his sentence was already determined, answered him nothing. The evidence gained from the last two witnesses proved nothing against him worthy of death; and Jesus himself remained calm and silent. The priests and rulers began to fear that they would fail to gain their object after all. They were disappointed and perplexed that they had failed to gain anything from the false witnesses upon which to condemn their prisoner. Their only hope now was to make Jesus speak out and say something which would condemn him before the people. (3SP 119.1)

The silence of Christ upon this occasion had already been described by Isaiah in prophetic vision: "He was oppressed, and he was afflicted, yet he opened not his mouth. He is brought as a lamb to the slaughter; and as a sheep before her shearers is dumb, so he openeth not his mouth." (3SP 119.2)

The high priest now raised his right hand toward Heaven in a most imposing manner, and with a solemn voice addressed Jesus: "I adjure thee by the living God that thou tell us whether thou be the Christ, the Son of God." Thus appealed to by the highest acknowledged authority in the nation, and in the name of the Most High, Jesus, to show proper respect for the law, answered, "Thou hast said." Every ear was bent to listen, and every eye was fixed upon his face, as with calm voice and dignified manner, he made this reply. A heavenly light seemed to illuminate his pale countenance as he added, "Nevertheless I say unto you, Hereafter shall ye see the Son of man sitting on the right hand of power, and coming in the clouds of heaven." (3SP 119.3)

For a moment the divinity of Christ flashed through his guise of humanity; and the high priest quailed before the penetrating eyes of the Saviour. That look seemed to read his hidden thoughts, and burn into his heart; and never in after-life did he forget that searching glance of the persecuted Son of God. This voluntary confession of Jesus, claiming his Sonship with God, was made in the most public manner, and under the most solemn oath. In it he presented to the minds of those present a reversal of the scene then being enacted before them, when he, the Lord of life and glory, would be seated at the right hand of God, the supreme Judge of Heaven and earth, from whose decision there could be no appeal. He brought before them a view of that day, when, instead of being surrounded and abused by a riotous mob, headed by the priests and judges of the land, he would come in the clouds of heaven, with power and great glory, escorted by legions of angels, to pronounce the sentence of his enemies. (3SP 120.1)

Jesus knew what would be the result of this announcement; that it would secure his condemnation. The object of the designing priests was now gained. Jesus had declared himself to be the Christ. The high priest, in order to give those present the impression that he was jealous for the insulted majesty of Heaven, rent his garments, and, lifting his hands toward heaven as if in holy horror, said, in a voice calculated to rouse the excited people to violence, "He hath spoken blasphemy; what further need have we of witnesses? behold, now ye have heard his blasphemy. What think ye?" The answer of the judges was, "He is guilty of death." (3SP 120.2)

The priests and judges, exulting in the advantage they had gained through the words of Jesus, but anxious to hide their malicious

Chapter 8 - In the Judgment Hall (3SP 123.1)

satisfaction, now pressed close to him, and, as if they could not believe that they had heard aright, simultaneously inquired, "Art thou the Christ? tell us." Jesus looked calmly at his hypocritical questioners, and answered, "If I tell you, ye will not believe. And if I ask you, ye will not answer me, nor let me go." Jesus could have traced down the prophecies, and given his accusers evidence that the very things were then taking place which had been predicted in regard to Messiah. He could have silenced them thus; but they would not then have believed. He could have pointed them to his mighty miracles; but they had set their hearts against the light of Heaven, and no power could change them. (3SP 121.1)

There were some in that assembly who heeded the words of Jesus and noted his Godlike bearing as he stood serenely before the infuriated judges. The gospel seed found lodgment that day in hearts where it was eventually to spring up and yield an abundant harvest. The reverence and awe which his words inspired in the hearts of many who heard them were to increase and develop into perfect faith in Jesus as the world's Redeemer. Some of the witnesses of that scene were themselves afterward placed in a similar position to that of Jesus in the judgment hall; and were tried for their lives because they were the disciples of Christ. (3SP 121.2)

When the condemnation of Jesus was pronounced by the judges, a satanic fury took possession of the people. The roar of voices was like that of wild beasts. They made a rush toward Jesus, crying, He is guilty, put him to death! and had it not been for the Roman soldiers, Jesus would not have lived to be hanged upon the cross of Calvary. He would have been torn in pieces before his judges, had not Roman authority interfered, and by force of arms withheld the violence of the mob. (3SP 122.1)

Although Jesus was bound, yet he was also guarded, and held by two men lest he should escape from the hands of his persecutors. The judges and rulers now entirely forgot the dignity of their office, and abused the Son of God with foul epithets, railing upon him in regard to his parentage, and declaring that his presumption in proclaiming himself the Messiah, notwithstanding his low birth, made him deserving of the most ignominious death. Most dissolute men engaged in this infamous abuse of the Saviour. An old garment was thrown over his head, and his jeering persecutors struck him in the face, crying, "Prophesy unto us, thou Christ, Who is he that smote thee?" Upon the garment being removed, one poor wretch spat in his face. But the Saviour directed no word or look of retaliation against the deluded souls around him, who had cast off all restraint because they perceived that the priests and rulers sanctioned their acts. (3SP 122.2)

Jesus realized that the hosts of Heaven were witnessing his humiliation, and that the least angel, if summoned to his aid, could have instantly dispersed that insulting throng, and delivered him from their power. Jesus himself could have stricken down the excited multitude like dead men, by a look or word of his divinity, or driven them frightened from his presence, as he had the defilers of the temple. But it was in the plan of redemption that he should suffer the scorn and abuse of wicked men, and he consented to all this when he became the Redeemer of man. The angels of God faithfully recorded every insulting look, word, and act directed against their beloved Commander; and the base men who scorned and spat upon the calm, pale face of Christ, were one day to look upon it in its glory, shining brighter than the sun. In that awful time they would pray to the rocks and the mountains: "Hide us from the face of Him who sitteth upon the throne, and from the wrath of the Lamb." (3SP 122.3)

Jesus was pushed hither and thither, and so insulted and abused that at last the Roman officers were ashamed and angry that a man against whom nothing had yet been proven should be subject to the brutal treatment of the worst class of persons. Accordingly they accused the Jewish authorities of assuming to exercise a power that did not belong to them, in trying a man for his life, and pronouncing his condemnation. They declared that in doing this they infringed upon the Roman power, and that it was even against the Jewish law to condemn any man to death on his own testimony. This intervention of Roman authority caused a lull in the rude excitement. (3SP 123.1)

Just then a hoarse voice rang through the hall, which sent a thrill of terror through the hearts of all present: He is innocent. Spare him, O Caiaphas! He has done nothing worthy of death! The tall form of Judas was now seen pressing his way through the startled crowd. His face was pale and haggard, and large drops of perspiration stood upon his forehead. He rushed to the throne of judgment, and threw down before the high priest the pieces of silver he had

Chapter 8 - In the Judgment Hall (3SP 123.2)

received as the price of his Lord's betrayal. He eagerly grasped the robe of Caiaphas, and implored him to release Jesus, declaring that he was innocent of all crime. Caiaphas angrily shook him off, but he was confused and knew not what to say. The perfidy of the priests was revealed before the people. It was evident to all that Judas had been bribed to deliver Jesus into the hands of those who sought his life. (3SP 123.2)

Judas continued to beseech Caiaphas to do nothing against Jesus, declaring that he was indeed the Son of God, and cursing himself that he had betrayed innocent blood. But the high priest, having recovered his self-possession, answered with chilling scorn, "What is that to us? see thou to that." He then represented to the people that Judas was some poor maniac, one of the mad followers of Jesus, and charged them not to let any influence prevail to release the prisoner, who was a base deceiver. (3SP 124.1)

Finding his prayers were in vain. Judas fell at the feet of Jesus, acknowledging him to be the Son of God, begging forgiveness for his sin, and imploring him to exercise his God-like power and deliver himself from his enemies. The Saviour did not reproach his betrayer either by look or word. He knew that he was suffering the bitterest remorse for his crime. He gazed compassionately upon Judas, and declared that for that hour he had come into the world. (3SP 124.2)

A murmur of surprise ran through the assembly at the heavenly forbearance manifested by Jesus. Again a conviction swept over their minds that this man was more than mortal. But the question then arose, If he was indeed the Son of God, why did he not free himself from his bonds and rise triumphant above his accusers? (3SP 125.1)

The love of money had perverted the nobler nature of Judas, making him a fit agent for Satan to use in the betrayal of Christ. When Judas had become annoyed at the implied rebuke of Jesus because of his covetous spirit upon the occasion of Mary anointing her Lord with costly ointment, he yielded to the tempter, and gave Satan easy access to his mind. But when he decided to sell his Master to the murderous priests and rulers, he had no thought that Jesus would permit himself to be taken. He thought the priests would be cheated of their bribe, and he, the betrayer, would secure the money to use for some purpose of his own, and Jesus would have a new opportunity to display his divine power in delivering himself from the wiles of his enemies. (3SP 125.2)

From the time of his betrayal in the garden, Judas had not lost sight of the Saviour. He eagerly looked for him to surprise his enemies by appearing before them in the character of the Son of God, setting at naught all their plots and power. But when he saw him meekly submitting to their abuse, suffering himself to be tried and condemned to death, his heart smote him, and he realized the full extent of his own crime—he had sold his divine Master to shame and death. He remembered how kind and considerate Jesus had ever been to him, and his heart filled with remorse and anguish. He now despised the covetousness which Jesus had reproved, and which had tempted him to sell the Saviour for a few pieces of silver. (3SP 125.3)

Perceiving that his entreaties to spare the life of Jesus availed nothing with the high priest, he rushed from the hall in despair, crying, It is too late! It is too late! He felt unable to live to see Jesus crucified, and, in an agony of remorse, went out and hanged himself. (3SP 126.1)

Afterward the money which Judas had cast down before the priest was used for the purchase of a public burial ground. "And the chief priests took the silver pieces, and said, It is not lawful for to put them into the treasury, because it is the price of blood. And they took counsel, and bought with them the potter's field, to bury strangers in. Wherefore that field was called, The field of blood, unto this day." (3SP 126.2)

If any testimony had been needed to prove the innocence of Jesus, it was given in the confession of Judas. Not only was it an evidence of the innocence of the Saviour, but the event was a direct fulfillment of prophecy. In prophetic vision Zechariah had looked down the ages and seen the trial of God's dear Son. The act of Judas is thus described: "And I said unto them, If ye think good, give me my price; and if not, forbear. So they weighed for my price thirty pieces of silver. And the Lord said unto me, Cast it unto the potter; a goodly price that I was prized at of them. And I took the thirty pieces of silver, and cast them to the potter in the house of the Lord." (3SP 126.3)

Chapter 9
Condemnation of Jesus

When Jesus was asked the question, Art thou the Son of God? he knew that to answer in the affirmative would make his death certain; a denial would leave a stain upon his humanity. There was a time to be silent, and a time to speak. He had not spoken until plainly interrogated. In his lessons to his disciples he had declared: "Whosoever, therefore, shall confess me before men, him will I confess also before my Father who is in Heaven." When challenged, Jesus did not deny his relationship with God. In that solemn moment his character was at stake and must be vindicated. He left on that occasion an example for man to follow under similar circumstances. He would teach him not to apostatize from his faith to escape suffering or even death. (3SP 127.1)

Had the Jews possessed the authority to do so, they would have executed Jesus at once upon the hasty condemnation of their judges; but such power had passed from them into the hands of the Romans, and it was necessary that the case be referred to the proper authorities of that government for final decision. The Jews were anxious to hasten the trial and execution of Jesus, because if it were not brought about at once there would be a delay of a week on account of the immediate celebration of the passover. In that case Jesus would be kept in bonds, and the intense excitement of the mob that was clamoring for his life, would have been allayed, and a natural reaction would have set in. The better part of the people would have become aroused in his behalf, and in all probability his release would be accomplished. The priests and rulers felt that there was no time to lose. (3SP 127.2)

The whole Sanhedrim, followed by the multitude, escorted Jesus to the judgment hall of Pilate, the Roman governor, to secure a confirmation of the sentence they had just pronounced. The Jewish priests and rulers could not themselves enter Pilate's hall for fear of ceremonial defilement, which would disqualify them for taking part in the paschal feast. In order to condemn the spotless Son of God, they were compelled to appeal for judgment to one whose threshold they dared not cross for fear of defilement. Blinded by prejudice and cruelty, they could not discern that their passover festival was of no value, since they had defiled their souls by the rejection of Christ. The great salvation that he brought was typified by the deliverance of the children of Israel, which event was commemorated by the feast of the passover. The innocent lamb slain in Egypt, the blood of which sprinkled upon the door-posts caused the destroying angel to pass over the homes of Israel, prefigured the sinless Lamb of God, whose merits can alone avert the judgment and condemnation of fallen man. The Saviour had been obedient to the Jewish law, and observed all its divinely appointed ordinances. He had just identified himself with the paschal lamb as its great antitype, by connecting the Lord's supper with the passover. What a bitter mockery then was the ceremony about to be observed by the priestly persecutors of Jesus! Pilate beheld, in the accused, a man bearing the marks of violence, but with a serene and noble countenance and dignified bearing. Many cases had been tried before the Roman governor, but never before had there stood in his presence a man like this. He discovered no trace of crime in his face; and something in the prisoner's appearance excited his sympathy and respect. He turned to the priests, who stood just without the door, and asked, "What accusation bring ye against this man?" (3SP 128.1)

They were not prepared for this question. They had not designed to state the particulars of the alleged crime of Jesus. They had expected that Pilate would, without delay, confirm their decision against the Saviour. However they answered him that they had tried the prisoner according to their law and found him deserving of death. Said they, "If he were not a malefactor we would not have delivered him up unto thee." But Pilate was not satisfied with the explanation of the Jews, and reminded them of their inability

Chapter 9 - Condemnation of Jesus (3SP 129.1)

to execute the law. He intimated that if their judgment only was necessary to procure his condemnation, it was useless to bring the prisoner to him. Said he, "Take ye him, and judge him according to your law." (3SP 129.1)

The treacherous priests felt that they were outwitted; they saw that it would not do to specify the grounds for their condemnation of Jesus. The charge of blasphemy would be regarded by Pilate as the expression of religious bigotry and priestly jealousy; and the case would be at once dismissed. But if they could excite the apprehensions of the Roman governor that Jesus was a leader of sedition, their purpose would be accomplished. Tumults and insurrections were constantly arising among the Jews against the Roman government, for many affirmed that it was against the Jewish law to pay tribute to a foreign power. The authorities had found it necessary to deal very rigorously with these revolts among the people, and were constantly on the watch for developments of that character, in order to suppress them at once. But Jesus had always been obedient to the reigning power. When the scheming priests sought to entrap him by sending spies to him with the question, "Is it lawful to render tribute to Caesar?" he had directed their attention to the image and superscription of Caesar upon the tribute money, and answered, "Render unto Caesar the things which are Caesar's." Jesus himself had paid tribute, and had taught his disciples to do so. (3SP 129.2)

In their extremity the priests called the false witnesses to their aid. "And they began to accuse him, saying, We found this fellow perverting the nation, and forbidding to give tribute to Caesar, saying that he himself is Christ, a king." (3SP 130.1)

Pilate was not deceived by this testimony. He now became confident that a deep plot had been laid to destroy an innocent man, who stood in the way of the Jewish dignitaries. He turned to the prisoner and "asked him, saying, Art thou the King of the Jews? And he answered him and said, Thou sayest it." Jesus stood before Pilate, pale, bruised, and faint from loss of sleep and food. He had been hurried from place to place, and subjected to insult and violence; yet his bearing was noble, and his countenance was lighted as though a sunbeam were shining upon it. (3SP 130.2)

When his answer was heard by Caiaphas, who stood at the threshold of the judgment hall, the high priest joined with others in calling Pilate to witness that Jesus had admitted his crime by this answer, which was a virtual acknowledgment that he was seeking to establish a throne in Judah in opposition to the power of Caesar. Priests, scribes, and rulers, all united in noisy denunciations of Jesus, and in importuning Pilate to pronounce sentence of death upon him. The lawless uproar of the infuriated priests and dignitaries of the temple confused the senses of the Roman governor. Finally, when some measure of quiet was secured, he again addressed Jesus, saying, "Answerest thou nothing? behold how many things they witness against thee. But Jesus yet answered nothing; so that Pilate marveled." The silence of the Saviour perplexed him. He saw in the prisoner no marks of a seditious character, and he had no confidence in the accusations of the priests. Hoping to gain the truth from him, and to escape from the clamor of the excited crowd, he requested Jesus to step with him into his house. When he had done so, and the two were alone, Pilate turned to Jesus, and in a respectful voice asked him, "Art thou the King of the Jews?" (3SP 131.1)

Jesus did not directly answer this question. He knew that conviction was awakened in the heart of Pilate, and he wished to give him an opportunity to acknowledge how far his mind had been influenced in the right direction. He therefore answered, "Sayest thou this thing of thyself, or did others tell it thee of me?" The Saviour wished a statement from Pilate whether his question arose from the accusations just made by the Jews, or from his desire to receive light from Christ. Pilate longed for a more intelligent faith. The dignified bearing of Jesus, and his calm self-possession when placed in a position where there would naturally be developed a spirit of hate and revenge, astonished Pilate and won his deep respect. The direct question just asked him by Jesus was immediately understood by him, which evidenced that his soul was stirred by conviction. But pride rose in the heart of the Roman judge and overpowered the Spirit of God. "Pilate answered, Am I a Jew? Thine own nation and the chief priests have delivered thee unto me; what hast thou done?" (3SP 131.2)

Pilate's golden opportunity had passed. Jesus, however, did not leave him without farther light. At his desire God sent an angel to Pilate's wife; and, in a dream, she was shown the pure life and holy character of the man who was about to be consigned to a cruel death. Jesus did not directly answer the question of Pilate as to what he had done; but he plainly stated to him his mission:– (3SP 132.1)

"My kingdom is not of this world; if my kingdom were of this world, then would my servants fight, that I should not be delivered to the Jews; but now is my kingdom not from hence. Pilate therefore said unto him, Art thou a king then? Jesus answered, Thou sayest that I am a king. To this end was I born, and for this cause came I into the world, that I should bear witness unto the truth. Every one that is of the truth heareth my voice." (3SP 132.2)

Jesus thus sought to convince Pilate that he was innocent of aspiring to kingly honors upon earth. Pilate had been confused by the disturbed and divided elements of the religious world, and his mind grasped eagerly at the words of Jesus declaring that he had come into the world to bear witness to the truth. Pilate had heard many voices cry, Here is the truth! I have the truth! But this man, arraigned as a criminal, who claimed to have the truth, stirred his heart with a great longing to know what it was, and how it could be obtained. He inquired of Jesus, "What is truth?" But he did not wait for a reply; the tumult of the excited crowd was continually increasing; their impatient cries jarred upon his ears, and recalled him to his judicial position. He went out to the Jews, who stood beyond the door of the hall, and declared in an emphatic voice, "I find in him no fault at all." (3SP 132.3)

Those words, traced by the pen of inspiration, will forever stand as a proof to the world of the base perfidy and falsehood of the Jews in their charges against Jesus. Even the heathen magistrate pronounced him innocent. As Pilate thus spoke, the rage and disappointment of the priests and elders knew no bounds. They had made great efforts to accomplish the death of Jesus, and now that there appeared to be a prospect of his release they seemed ready to tear him in pieces. They lost all reason and self-control, and gave vent to curses and maledictions against him, behaving more like demons than men. They were loud in their censures of Pilate, and threatened the vengeance of the Roman law against him if he refused to condemn one who, they affirmed, had set himself up against Caesar. (3SP 133.1)

During all this uproar, Jesus stood unmoved, uttering no word in answer to the abuse that was heaped upon him. He had spoken freely to Pilate when alone with him, that the light of his truth might illuminate the darkened understanding of the Roman governor; and now he could say nothing more to prevent him from committing the fearful act of condemning to death the Son of God. Pilate turned again to Jesus and inquired, "Hearest thou not how many things they witness against thee? And he answered him to never a word; insomuch that the governor marveled greatly." (3SP 133.2)

Angry voices were now heard, declaring that the seditious influence of Jesus was well known throughout all the country. Said they, "He stirreth up the people, teaching throughout all Jewry, beginning from Galilee to this place." Pilate at this time had no thought of condemning Jesus, because he was certain that he was the victim of the envious and designing priests. As he afterward stated to Jesus, he had the power to condemn or to release him; but he dreaded the ill-will of the people; so when he heard that Jesus was a Galilean and was under the jurisdiction of Herod, he embraced the opportunity to spare himself from farther difficulty, and refused to decide the case, sending him to Herod, who was then in Jerusalem. (3SP 134.1)

Jesus was faint and weary from loss of sleep and food, and the ill-treatment he had received; yet his suffering condition awakened no pity in the hearts of his persecutors. He was dragged away to the judgment hall of Herod amid the hooting and insults of the merciless mob. Besides escaping responsibility in regard to the trial of Jesus, Pilate thought this would be a good opportunity to heal an old quarrel between himself and Herod. He thought that this act on his part would be regarded by Herod as an acknowledgment of his superior authority, and would thus bring about a reconciliation. In this he was not wrong, for the two magistrates made friends over the trial of the Saviour. (3SP 134.2)

When Herod had first heard of Jesus and the mighty works wrought by him, he was terror-stricken, and said, "It is John whom I beheaded; he is risen from the dead;" "therefore mighty works do show forth themselves in him." Herod had never before met Jesus, but he had long desired to see him, and witness his marvelous power. He was pleased that he was brought to him a prisoner, for he made no doubt that he could force him to work a miracle as a condition of saving his life. Herod's conscience was far less sensitive than when he had trembled with horror at the request of Herodias for the

Chapter 9 - Condemnation of Jesus (3SP 135.1)

head of John the Baptist. For a time he had felt the keen stings of remorse for the terrible act he had committed to gratify the revenge of a cruel woman; but his moral perceptions had become more and more degraded by his licentious life, till his sins appeared but trifles in his eyes. The men who are capable of the worst crimes are those who have once been convicted by the Spirit of truth, and have turned away from the light into the darkness of iniquity. Herod had very nearly become a disciple of John; but at the very point of decision, he had fallen into the snare of Satan and put to death one whom he knew to be a true prophet. (3SP 135.1)

As the Saviour was brought before Herod, the rabble surged and pressed about, crying out against the prisoner, some charging him with one crime and some with another. Herod commanded silence and directed that Jesus be unbound, for he wished to interrogate him. He looked with curiosity, mingled with an impulse of pity, upon the pale, sad face of the Saviour, which was marked with deep wisdom and purity, but showed extreme weariness and suffering. Herod, as well as Pilate, knew from his acquaintance with the character of the Jews, that malice and envy had caused them to condemn this innocent man. (3SP 135.2)

Herod urged Jesus to save his life by working a miracle that would give evidence of his divine power. But the Saviour had no such work to do. He had taken upon himself the nature of man, and was not to perform a miracle to gratify the curiosity of wicked men, nor to save himself one jot of the pain and humiliation that man would suffer under similar circumstances. Herod urged him to prove that he was not an impostor by demonstrating his power before the crowd. He summoned for the purpose maimed, crippled, and deformed persons, and, in an authoritative manner, commanded Jesus to heal these subjects in his presence, urging that if he had really worked such remarkable cures as were reported of him, he still had power to do like wonders, and could now turn it to his own profit by procuring his release. (3SP 136.1)

But Jesus stood calmly before the haughty ruler as one who neither saw nor heard. Herod repeatedly urged his proposition upon Jesus, and reiterated the fact that he had the power to release or to condemn him. He even dared to boast of the punishment he had inflicted upon the prophet John for presuming to reprove him. To all this, Jesus made no answer either by word or look. Herod was irritated by the profound silence of the prisoner, which indicated an utter indifference to the royal personage before whom he had been summoned. Open rebuke would have been more palatable to the vain and pompous ruler than to be thus silently ignored. (3SP 136.2)

Had Jesus desired to do so, he could have spoken words which would have pierced the ears of the hardened king. He could have stricken him with fear and trembling by laying before him the full iniquity of his life, and the horror of his approaching doom. But Jesus had no light to give one who had gone directly contrary to the knowledge he had received from the greatest of prophets. The ears of Christ had ever been open to the earnest plea of even the worst sinners; but he had no ear for the commands of Herod. Those eyes, that had ever rested with pity and forgiveness upon the penitent sinner, however defiled and lowly, had no look to bestow upon Herod. Those lips, that had dropped precious words of instruction, and were ever ready to answer the questions of those who sought knowledge, and to speak comfort and pardon to the sinful and desponding, had no words for proud and cruel Herod. That heart, ever touched by the presence of human woe, was closed to the haughty king who felt no need of a Saviour. (3SP 137.1)

The silence of Jesus could no longer be borne by Herod; his face grew dark with passion, and he angrily threatened Jesus; but the captive still remained unmoved. Herod then turned to the multitude and denounced him as an impostor. His accusers well knew that he was no impostor; they had seen too many evidences of his power to be thus misled. They knew that even the grave had opened at his command, and the dead had walked forth, clothed again with life. They had been greatly terrified when Herod commanded him to work a miracle; for of all things they dreaded an exhibition of his divine power, which would prove a death-blow to their plans, and would perhaps cost them their lives. Therefore the priests and rulers began to cry out vehemently against him, accusing him of working miracles through the power given him of Beelzebub, the prince of devils. (3SP 137.2)

Some cried out that he claimed to be the Son of God, the King of Israel. Herod, hearing this, said, in derision, A king, is he? Then crown him, and put upon him a royal robe, and worship your king. Then turning to Jesus he angrily declared that if he refused to speak, he should be delivered into the hands of the soldiers, who would have little respect for his claims or his person; if he was an impostor it would be no more than he deserved; but if he was the Son of God he could save himself by working a miracle. No sooner were these words uttered than the mob, at the instigation of the priests, made a rush toward Jesus. Had not the Roman soldiers forced them back, the Saviour would have been torn in pieces. (3SP 138.1)

At the suggestion of Herod, a crown was now plaited from a vine bearing sharp thorns, and this was placed upon the sacred brow of Jesus; and an old tattered purple robe, once the garment of a king, was placed upon his noble form, while Herod and the Jewish priests encouraged the insults and cruelty of the mob. Jesus was then placed upon a large block, which was derisively called a throne, an old reed was placed in his hand as a scepter, and, amid satanic laughter, curses, and jeers, the rude throng bowed to him mockingly as to a king. Occasionally some murderous hand snatched the reed that had been placed in his hand, and struck him on the head with it, forcing the thorns into his temples, and causing the blood to flow down his face and beard. (3SP 138.2)

Satan instigated the cruel abuse of the debased mob, led on by the priests and rulers, to provoke, if possible, retaliation from the world's Redeemer, or to drive him to deliver himself by a miracle from the hands of his persecutors, and thus break up the plan of salvation. One stain upon his human life, one failure of his humanity to bear the terrible test imposed upon it, would make the Lamb of God an imperfect offering, and the redemption of man would be a failure. But he who could command the heavenly hosts, and in an instant call to his aid legions of holy angels, one of whom could have immediately overpowered that cruel mob,–he who could have stricken down his tormentors by the flashing forth of his divine majesty,–submitted to the coarsest insult and outrage with dignified composure. As the acts of his torturers degraded them below humanity, into the likeness of Satan, so did the meekness and patience of Jesus exalt him above the level of humanity. (3SP 139.1)

When Herod saw that Jesus submitted passively to all the indignity that was heaped upon him, preserving an unparalleled serenity through it all, he was moved by a sudden fear that after all this might not be a common man who stood before him. He was greatly perplexed when he looked upon the pure, pale face of the prisoner, and questioned if he might not be a God come down to earth. The very silence of Jesus spoke conviction to the heart of the king, such as no words could have done. Herod noticed that while some bowed before Jesus in mockery, others, who came forward for the same purpose, looked into the sufferer's face and saw expressed there a look so like a king that they turned back, ashamed of their own audacity. Herod was ill at ease, and, hardened as he was, dared not ratify the condemnation of the Jews; and he therefore sent Jesus back to Pilate. (3SP 139.2)

The Saviour, tottering with weariness, pale and wounded, wearing a robe of mockery and a crown of thorns, was mercilessly hurried back to the court of the Roman governor. Pilate was very much irritated; for he had congratulated himself on being rid of a fearful responsibility when he referred the accusers of Jesus to Herod. He now impatiently inquired of the Jews what they would have him do. He reminded them that he had already examined the prisoner and found no blame in him; that his accusers had failed to sustain a single charge against him; that he had sent Jesus to Herod, a tetrarch of Galilee, and one of their own nation, who also found nothing worthy of death against the prisoner. Said Pilate, "I will therefore chastise him and release him." (3SP 140.1)

Here Pilate exposed his weakness. He had declared that Jesus was innocent of the crimes of which he was accused, yet he was willing to make a partial sacrifice of justice and principle in order to compromise with an unfeeling mob; he was willing to suffer an innocent man to be scourged, that their inhuman wrath might be appeased. But the fact that he proposed to make terms with them placed Pilate at a disadvantage with the ungovernable crowd, who now presumed upon his indecision, and clamored the more for the life of the prisoner. Pilate turned to the people, and represented to them that the priests and elders had not substantiated in any degree the charges brought against Jesus. He hoped by this means to raise their sympathy for him, so they would be willing to release him. Meanwhile Jesus had fallen through exhaustion upon the marble pavement. Just then a messenger pressed through the crowd, and placed in Pilate's hand a letter from his wife, which ran thus:– (3SP 140.2)

"Have thou nothing to do with that just

Chapter 9 - Condemnation of Jesus (3SP 141.1)

man; for I have suffered many things this day in a dream because of him." Pilate's wife was not a Jew; but the angel of God had sent this warning to her, that, through her, Pilate might be prevented from committing the terrible crime of delivering up to death the divine Son of God. (3SP 141.1)

Pilate turned pale when he read the message; but the priests and rulers had occupied the interval in farther inflaming minds of the people, till they were wrought up to a state of insane fury. The governor was forced to action; he turned to the crowd and spoke with great earnestness: "Whom will ye that I release unto you? Barabbas, or Jesus who is called Christ?" It was customary at this feast for the governor to release one prisoner, whomsoever the people desired to be set at liberty. Pilate seized this as an opportunity to save Jesus; and by giving them a choice between the innocent Saviour and the notable robber and murderer, Barabbas, he hoped to rouse them to a sense of justice. But great was his astonishment when the cry, "Away with this man, and release unto us Barabbas!" was started by the priests, and taken up by the mob, resounding through the hall like the hoarse cry of demons. (3SP 141.2)

Pilate was dumb with surprise and disappointment; but by appealing to the people, and yielding his own judgment, he had compromised his dignity, and lost control of the crowd. The priests saw that though he was convinced of the innocence of Jesus, he could be intimidated by them, and they determined to carry their point. So when Pilate inquired, "What shall I do then with Jesus, who is called Christ?" they with one accord cried out, "Let him be crucified!" (3SP 142.1)

"And the governor said, Why, what evil hath he done? But they cried out the more, saying, Let him be crucified." Here Pilate again revealed his weakness, in submitting the sentence of Jesus to a lawless and infuriated mob. How true were the words of the prophet: "Judgment is turned away backward, and justice standeth afar off; for truth is fallen in the street, and equity cannot enter." The governor's cheek paled as he heard the terrible cry: "Crucify him!" He had not thought it would come to that–a man whom he had repeatedly pronounced innocent, to be consigned to the most dreaded of deaths. He now saw what a terrible thing he had done in placing the life of a just man in the balance against the decision of those, who, from envy and malice, had delivered him up to trial. Pilate had taken step after step in the violation of his conscience, and in excusing himself from judging with equity and fairness, as his position demanded he should do, until now he found himself almost helpless in the hands of the Jews. (3SP 142.2)

Again he asked the question, "Why, what evil hath he done?" and again they cried out, "Crucify him!" Once more Pilate expostulated with them against putting to death one against whom they could prove nothing. Again, to conciliate them, he proposed to chastise him and let him go. It was not enough that the Saviour of the world, faint with weariness and covered with wounds, must be subjected to the shameful humiliation of such a trial; but his sacred flesh must be bruised and mangled to gratify the satanic fury of the priests and rulers. Satan, with his hellish army had gained possession of them. (3SP 142.3)

Pilate, in the vain hope of exciting their pity, that they might decide this was sufficient punishment, now caused Jesus to be scourged in the presence of the multitude. The pale sufferer, with a crown of thorns upon his head, and stripped to the waist, revealing the long, cruel stripes, from which the blood flowed freely, was then placed side by side with Barabbas. Although the face of Jesus was stained with blood, and bore marks of exhaustion and pain, yet his noble character could not be hidden, but stood out in marked contrast with that of the robber chief, whose every feature proclaimed him to be a debased and hardened desperado. (3SP 143.1)

Pilate was filled with sympathy and amazement as he beheld the uncomplaining patience of Jesus. Gentleness and resignation were expressed in every feature; there was no cowardly weakness in his manner, but the strength and dignity of long-suffering. Pilate did not doubt that the sight of this man, who had borne insult and abuse in such a manner, when contrasted with the repulsive criminal by his side, would move the people to sympathy, and they would decide that Jesus had already suffered enough. But he did not understand the fanatical hatred of the priests for Christ, who, as the Light of the world, had made apparent their darkness and error. (3SP 143.2)

Pilate, pointing to the Saviour, in a voice of solemn entreaty said to priests, rulers, and people, "Behold the man." "I bring him forth to you that ye may know that I find no fault in him."

But the priests had moved the mob to mad fury; and, instead of pitying Jesus in his suffering and forbearance, they cried, "Crucify him, crucify him!" and their hoarse voices were like the roaring of wild beasts. Pilate, losing all patience with their unreasoning cruelty, cried out despairingly, "Take ye him, and crucify him; for I find no fault in him." (3SP 144.1)

The Roman governor, familiarized with cruel scenes, educated amid the din of battle, was moved with sympathy for the suffering prisoner, who, contemned and scourged, with bleeding brow and lacerated back, still had more the bearing of a king upon his throne than that of a condemned criminal. But the hearts of his own people were hardened against him. The priests declared, "We have a law, and by our law he ought to die, because he made himself the Son of God." (3SP 144.2)

Pilate was startled by these words; he had no correct idea of Christ and his mission; but he had an indistinct faith in God and in beings superior to humanity. The thought that had once before passed through his mind now took more definite shape, and he questioned if it might not be a divine personage who stood before him, clad in the purple robe of mockery, and crowned with thorns, yet with such a noble bearing that the stanch Roman trembled with awe as he gazed upon him. (3SP 144.3)

"When Pilate therefore heard that saying, he was the more afraid; and went again into the judgment hall, and saith unto Jesus, Whence art thou? But Jesus gave him no answer." Jesus had already told Pilate that he was the Messiah, that his kingdom was not of this world; and he had no farther words for a man who so abused the high office of judge as to yield his principles and authority to the demands of a blood-thirsty rabble. Pilate was vexed at the silence of Jesus, and haughtily addressed him:– (3SP 145.1)

"Speakest thou not unto me? knowest thou not that I have power to crucify thee, and have power to release thee? Jesus answered, Thou couldest have no power at all against me, except it were given thee from above; therefore he that delivered me unto thee hath the greater sin." Jesus here laid the heaviest burden of guilt upon the Jewish judges, who had received unmistakable evidence of the divinity of Him whom they had condemned to death, both from the prophecies and his own teachings and miracles. What a scene was this to hand down to the world through all time! The pitying Saviour, in the midst of his intense suffering and grief, excuses as far as possible the act of Pilate, who might have released him from the power of his enemies. (3SP 145.2)

Pilate was now more convinced than before of the superiority of the man before him, and tried again and again to save him. "But the Jews cried out, saying, If thou let this man go, thou art not Caesar's friend; whosoever maketh himself a king speaketh against Caesar." This was touching Pilate in a weak point. He had been looked upon with some suspicion by the government; and he knew that a report of unfaithfulness on his part would be likely to cost him his position. He knew that if the Jews became his enemies he could hope for no mercy at their hands; for he had before him an example of the perseverance with which they sought to destroy one whom they hated without reason. (3SP 145.3)

The implied threat in the declaration of the priests, regarding his allegiance to Caesar, intimidated Pilate, so that he yielded to the demands of the mob, and delivered Jesus up to the crucifixion rather than risk losing his position. But the very thing he dreaded came upon him afterward in spite of his precautions. His honors were stripped from him; he was cast down from his high office; and, stung by remorse and wounded pride, he committed suicide not long after the crucifixion. (3SP 146.1)

"When Pilate saw that he could prevail nothing, but that rather a tumult was made, he took water, and washed his hands before the multitude, saying, I am innocent of the blood of this just person; see ye to it." Caiaphas answered defiantly, "His blood be on us, and on our children;" and his words were echoed by the priests and rulers, and taken up by the crowd in an inhuman roar of voices. "Then answered all the people and said, His blood be on us, and on our children." (3SP 146.2)

At this exhibition of satanic madness, the light of conviction shone more clearly upon the mind of Pilate. He had never before witnessed such rash presumption and heartless cruelty. And in strong contrast with the ungovernable passion of his persecutors was the dignified repose of Jesus. In his own mind Pilate said, He is a God, and thought he could discern a soft light shining about his head. Looking thus upon Christ he turned pale with fear and self-condemnation; then, confronting the people with a troubled countenance, he said, I am clear of his blood. Take ye him and crucify him; but

Chapter 9 - Condemnation of Jesus (3SP 146.3)

mark ye, priests and rulers, I pronounce him a just man, and may He whom he claims as his Father judge you for this day's work, and not me. Then turning to Jesus he continued, Forgive me for this act; I am not able to save you. (3SP 146.3)

Only a short time before, the governor had declared to his prisoner that he had power to release or to condemn him; but he now thought that he could not save him, and also his own position and honor; and he preferred to sacrifice an innocent life rather than his own worldly power. Had he acted promptly and firmly at the first, carrying out his convictions of right, his will would not have been overborne by the mob; they would not have presumed to dictate to him. His wavering and indecision proved his irredeemable ruin. How many, like Pilate, sacrifice principle and integrity, in order to shun disagreeable consequences. Conscience and duty point one way, and self-interest points another; and the current, setting strongly in the wrong direction, sweeps away into the thick darkness of guilt him who compromises with evil. (3SP 147.1)

Satan's rage was great as he saw that all the cruelty which he had led the Jews to inflict upon Jesus had not forced the least murmur from his lips. Although he had taken upon himself the nature of man, he was sustained by a Godlike fortitude, and departed in no particular from the will of his Father. (3SP 147.2)

Wonder, O Heavens! and be astonished, O earth! Behold the oppressor and the oppressed. A vast multitude inclose the Saviour of the world. Mocking and jeering are mingled with the coarse oaths of blasphemy. His lowly birth and his humble life are commented upon by unfeeling wretches. His claim to be the Son of God is ridiculed by the chief priests and elders, and the vulgar jest and insulting sneer are passed from lip to lip. Satan has full control of the minds of his servants. In order to do this effectually, he had commenced with the chief priests and the elders, and imbued them with a religious frenzy. This they had communicated to the rude and uncultivated mob, until there was a corrupt harmony in the feelings of all, from the hypocritical priests and elders down to the most debased. Christ, the precious Son of God, was led forth and delivered to the people to be crucified. (3SP 148.1)

*****

Chapter 10
Calvary

They hurried Jesus away with loud shouts of triumph; but their noise ceased for a time when they passed a retired place, and saw at the foot of a lifeless tree the dead body of Judas, who had betrayed Christ. It was a most revolting spectacle; his weight had broken the cord by which he had hung himself to the tree, and, in falling, his body had become horribly mangled, and was then being devoured by dogs. The mutilated remains were ordered to be buried at once, and the crowd passed on; but there was less noisy mockery, and many a pale face revealed the fearful thoughts within. Retribution seemed already to be visiting those who were guilty of the blood of Jesus. (3SP 148.2)

By this time the news of the condemnation of Jesus had spread through all Jerusalem, striking terror and anguish to thousands of hearts, but bringing a malicious joy to many who had been reproved by the teachings of the Saviour. The priests had been bound by a promise not to molest any of his disciples if Jesus were delivered up to them; so all classes of people flocked to the scene of outrage, and Jerusalem was left almost empty. Nicodemus, and Joseph of Arimathea, had not been summoned to the Sanhedrim council, and their voices had nothing to do with condemning Jesus. They were present at his crucifixion, but unable to change or modify his terrible sentence. (3SP 149.1)

The disciples and believers from the region round about joined the throng that followed Jesus to Calvary. The mother of Jesus was also there, supported by John, the beloved disciple. Her heart was stricken with unutterable anguish; yet she, with the disciples, hoped that the painful scene would change, and Jesus would assert his power, and appear before his enemies as the Son of God. Then again her mother's heart would sink as she remembered words in which he had briefly referred to the things which were that day being enacted. (3SP 149.2)

Jesus had scarcely passed the gate of Pilate's house when the cross which had been prepared for Barabbas was brought out and laid upon his bruised and bleeding shoulders. Crosses were also placed upon the companions of Barabbas, who were to suffer death at the same time with Jesus. The Saviour had borne his burden but a few rods, when, from loss of blood and excessive weariness and pain, he fell fainting to the ground. As he lay beneath the heavy burden of the cross, how the heart of the mother of Christ longed to place a supporting hand beneath his wounded head, and bathe that brow that had once been pillowed upon her bosom. But, alas, that mournful privilege was denied her. (3SP 150.1)

When Jesus revived, the cross was again placed upon his shoulders and he was forced forward. He staggered on for a few steps, bearing his heavy load, then fell as one lifeless to the ground. He was at first pronounced to be dead, but finally he again revived. The priests and rulers felt no compassion for their suffering victim; but they saw that it was impossible for him to carry the instrument of torture farther. They were puzzled to find any one who would humiliate himself to bear the cross to the place of execution. The Jews could not do it because of defilement, and their consequent inability to keep the coming passover festival. (3SP 150.2)

While they were considering what to do, Simon, a Cyrenian, coming from an opposite direction, met the crowd, was seized at the instigation of the priests, and compelled to carry the cross of Christ. The sons of Simon were disciples of Jesus, but he himself had never been connected with him. This occasion was a profitable one for him. The cross he was forced to bear became the means of his conversion. His sympathies were deeply stirred in favor of Jesus; and the events of Calvary, and the words uttered by Jesus, caused him to acknowledge that he was the Son of God. Simon ever after felt grateful to God for the singular providence which placed him in a position to receive evidence for himself that Jesus was the world's Redeemer. (3SP 150.3)

Chapter 10 - Calvary (3SP 151.1)

When Jesus was thought to be dying beneath the burden of the cross, many women, who, though not believers in Christ, were touched with pity for his sufferings, broke forth into a mournful wailing. When Jesus revived, he looked upon them with tender compassion. He knew they were not lamenting him because he was a teacher sent from God, but from motives of common humanity. He looked upon the weeping women and said, "Daughters of Jerusalem, weep not for me, but for yourselves, and for your children." (3SP 151.1)

Jesus did not despise their tears, but the sympathy which they expressed wakened a deeper chord of sympathy in his own heart for them. He forgot his own grief in contemplating the future fate of Jerusalem. Only a short time ago the people had cried out, "His blood be on us and on our children." How blindly had they invoked the doom they were soon to realize! Many of the very women who were weeping about Jesus were to perish with their children in the siege of Jerusalem. (3SP 151.2)

Jesus referred not only to the destruction of Jerusalem, but to the end of the world. Said he, "Then shall they begin to say to the mountains, Fall on us; and to the hills, Cover us. For if they do these things in a green tree, what shall be done in the dry?" The innocent were represented by the green tree. If God suffered his wrath because of the sins of the world to fall upon the Redeemer, in that he was permitted to suffer death by crucifixion, what might be expected to come upon the impenitent and unbelieving, who had slighted the mercies of God, purchased for them by the death of his Son? The mind of Jesus wandered from the destruction of Jerusalem to a wider judgment, when all the impenitent would suffer condemnation for their sins; when the Son of man should come, attended not by a murderous mob, but by the mighty hosts of God. (3SP 151.3)

A great multitude followed the Saviour to Calvary, many mocking and deriding; but some were weeping and recounting his praise. Those whom he had healed of various infirmities, and those whom he had raised from the dead, declared his marvelous works with earnest voice, and demanded to know what Jesus had done that he should be treated as a malefactor. Only a few days before, they had attended him with joyful hosannas, and the waving of palm-branches, as he rode triumphantly to Jerusalem. But many who had then shouted his praise, because it was popular to do so, now swelled the cry of "Crucify him! Crucify him!" (3SP 152.1)

Upon the occasion of Christ riding into Jerusalem, the disciples had been raised to the highest pitch of expectation. They had pressed close about their Master, and had felt that they were highly honored to be connected with him. Now they followed him in his humiliation at a distance. They were filled with inexpressible grief, and disappointed hopes. How were the words of Jesus verified: "All ye will be offended because of me this night; for it is written, I will smite the shepherd, and the sheep of the flock shall be scattered abroad." Yet the disciples still had faint hope that their Master would manifest his power at the last moment, and deliver himself from his enemies. (3SP 152.2)

Upon arriving at the place of execution, the condemned were bound to the instruments of torture. While the two thieves wrestled in the hands of those who stretched them upon the cross, Jesus made no resistance. The mother of Jesus looked on with agonizing suspense, hoping that he would work a miracle to save himself. Surely He who had given life to the dead would not suffer himself to be crucified. What torture must this woman have endured as she witnessed the shame and suffering of her son, yet was not able to minister to him in his distress! Bitter grief and disappointment filled her heart. Must she give up her faith that he was the true Messiah? Would the Son of God allow himself to be thus cruelly slain? She saw his hands stretched upon the cross–those dear hands that had ever dispensed blessings, and had been reached forth so many times to heal the suffering. And now the hammer and nails were brought, and as the spikes were driven through the tender flesh and fastened to the cross, the heart-stricken disciples bore away from the cruel scene the fainting form of the mother of Christ. (3SP 153.1)

Jesus made no murmur of complaint; his face remained pale and serene, but great drops of sweat stood upon his brow. There was no pitying hand to wipe the death-dew from his face, nor words of sympathy and unchanging fidelity to stay his human heart. He was treading the wine-press all alone; and of all the people there was none with him. While the soldiers were doing their fearful work, and he was enduring the most acute agony, Jesus prayed for his enemies–"Father, forgive them; for they know not what they do." His mind was borne from his own suffering to the crime of his persecutors, and the terrible but just retribution that would be theirs. He pitied them in their ignorance and guilt. No curses were called down upon the soldiers who were handling him so roughly, no vengeance was invoked upon the priests and rulers who were the cause of all his suffering, and were then gloating over the accomplishment of their purpose, but only a plea for their forgiveness–"for they know not what they do." (3SP 153.2)

Had they known that they were putting to exquisite torture one who had come to save the sinful race from eternal ruin, they would have been seized with horror and remorse. But their ignorance did not remove their guilt; for it was their privilege to know and accept Jesus as their Saviour. They rejected all evidence, and not only sinned against Heaven in crucifying the King of Glory, but against the commonest feelings of humanity in putting to a torturous death an innocent man. Jesus was earning the right to become the Advocate for man in the Father's presence. That prayer of Christ for his enemies embraced the world, taking in every sinner who should live, until the end of time. (3SP 154.1)

After Jesus was nailed to the cross, it was lifted by several powerful men, and thrust with great violence into the place prepared for it, causing the most excruciating agony to the Son of God. Pilate then wrote an inscription in three different languages and placed it upon the cross, above the head of Jesus. It ran thus: "This is Jesus, the King of the Jews." This inscription, placed so conspicuously upon the cross, irritated the Jews. In Pilate's court they had cried, Crucify him! We have no king but Caesar! They declared that whoever claimed other than Caesar for a king was a traitor. But they had overreached themselves in disclaiming any desire to have a king of their own nation. Pilate, in his inscription, wrote out the sentiments which they had expressed. It was a virtual declaration, and so understood by all, that the Jews acknowledged that on account of their allegiance to the Roman power, any man who aspired to be king of the Jews, however innocent in other respects, should be judged by them worthy of death. There was no other offense named in the inscription; it simply stated that Jesus was the king of the Jews. (3SP 154.2)

The Jews saw this, and asked Pilate to change the inscription. Said the chief priests, "Write not, The King of the Jews; but that he said, I am King of the Jews." But Pilate, angry with himself because of his former weakness, and thoroughly despising the jealous and artful priests and rulers, coldly replied, "What I have written I have written." (3SP 155.1)

And now a terrible scene was enacted. Priests, rulers, and scribes forgot the dignity of their sacred offices, and joined with the rabble in mocking and jeering the dying Son of God, saying, "If thou be the King of the Jews, save thyself." And some deridingly repeated among themselves: "He saved others; himself he cannot save. If he be the King of Israel, let him now come down from the cross, and we will believe him. He trusted in God; let him deliver him now, if he will have him; for he said, I am the Son of God." "And they that passed by railed on him, wagging their heads, and saying, Ah, thou that destroyest the temple, and buildest it in three days, save thyself, and come down from the cross." (3SP 155.2)

These men, who professed to be the expounders of prophecy, were themselves repeating the very words which inspiration had foretold they would utter upon this occasion; yet, in their blindness, they did not perceive that they were fulfilling prophecy. The dignitaries of the temple, the hardened soldiers, the vile thief upon the cross, and the base and cruel among the multitude, all united in their abuse of Christ. (3SP 156.1)

The thieves who were crucified with Jesus suffered like physical torture with him; but one was only hardened and rendered desperate and defiant by his pain. He took up the mocking of the priests, and railed upon Jesus, saying, "If thou be Christ, save thyself and us." The other malefactor was not a hardened criminal; his morals had been corrupted by association with the base, but his crimes were not so great as were those of many who stood beneath the cross reviling the Saviour. (3SP 156.2)

In common with the rest of the Jews, he had believed that Messiah was soon to come. He had heard Jesus, and been convicted by his teachings; but through the influence of the priests and rulers he had turned away from him. He had sought to drown his convictions in the fascinations of pleasure. Corrupt associations had led him farther and farther into wickedness, until he was arrested for open crime and condemned to die upon the cross. During that day of trial he had been in company with Jesus in the judgment hall and on the way to Calvary. He had heard Pilate declare him to be a just man; he

Chapter 10 - Calvary (3SP 156.3)

had marked his Godlike deportment and his pitying forgiveness of his tormentors. In his heart he acknowledged Jesus to be the Son of God. (3SP 156.3)

When he heard the sneering words of his companion in crime, he "rebuked him, saying, Dost thou not fear God, seeing thou art in the same condemnation? And we indeed justly; for we receive the due reward of our deeds; but this man hath done nothing amiss." Then, as his heart went out to Christ, heavenly illumination flooded his mind. In Jesus, bruised, mocked, and hanging upon the cross, he saw his Redeemer, his only hope, and appealed to him in humble faith: "Lord, remember me when thou comest into thy kingdom! And Jesus said unto him, Verily I say unto thee today, [By placing the comma after the word today, instead of after the word thee, as in the common versions, the true meaning of the text is more apparent.] shalt thou be with me in Paradise." (3SP 157.1)

Jesus did not promise the penitent thief that he should go with him, upon the day of their crucifixion, to Paradise; for he himself did not ascend to his Father until three days afterward. See *John 20:17*. But he declared unto him, "I say unto thee today –" meaning to impress the fact upon his mind, that at that time, while enduring ignominy and persecution, he had the power to save sinners. He was man's Advocate with the Father, having the same power as when he healed the sick and raised the dead to life; it was his divine right to promise that day to the repentant, believing malefactor, "Thou shalt be with me in Paradise." (3SP 157.2)

The criminal upon the cross, notwithstanding his physical suffering, felt in his soul the peace and comfort of acceptance with God. The Saviour, lifted upon the cross, enduring pain and mockery, rejected by the priests and elders, is sought by a guilty, dying soul with a faith discerning the world's Redeemer in Him who is crucified like a malefactor. For such an object did the Son of God leave Heaven, to save lost and perishing sinners. While the priests and rulers, in their self-righteous scorn, fail to see his divine character, he reveals himself to the penitent thief as the sinner's Friend and Saviour. He thus teaches that the vilest sinner may find pardon and salvation through the merits of the blood of Christ. (3SP 158.1)

The Spirit of God illuminated the mind of this criminal, who took hold of Christ by faith, and, link after link, the chain of evidence that Jesus was the Messiah was joined together, until the suffering victim, in like condemnation with himself, stood forth before him as the Son of God. While the leading Jews deny him, and even the disciples doubt his divinity, the poor thief, upon the brink of eternity, at the close of his probation, calls Jesus his Lord! Many were ready to call him Lord when he wrought miracles, and also after he had risen from the grave; but none called him Lord as he hung dying upon the cross, save the penitent thief, who was saved at the eleventh hour. (3SP 158.2)

This was a genuine conversion under peculiar circumstances, for a special and peculiar purpose. It testified to all beholders that Jesus was not an impostor, but sustained his character, and carried out his mission to the closing scene of his earthly life. Never in his entire ministry were words more grateful to his ears than the utterance of faith from the lips of the dying thief, amid the blasphemy and taunts of the mob. But let no one neglect present opportunities and delay repentance, presuming on the eleventh-hour conversion of the thief, and trusting to a death-bed repentance. Every ray of light neglected leaves the sinner in greater darkness than before, till some fearful deception may take possession of his mind, and his case may become hopeless. Yet there are instances, like that of the poor thief, where enlightenment comes at the last moment, and is accepted with an intelligent faith. Such penitents find favor with Christ. (3SP 159.1)

With amazement the angels beheld the infinite love of Jesus, who, suffering the most excruciating agony of mind and body, thought only of others, and encouraged the penitent soul to believe. While pouring out his life in death, he exercised a love for man stronger than death. In Christ's humiliation, he, as a prophet, had addressed the daughters of Jerusalem; as priest and Advocate, he had pleaded with the Father to forgive the sins of his destroyers; as a loving Saviour, he had forgiven the iniquity of the penitent thief who called upon him. Many who witnessed those scenes upon Calvary were afterward established by them in the faith of Christ. (3SP 159.2)

The serpent lifted up in the wilderness represented the Son of man lifted upon the cross, Christ said to Nicodemus, "As Moses lifted up the serpent in the wilderness, even so must the Son of man be lifted up, that whosoever believeth in him should not perish, but have eternal life."

In the wilderness all who looked upon the elevated brazen serpent lived, while those who refused to look died. The two thieves upon the cross represent the two great classes of mankind. All have felt the poison of sin, represented by the sting of the fiery serpent in the wilderness. Those who look upon and believe in Jesus Christ, as the thief looked upon him when lifted upon the cross, shall live forever; but those who refuse to look upon him and believe in him, as the hardened thief refused to look upon and believe in the crucified Redeemer, shall die without hope. (3SP 159.3)

The enemies of Jesus now awaited his death with impatient hope. That event they imagined would forever hush the rumors of his divine power, and the wonders of his miracles. They flattered themselves that they should then no longer tremble because of his influence. The unfeeling soldiers who had stretched the body of Jesus upon the cross, divided his clothing among themselves, contending over one garment, which was woven without seam. They finally decided the matter by casting lots for it. The pen of inspiration had accurately described this scene hundreds of years before it took place: "For dogs have compassed me; the assembly of the wicked have inclosed me; they pierced my hands and my feet." "They parted my raiment among them, and for my vesture they did cast lots." (3SP 160.1)

The eyes of Jesus wandered over the multitude that had collected together to witness his death, and he saw at the foot of the cross John supporting Mary, the mother of Christ. She had returned to the terrible scene, not being able to longer remain away from her son. The last lesson of Jesus was one of filial love. He looked upon the grief-stricken face of his mother, and then upon John; said he, addressing the former: "Woman, behold thy son." Then, to the disciple: "Behold, thy mother," John well understood the words of Jesus, and the sacred trust which was committed to him. He immediately removed the mother of Christ from the fearful scene of Calvary. From that hour he cared for her as would a dutiful son, taking her to his own home. O pitiful, loving Saviour! Amid all his physical pain, and mental anguish, he had a tender, thoughtful care for the mother who had borne him. He had no money to leave her, by which to insure her future comfort, but he was enshrined in the heart of John, and he gave his mother unto the beloved disciple as a sacred legacy. This trust was to prove a great blessing to John, a constant reminder of his beloved Master. (3SP 160.2)

The perfect example of Christ's filial love shines forth with undimmed luster from the mist of ages. While enduring the keenest torture, he was not forgetful of his mother, but made all provision necessary for her future. The followers of Christ should feel that it is a part of their religion to respect and provide for their parents. No pretext of religious devotion can excuse a son or daughter from fulfilling the obligations due to a parent. (3SP 161.1)

The mission of Christ's earthly life was now nearly accomplished. His tongue was parched, and he said, "I thirst." They saturated a sponge with vinegar and gall and offered it him to drink; and when he had tasted it, he refused it. And now the Lord of life and glory was dying, a ransom for the race. It was the sense of sin, bringing the Father's wrath upon him as man's substitute, that made the cup he drank so bitter, and broke the heart of the Son of God. Death is not to be regarded as an angel of mercy. Nature recoils from the thought of dissolution, which is the consequence of sin. (3SP 161.2)

But it was not the dread of death which caused the inexpressible agony of Jesus. To believe this would be to place him beneath the martyrs in courage and endurance; for many of those who have died for their faith, yielded to torture and death, rejoicing that they were accounted worthy to suffer for Christ's sake. Christ was the prince of sufferers; but it was not bodily anguish that filled him with horror and despair; it was a sense of the malignity of sin, a knowledge that man had become so familiar with sin that he did not realize its enormity, that it was so deeply rooted in the human heart as to be difficult to eradicate. (3SP 162.1)

As man's substitute and surety, the iniquity of men was laid upon Christ; he was counted a transgressor that he might redeem them from the curse of the law. The guilt of every descendant of Adam of every age was pressing upon his heart; and the wrath of God, and the terrible manifestation of his displeasure because of iniquity, filled the soul of his Son with consternation. The withdrawal of the divine countenance from the Saviour, in this hour of supreme anguish, pierced his heart with a sorrow that can never be fully understood by man. Every pang endured by the Son of God upon the cross, the blood drops that flowed from his head, his hands, and feet, the convulsions of agony which racked his frame, and the unutterable anguish

Chapter 10 - Calvary (3SP 162.2)

that filled his soul at the hiding of his Father's face from him, speak to man, saying, It is for love of thee that the Son of God consents to have these heinous crimes laid upon him; for thee he spoils the domain of death, and opens the gates of Paradise and immortal life. He who stilled the angry waves by his word, and walked the foam-capped billows, who made devils tremble, and disease flee from his touch, who raised the dead to life and opened the eyes of the blind,–offers himself upon the cross as the last sacrifice for man. He, the sin-bearer, endures judicial punishment for iniquity, and becomes sin itself for man. (3SP 162.2)

Satan, with his fierce temptations, wrung the heart of Jesus. Sin, so hateful to his sight, was heaped upon him till he groaned beneath its weight. No wonder that his humanity trembled in that fearful hour. Angels witnessed with amazement the despairing agony of the Son of God, so much greater than his physical pain that the latter was hardly felt by him. The hosts of Heaven veiled their faces from the fearful sight. (3SP 163.1)

Inanimate nature expressed a sympathy with its insulted and dying Author. The sun refused to look upon the awful scene. Its full, bright rays were illuminating the earth at midday, when suddenly it seemed to be blotted out. Complete darkness enveloped the cross, and all the vicinity about, like a funeral pall. There was no eclipse or other natural cause for this darkness, which was deep as midnight without moon or stars. The dense blackness was an emblem of the soul-agony and horror that encompassed the Son of God. He had felt it in the garden of Gethsemane, when from his pores were forced drops of blood, and where he would have died had not an angel been sent from the courts of Heaven to invigorate the divine sufferer, that he might tread his blood-stained path to Calvary. (3SP 163.2)

The darkness lasted three full hours. No eye could pierce the gloom that enshrouded the cross, and none could penetrate the deeper gloom that flooded the suffering soul of Christ. A nameless terror took possession of all who were collected about the cross. The silence of the grave seemed to have fallen upon Calvary. The cursing and reviling ceased in the midst of half-uttered sentences. Men, women, and children prostrated themselves upon the earth in abject terror. Vivid lightnings, unaccompanied by thunder, occasionally flashed forth from the cloud, and revealed the cross and the crucified Redeemer. (3SP 164.1)

Priests, rulers, scribes, executioners, and the mob, all thought their time of retribution had come. After a while, some whispered to others that Jesus would now come down from the cross. Some attempted to grope their way back to the city, beating their breasts and wailing in fear. (3SP 164.2)

At the ninth hour the terrible darkness lifted from the people, but still wrapt the Saviour as in a mantle. The angry lightnings seemed to be hurled at him as he hung upon the cross. Then "Jesus cried with a loud voice, saying, Eloi, eloi, lama sabacthani? which is, being interpreted, My God, my God, why hast thou forsaken me?" As the outer gloom settled about Christ, many voices exclaimed, The vengeance of God is upon him! The bolts of God's wrath are hurled upon him because he claimed to be the Son of God! When the Saviour's despairing cry rang out, many who had believed on him were filled with terror; hope left them; if God had forsaken Jesus, what was to become of his followers, and the doctrine they had cherished? (3SP 164.3)

The darkness now lifted itself from the oppressed spirit of Christ, and he revived to a sense of physical suffering, and said, "I thirst." Here was a last opportunity for his persecutors to sympathize with and relieve him; but when the gloom was removed their terror abated, and the old dread returned that Jesus might even yet escape them, "and one ran and filled a sponge full of vinegar, and put it on a reed, and gave him to drink, saying, Let alone; let us see whether Elias will come to take him down." (3SP 165.1)

In yielding up his precious life, Christ was not cheered by triumphant joy; all was oppressive gloom. There hung upon the cross the spotless Lamb of God, his flesh lacerated with stripes and wounds; those precious hands, that had ever been ready to relieve the oppressed and suffering, extended upon the cross, and fastened by the cruel nails; those patient feet, that had traversed weary leagues in the dispensing of blessings and in teaching the doctrine of salvation to the world, bruised and spiked to the cross; his royal head wounded by a crown of thorns; those pale and quivering lips, that had ever been ready to respond to the plea of suffering humanity, shaped to the mournful words, "My God, my God, why hast thou forsaken me?" (3SP 165.2)

In silence the people watch for the end of

this fearful scene. Again the sun shines forth; but the cross is enveloped in darkness. Priests and rulers look toward Jerusalem; and lo, the dense cloud has settled upon the city, and over Judah's plains, and the fierce lightnings of God's wrath are directed against the fated city. Suddenly the gloom is lifted from the cross, and in clear trumpet tones, that seem to resound throughout creation, Jesus cries, "It is finished;" "Father, into thy hands I commend my spirit." A light encircled the cross, and the face of the Saviour shone with a glory like unto the sun. He then bowed his head upon his breast, and died. (3SP 165.3)

All the spectators stood paralyzed, and with bated breath gazed upon the Saviour. Again darkness settled upon the face of the earth, and a hoarse rumbling like heavy thunder was heard. This was accompanied by a violent trembling of the earth. The multitude were shaken together in heaps, and the wildest confusion and consternation ensued. In the surrounding mountains, rocks burst asunder with loud crashing, and many of them came tumbling down the heights to the plains below. The sepulchers were broken open, and the dead were cast out of their tombs. Creation seemed to be shivering to atoms. Priests, rulers, soldiers, and executioners were mute with terror, and prostrate upon the ground. (3SP 166.1)

The darkness was again lifted from Calvary, and hung like a pall over Jerusalem. At the moment in which Christ died, there were priests ministering in the temple before the vail which separated the holy from the most holy place. Suddenly they felt the earth tremble beneath them, and the vail of the temple, a strong, rich drapery that had been renewed yearly, was rent in twain from top to bottom by the same bloodless hand that wrote the words of doom upon the walls of Belshazzar's palace. The most holy place, that had been sacredly entered by human feet only once a year, was revealed to the common gaze. God had ever before protected his temple in a wonderful manner; but now its sacred mysteries were exposed to curious eyes. No longer would the presence of God overshadow the earthly mercy-seat. No longer would the light of his glory flash forth upon, nor the cloud of his disapproval shadow, the precious stones in the breastplate of the high priest. (3SP 166.2)

When Christ died upon the cross of Calvary, a new and living way was opened to both Jew and Gentile. The Saviour was henceforth to officiate as Priest and Advocate in the Heaven of heavens. From henceforth the blood of beasts offered for sin was valueless; for the Lamb of God had died for the sins of the world. The darkness upon the face of nature expressed her sympathy with Christ in his expiring agony. It evidenced to humanity that the Sun of Righteousness, the Light of the world, was withdrawing his beams from the once favored city of Jerusalem, and from the world. It was a miraculous testimony given of God, that the faith of after generations might be confirmed. (3SP 167.1)

Jesus did not yield up his life till he had accomplished the work which he came to do; and he exclaimed with his parting breath, "It is finished!" Angels rejoiced as the words were uttered; for the great plan of redemption was being triumphantly carried out. There was joy in Heaven that the sons of Adam could now, through a life of obedience, be exalted finally to the presence of God. Satan was defeated, and knew that his kingdom was lost. (3SP 167.2)

When the Christian fully comprehends the magnitude of the great sacrifice made by the Majesty of Heaven, then will the plan of salvation be magnified before him, and to meditate upon Calvary will awaken the deepest and most sacred emotions of his heart. Contemplation of the Saviour's matchless love should absorb the mind, touch and melt the heart, refine and elevate the affections, and completely transform the whole character. The language of the apostle is, "I determined not to know anything among you, save Jesus Christ, and him crucified." And we may look toward Calvary and exclaim, "God forbid that I should glory, save in the cross of our Lord Jesus Christ, by whom the world is crucified unto me, and I unto the world." (3SP 168.1)

With the death of Christ the hopes of his disciples seemed to perish. They looked upon his closed eyelids and drooping head, his hair matted with blood, his pierced hands and feet, and their anguish was indescribable. They had not believed until the last that he would die, and they could hardly credit their senses that he was really dead. The Majesty of Heaven had yielded up his life, forsaken of the believers, unattended by one act of relief or word of sympathy; for even the pitying angels had not been permitted to minister to their beloved Commander. (3SP 168.2)

Chapter 10 - Calvary (3SP 168.3)

Evening drew on, and an unearthly stillness hung over Calvary. The crowd dispersed, and many returned to Jerusalem greatly changed in spirit from what they had been in the morning. Many of them had then collected at the crucifixion from curiosity, and not from hatred toward Christ. Still they accepted the fabricated reports of the priests concerning him, and looked upon him as a malefactor. At the execution they had imbibed the spirit of the leading Jews, and, under an unnatural excitement, had united with the mob in mocking and railing against him. (3SP 168.3)

But when the earth was draped with blackness, and they stood accused by their own consciences, reason again resumed her sway, and they felt guilty of doing a great wrong. No jest nor mocking laughter was heard in the midst of that fearful gloom; and when it was lifted, they solemnly made their way to their homes, awestruck and conscience-smitten. They were convinced that the accusations of the priests were false, that Jesus was no pretender; and a few weeks later they were among the thousands who became thorough converts to Christ, when Peter preached upon the day of Pentecost, and the great mystery of the cross was explained with other mysteries in regard to Messiah. (3SP 169.1)

The Roman officers in charge were standing about the cross when Jesus cried out, "It is finished," in a voice of startling power, and then instantly died with that cry of victory upon his lips. They had never before witnessed a death like that upon the cross. It was an unheard-of thing for one to die thus within six hours after crucifixion. Death by crucifixion was a slow and lingering process; nature became more and more exhausted until it was difficult to determine when life had become extinct. But for a man dying thus to summon such power of voice and clearness of utterance as Jesus had done, immediately before his death, was such an astonishing event that the Roman officers, experienced in such scenes, marveled greatly; and the centurion who commanded the detachment of soldiers on duty there, immediately declared, "Truly this was the Son of God." Thus three men, differing widely from one another, openly declared their belief in Christ upon the very day of his death–he who commanded the Roman guard, he who bore the cross of his Saviour, and he who died upon the cross by his side. (3SP 169.2)

The spectators, and the soldiers who guarded the cross, were convinced, so far as their minds were capable of grasping the idea, that Jesus was the Redeemer for whom Israel had so long looked. But the darkness that mantled the earth could not be more dense than that which enveloped the minds of the priests and rulers. They were unchanged by the events they had witnessed, and their hatred of Jesus had not abated with his death. (3SP 170.1)

At his birth the angel star in the heavens had known Christ, and had conducted the seers to the manger where he lay. The heavenly hosts had known him, and sung his praise over the plains of Bethlehem. The sea had acknowledged his voice, and was obedient to his command. Disease and death had recognized his authority, and yielded their prey to his demand. The sun had known him, and hidden its face of light from the sight of his dying anguish. The rocks had known him, and shivered into fragments at his dying cry. Although inanimate nature recognized, and bore testimony of Christ, that he was the Son of God, yet the priests and rulers knew not the Saviour, rejected the evidence of his divinity, and steeled their hearts against his truths. They were not so susceptible as the granite rocks of the mountains. (3SP 170.2)

The Jews were unwilling that the bodies of those who had been executed should remain that night upon the cross. They dreaded to have the attention of the people directed any farther to the events attending the death of Jesus. They feared the results of that day's work upon the minds of the public. So, under pretext that they did not wish the sanctity of the Sabbath to be defiled by the bodies remaining upon the cross during that holy day, which was the one following the crucifixion, the leading Jews sent a request to Pilate that he would permit them to hasten the death of the victims, so that their bodies might be removed before the setting of the sun. (3SP 171.1)

Pilate was as unwilling as they were that the spectacle of Jesus upon the cross should remain a moment longer than was necessary. The consent of the governor having been obtained, the legs of the two that were crucified with Jesus were broken to hasten their death; but Jesus was already dead, and they broke not his legs. The rude soldiers, who had witnessed the looks and words of Jesus upon his way to Calvary, and while dying upon the cross, were softened by what they had witnessed, and were restrained from marring him by breaking his limbs. Thus was prophecy fulfilled, which declared that a bone of him should not be broken; and the law of the passover, requiring the sacrifice to be perfect and whole, was also fulfilled in the offering of the Lamb of God. "They shall leave none of it unto the morning, nor break any bone of it; according to all the ordinances of the passover they shall keep it." (3SP 171.2)

A soldier, at the suggestion of the priests who wished to make the death of Jesus sure, thrust his spear into the Saviour's side, inflicting a wound which would have caused instant death if he had not already been dead. From the wide incision made by the spear there flowed two copious and distinct streams, one of blood, the other of water. This remarkable fact was noted by all the beholders, and John states the occurrence very definitely; he says: "One of the soldiers with a spear pierced his side, and forthwith came there out blood and water. And he that saw it bare record, and his record is true; and he knoweth that he saith true, that ye might believe. For these things were done that the scripture should be fulfilled, A bone of him shall not be broken. And again another scripture saith, They shall look on him whom they pierced." (3SP 172.1)

After the resurrection, the priests and rulers caused the report to be circulated that Jesus did not die upon the cross, that he merely fainted and was afterward resuscitated. Another lying report affirmed that it was not a real body of flesh and bone but the likeness of a body that was laid in the tomb. But the testimony of John concerning the pierced side of the Saviour, and the blood and water that flowed from the wound, refutes these falsehoods that were brought into existence by the unscrupulous Jews. (3SP 172.2)

Chapter 11
At the Sepulcher

Treason against the Roman government was the alleged crime for which Jesus was executed, and persons put to death for this offense were taken down by the common soldiers and consigned to a burial ground reserved exclusively for that class of criminals who had suffered the extreme penalty of the law. (3SP 173.1)

John was at a loss to know what measures he should take in regard to the body of his beloved Master. He shuddered at the thought of its being handled by rough and unfeeling soldiers, and placed in a dishonored burial place. He knew he could obtain no favors from the Jewish authorities, and he could hope little from Pilate. But Joseph and Nicodemus came to the front in this emergency. Both of these men were members of the Sanhedrim, and acquainted with Pilate. Both were men of wealth and influence. They were determined that the body of Jesus should have an honorable burial. (3SP 173.2)

Joseph went boldly to Pilate, and begged from him the body of Jesus for burial. His prayer was speedily granted by Pilate, who firmly believed Jesus to have been innocent. Pilate now for the first time heard from Joseph that Jesus was really dead. The knowledge had been purposely kept from him, although various conflicting reports had reached his ears concerning the strange events attending the crucifixion. Now he learned that the Saviour died at the very moment when the mysterious darkness that enshrouded the earth had passed away. Pilate was surprised that Jesus had died so soon; for those who were crucified frequently lingered days upon the cross. The account which Pilate now received of the death of Jesus caused him more firmly to believe that he was no ordinary man. The Roman governor was strangely agitated, and regretted most keenly the part he had taken in the condemnation of the Saviour. (3SP 173.3)

The priests and rulers had charged Pilate and his officers to guard against any deception which the disciples of Jesus might attempt to practice upon them in regard to the body of their Master. Pilate, therefore, before granting the request of Joseph, sent for the centurion who was in command of the soldiers at the cross, and heard for a certainty from his lips that Jesus was dead; and in compliance with Pilate's earnest request he recounted the fearful scenes of Calvary, corroborating the testimony of Joseph. (3SP 174.1)

Pilate then gave an official order that the body of Jesus should be given to Joseph. While the disciple John was anxious and troubled about the sacred remains of his beloved Master, Joseph of Arimathea returned with the commission from the governor; and Nicodemus, anticipating the result of Joseph's interview with Pilate, came with a costly mixture of myrrh and aloes of about one hundred pounds' weight. The most honored in all Jerusalem could not have been shown more respect in death. (3SP 174.2)

The women of Galilee had remained with the disciple John to see what disposition would be made of the body of Jesus, which was very precious to them, although their faith in him as the promised Messiah had perished with him. The disciples were plunged in sorrow; they were so overwhelmed by the events which had transpired that they were unable to recall the words of Jesus stating that just such things would take place concerning him. The women were astonished to see Joseph and Nicodemus, both honored and wealthy councilors, as anxious and interested as themselves for the proper disposal of the body of Jesus. (3SP 174.3)

Neither of these men had openly attached himself to the Saviour while he was living, although both believed on him. They knew that if they declared their faith they would be excluded from the Sanhedrim council, on account of the prejudice of the priests and elders toward Jesus. This would have cut them off from all power to aid or protect him by using their influence in the council. Several times they had shown the fallacy of the grounds of his condemnation, and protested against his arrest, and the council had broken up without accomplishing that for which it had been called together; for it was impossible to procure the condemnation of Jesus without the unanimous consent of the Sanhedrim. The object of the priests had finally been obtained by calling a secret council, to which Joseph and Nicodemus were not summoned. (3SP 175.1)

The two councilors now came boldly forth to the aid of the disciples. The help of these rich and honored men was greatly needed at that time. They could do for the slain Saviour what it was impossible for the poorer disciples to do; and their influential positions protected them, in a great measure, from censure and remonstrance. While the acknowledged disciples of Christ were too thoroughly disheartened and intimidated to show themselves openly to be his followers, these men came boldly to the front and acted their noble part. (3SP 175.2)

Gently and reverently they removed with their own hands the body of Jesus from the instrument of torture, their sympathetic tears falling fast as they looked upon his bruised and lacerated form, which they carefully bathed and cleansed from the stain of blood. Joseph owned a new tomb, hewn from stone, which he was reserving for himself; it was near Calvary, and he now prepared this sepulcher for Jesus. The body, together with the spices brought by Nicodemus, was carefully wrapped in a linen sheet, and the three disciples bore their precious burden to the new sepulcher, wherein man had never before lain. There they straightened those mangled limbs, and folded the bruised hands upon the pulseless breast. The Galilean women drew near, to see that all had been done that could be done for the lifeless form of their beloved Teacher. Then they saw the heavy stone rolled against the entrance of the sepulcher, and the Son of God was left at rest. The women were last at the cross, and last at the tomb of Christ. While the evening shades were gathering, Mary Magdalene and the other Marys lingered about the sacred resting-place of their Lord, shedding tears of sorrow over the fate of Him whom they loved. (3SP 176.1)

Although the Jewish rulers had carried out their fiendish purpose in putting to death the Son of God, their apprehensions were not quieted, nor was their jealousy of Christ dead. Mingled with the joy of gratified revenge, there was an ever-present fear that his dead body lying in Joseph's tomb would come forth to life. They had labored to believe that he was a deceiver; but it was in vain. They everywhere heard inquiries of Jesus of Nazareth from those who had not heard of his death, and had brought their sick and dying friends to the passover to be healed by the great Physician. The priests knew in their hearts that Jesus had been all-powerful; they had witnessed his miracle at the grave of Lazarus; they knew that he had there raised the dead to life, and they trembled for fear he would himself rise from the dead. (3SP 176.2)

They had heard him declare that he had power to lay down his life and to take it up again; they remembered that he had said, "Destroy this temple, and in three days I will raise it up;" they put this and that together, and were afraid. When Judas had betrayed his Master to the priests, he had repeated to them the declaration which Jesus had privately made to his disciples while on their way to the city. He had said, "Behold, we go up to Jerusalem; and the Son of man shall be betrayed unto the chief priests and unto the scribes, and they shall condemn him to death, and shall deliver him to the Gentiles to mock, and to scourge, and to crucify him; and the third day he shall rise again." They remembered many things which he had said, that they now recognized as plain prophecies of the events which had taken place. They did not desire to think of these things, but they could not shut them from their understanding. Like their father, the devil, they believed and trembled. (3SP 177.1)

Now that the frenzy of excitement was passed, the image of Christ would intrude upon their minds, as he stood serene and uncomplaining before his enemies, suffering their taunts and abuse without a murmur. They remembered the prayer for forgiveness, offered in behalf of those who nailed him to the cross, his forgetfulness of his own suffering, and his merciful response to the prayer of the dying thief, the darkness which covered the earth, its sudden lifting, and his triumphant cry, "It is finished," which seemed to resound through the universe, his immediate death, the quaking of the earth and the shivering of the rocks, the opening of the graves and the rending of the vail of the temple. All these remarkable circumstances pressed upon their minds the overpowering evidence that Jesus was the Son of God. (3SP 177.2)

When Judas had reported to the priests the words of Jesus in regard to his approaching

Chapter 11 - At the Sepulcher (3SP 178.1)

death, they had ridiculed the idea of his foreknowledge of events. All his predictions had been so far fulfilled, and they felt no surety that his entire prediction would not come to pass. If Jesus rose from the dead, they feared that their lives would pay the penalty of their crime. They could not sleep, for they were more troubled about Jesus in death than they had been during his life. They had then thought that their only hope of prosperity and influence was in silencing his reproving voice; now they trembled in view of the miraculous power he had possessed. (3SP 178.1)

They rested but little upon the Sabbath. Though they would not step over a Gentile's threshold for fear of defilement, yet they held a council concerning the body of Christ. They knew that the disciples would not attempt to remove him until after the Sabbath; but they were anxious that all precautions should be taken at its close. Therefore "the chief priests and Pharisees came together unto Pilate, saying, Sir, we remember that that deceiver said, while he was yet alive, After three days I will rise again. Command, therefore, that the sepulcher be made sure until the third day, lest his disciples come by night, and steal him away, and say unto the people, He is risen from the dead; so the last error shall be worse than the first." Pilate was as unwilling as were the Jews that Jesus should rise with power to punish the guilt of those who had destroyed him, and he placed a band of Roman soldiers at the command of the priests. Said he, "Ye have a watch; go your way, make it as sure as ye can. So they went, and made the sepulcher sure, sealing the stone and setting a watch." (3SP 178.2)

The discipline of the Roman army was very severe. A sentinel found sleeping at his post was punishable with death. The Jews realized the advantage of having such a guard about the tomb of Jesus. They placed a seal upon the stone that closed the sepulcher, that it might not be disturbed without the fact being known, and took every precaution against the disciples practicing any deception in regard to the body of Jesus. But all their plans and precautions only served to make the triumph of the resurrection more complete, and to more fully establish its truth. (3SP 179.1)

How must God and his holy angels have looked upon all those preparations to guard the body of the world's Redeemer! How weak and foolish must those efforts have seemed! The words of the psalmist picture this scene: "Why do the heathen rage, and the people imagine a vain thing? The kings of the earth set themselves, and the rulers take counsel together against the Lord, and against his Anointed, saying, Let us break their bands asunder, and cast away their cords from us. He that sitteth in the heavens shall laugh; the Lord shall have them in derision." Roman guards and Roman arms were powerless to confine the Lord of life within the narrow inclosure of the sepulcher. Christ had declared that he had power to lay down his life and to take it up again. The hour of his victory was near. (3SP 179.2)

God had ruled the events clustering around the birth of Christ. There was an appointed time for him to appear in the form of humanity. A long line of inspired prophecy pointed to the coming of Christ to our world, and minutely described the manner of his reception. Had the Saviour appeared at an earlier period in the world's history, the advantages gained to Christians would not have been so great, as their faith would not have been developed and strengthened by dwelling upon the prophecies which stretched into the far future, and recounted the events which were to transpire. (3SP 180.1)

Because of the wicked departure of the Jews from God, he had allowed them to come under the power of a heathen nation. Only a certain limited power was granted the Jews; even the Sanhedrim was not allowed to pronounce final judgment upon any important case which involved the infliction of capital punishment. A people controlled, as were the Jews, by bigotry and superstition, are most cruel and unrelenting. The wisdom of God was displayed in sending his Son to the world at a time when the Roman power held sway. Had the Jewish economy possessed full authority, we should not now have a history of the life and ministry of Christ among men. The jealous priests and rulers would have quickly made away with so formidable a rival. He would have been stoned to death on the false accusation of breaking the law of God. The Jews put no one to death by crucifixion; that was a Roman method of punishment; there would therefore have been no cross upon Calvary. Prophecy would not then have been fulfilled; for Christ was to be lifted up in the most public manner on the cross, as the serpent was lifted up in the wilderness. (3SP 180.2)

The Roman power was the instrument in

Chapter 11 - At the Sepulcher

God's hand to prevent the Light of the world from going out in darkness. The cross was lifted, according to the plan of God, in the sight of all nations, tongues, and people, calling their attention to the Lamb of God that taketh away the sins of the world. (3SP 181.1)

Had the coming of Christ been deferred many years later, until the Jewish power had become still less, prophecy would have failed of its fulfillment; for it would not have been possible for the Jews, with their waning power, to have influenced the Roman authorities to sign the death-warrant of Jesus upon the lying charges presented, and there would have been no cross of Christ erected upon Calvary. Soon after the Saviour's execution the method of death by crucifixion was abolished. The scenes which took place at the death of Jesus, the inhuman conduct of the people, the supernatural darkness which veiled the earth, and the agony of nature displayed in the rending of the rocks and the flashing of the lightning, struck them with such remorse and terror, that the cross, as an instrument of death, soon fell into disuse. At the destruction of Jerusalem, when mob power again obtained control, crucifixion was again revived for a time, and many crosses stood upon Calvary. (3SP 181.2)

Christ coming at the time and in the manner which he did was a direct and complete fulfillment of prophecy. The evidence of this, given to the world through the testimony of the apostles and that of their contemporaries, is among the strongest proofs of the Christian faith. We were not eye-witnesses of the miracles of Jesus, which attest his divinity; but we have the statements of his disciples who were eye-witnesses of them, and we see by faith through their eyes, and hear through their ears; and our faith with theirs grasps the evidence given. (3SP 182.1)

The apostles accepted Jesus upon the testimony of prophets and righteous men, stretching over a period of many centuries. The Christian world have a full and complete chain of evidence running through both the Old and the new testament; in the one pointing to a Saviour to come, and in the other fulfilling the conditions of that prophecy. All this is sufficient to establish the faith of those who are willing to believe. The design of God was to leave the race a fair opportunity to develop faith in the power of God and of his Son and in the work of the Holy Spirit. (3SP 182.2)

Chapter 12
The Conflict Ended

When Christ cried out, "It is finished," all Heaven triumphed. The controversy between Christ and Satan in regard to the execution of the plan of salvation was ended. The spirit of Satan and his works had taken deep root in the affections of the children of men. For Satan to have come into power would have been death to the world. The implacable hatred he felt toward the Son of God was revealed in his manner of treating him while he was in the world. Christ's betrayal, trial, and crucifixion were all planned by the fallen foe. His hatred, carried out in the death of the Son of God, placed Satan where his true diabolical character was revealed to all created intelligences that had not fallen through sin. (3SP 183.1)

The holy angels were horror-stricken that one who had been of their number could fall so far as to be capable of such cruelty. Every sentiment of sympathy or pity which they had ever felt for Satan in his exile, was quenched in their hearts. That his envy should be exercised in such a revenge upon an innocent person was enough to strip him of his assumed robe of celestial light, and to reveal the hideous deformity beneath; but to manifest such malignity toward the divine Son of God, who had, with unprecedented self-denial, and love for the creatures formed in his image, come from Heaven and assumed their fallen nature, was such a heinous crime against Heaven that it caused the angels to shudder with horror, and severed forever the last tie of sympathy existing between Satan and the heavenly world. Satan had put forth extraordinary efforts against Jesus from the time he appeared as a babe in Bethlehem. He had sought in every possible manner to prevent him from developing a perfect childhood, a faultless manhood, a holy ministry, and an infinite sacrifice in yielding up his life without a murmur for the sins of men. But Satan had been unable to discourage him, or to drive him from the work he had come on earth to do. The storm of Satan's wrath beat upon him from the desert to Calvary; but the more mercilessly it fell, the more firmly did the Son of God cling to the hand of his Father, and press on in the bloodstained path before him. All the efforts of Satan to oppress and overwhelm him, only brought out in a purer light the spotless character of Christ. (3SP 183.2)

In the controversy between Christ and Satan, the character of God was now fully vindicated in his act of banishing from Heaven the fallen angel, who had once been exalted next to Christ. All Heaven, and the worlds that had not fallen through sin, had been witnesses to the controversy between Christ and Satan. With what intense interest had they followed the closing scenes of the conflict! They had beheld the Saviour enter the garden of Gethsemane, his soul bowed down by a horror of darkness that he had never before experienced. An overmastering agony had wrenched from his lips the bitter cry for that cup, if possible, to pass from him. A terrible amazement, as he felt his Father's presence withdrawn from him, had filled his divine spirit with a shuddering dread. He was sorrowful, with a bitterness of sorrow exceeding that of the last great struggle with death; the sweat of blood was forced from his pores, and fell in drops upon the ground. Thrice the same prayer for deliverance had been wrung from his lips. Heaven had been unable to longer endure the sight, and had sent a messenger of consolation to the prostrate Son of God, fainting and dying under the accumulated guilt of the world. (3SP 184.1)

Heaven had beheld the victim betrayed and hurried from one earthly tribunal to another with mockery and violence. It had heard the sneers of his persecutors because of his lowly birth, and his denial with cursing and swearing by one of his best-loved disciples. It had seen the frenzied work of Satan, and his power over the hearts of men. Oh, fearful scene! the Saviour seized at midnight in Gethsemane as a murderer, dragged to and fro from palace to judgment hall, arraigned twice before the priests, twice before the Sanhedrim, twice before Pilate, and once

Chapter 12 - The Conflict Ended (3SP 188.1)

before Herod, mocked, scourged, and condemned, led out to be crucified, bearing the heavy burden of the cross amid the wailing of the daughters of Jerusalem and the jeering of the crowd! (3SP 185.1)

Heaven had viewed with grief and amazement Christ hanging upon the cross, blood flowing from his wounded temples, and sweat tinged with blood standing upon his brow. From his hands and feet the blood had fallen, drop by drop, upon the rock drilled for the foot of the cross. The wounds made by the nails had gaped as the weight of his body dragged upon his hands. His labored breath had grown quick and deep, as his soul panted under the burden of the sins of the world. All Heaven had been filled with admiration when the prayer of Christ was offered in the midst of his terrible suffering–"Father, forgive them; for they know not what they do." Yet there stood men, formed in the image of God, joining with Satan to crush out the last spark of life from the heart of the Son of God. (3SP 185.2)

In Christ was the embodiment of God himself. The plan and execution of man's salvation is a demonstration of divine wisdom and power mysterious to finite minds. The unfathomable love of God for the human race, in giving his Son to die for them, was made manifest. Christ was revealed in all his self-sacrificing love and purity; man could now obtain immortal life through his merits. When the justice of God was expressed in judicial sentence, declaring the final disposition of Satan, that he should be utterly consumed with all those who ranked under his banner, all Heaven rang with hallelujahs, and "Worthy is the Lamb that was slain to have all authority and power, and dominion, and glory." (3SP 186.1)

When we dwell upon the justice of God, we look upon only one side of his character; for in his greatness and might he has condescended to our feebleness in sending his Son to the world that man may not perish. In the cross we may read his tender mercy and forgiveness, harmoniously combined with his stern, unwavering justice. The severity of God is felt when we are separated from him; but when we repent of our sins, and make our peace with him through the virtue of the cross, we find him a merciful Father, reconciled to men through his Son. (3SP 186.2)

The body of Jesus was hastily placed in the tomb because of the near approach of the Sabbath, that the disciples might keep the day according to the commandment. The two Marys were the last at the sepulcher. This was a never-to-be-forgotten Sabbath to the sorrowing disciples, and also to the priests, rulers, scribes, and people. The passover was observed as it had been for centuries, while the antitypical Lamb, which it prefigured, had been slain by wicked hands, and lay in Joseph's tomb. Crowds of worshipers filled the courts of the temple and presented their morning and evening sacrifices as heretofore. Many minds were busy with thoughts started by the scenes of Calvary. Many sleepless eyes, from the crucifixion to the resurrection, were constantly searching the prophecies; some to learn the full meaning of the feast they were then celebrating; some to find evidence that Jesus was not what he claimed to be; and others, with disappointed hopes and sorrowful hearts, searched for convincing proof that he was the Messiah. Though searching with different objects in view, they were all convicted of the same truth–that prophecy had been fulfilled in the events of the past few days, and that the crucified one was indeed the world's Redeemer. (3SP 186.3)

The priests who ministered before the altar had gloomy presentiments as they looked upon the vail, rent by unseen hands from top to bottom, and which there had not been time to replace or to fully repair. The uncovering of the sacred mysteries of the most holy place brought to them a shuddering dread of coming calamity. Many of the officiating priests were deeply convicted of the true character of Jesus; their searching of the prophecies had not been in vain, and after he was raised from the dead they acknowledged him as the Son of God. (3SP 187.1)

The faith of the disciples was clouded with doubt. They were too thoroughly perplexed and uncertain to recall the words of Jesus, warning them beforehand of the things which would take place. They were indeed as sheep scattered without a shepherd. But they had never loved their Lord as now. They had never felt his worth and their need of him as when they were deprived of his society. (3SP 188.1)

Nicodemus, when he saw Jesus lifted upon the cross, remembered his words in that private interview at night in the mountains. On that Sabbath, while Christ lay silent in the grave, he had a favorable opportunity for reflection. A clearer light now illuminated his mind and the

Chapter 12 - The Conflict Ended (3SP 188.2)

words which Jesus had addressed to him were no longer mysterious. He felt that he had lost much by not connecting himself with Jesus while he was upon earth. When the Saviour was lifted upon the cross, Nicodemus remembered that he had told him that the Son of man should be lifted up as the serpent was lifted up in the wilderness. The prayer of Christ for his murderers, and his answer to the petition of the dying thief, while he himself was suffering the excruciating tortures of a death upon the cross, spoke with powerful distinctness to the heart of the learned councilor. And that last cry: "It is finished," spoken like the words of a conqueror, together with the reeling earth, the darkened heavens, the rent vail, the shivered rocks, forever settled the faith of Nicodemus. (3SP 188.2)

Joseph had believed on Jesus, though he had kept silent. Now all the fears of both these men were overcome by the courage of a firm and unwavering faith. During that memorable passover the scenes of the crucifixion were the theme of thought, and the topic of conversation. Hundreds had brought with them to the passover their afflicted relatives and friends, expecting to see Jesus and prevail upon him to heal and save them. Great was their disappointment to find that he was not at the feast; and when they were told that he had been executed as a criminal, their indignation and grief knew no bounds. No hope of their ever meeting him again, of hearing his words of reproof and warning, of comfort and hope in the streets of Jerusalem, by the lake, in the synagogues, and in the groves. (3SP 188.3)

The events of his death were recounted to these strangers by two parties. Those who helped put him to death made their false statements; and those who loved him, those whom he had healed and comforted, related the terrible truth, together with their own experience, and the wonders he had done for them. The sufferers who had come with the expectation of being healed by the Saviour sank under their disappointment. The streets and the temple courts were filled with mourning. The sick were dying for want of the healing touch of Jesus of Nazareth. Physicians were consulted in vain; there was no skill like that of Him who lay in state in Joseph's tomb. The afflicted, who had long looked forward to this time as their only hope of relief, asked in vain for the Healer they had sought. (3SP 189.1)

Many whose voices had swelled the cry of "Crucify him, crucify him!" now realized the calamity that had fallen upon them, and would have as eagerly cried, "Give us Jesus!" had he still been alive. The mourning cries of the sick and dying, who now had no one to save them, brought home the truth to thousands of minds, that a great light had gone out of the world. The death of Jesus left a blank which could not be supplied. The priests and rulers were ill at ease; they heard the people calling for Jesus of Nazareth, and they avoided them as much as possible. (3SP 189.2)

Upon this occasion those who were suspected of being attacked by the leprosy were examined by the priests. Many were forced to hear their husbands, wives, or children pronounced unclean, and doomed to go forth from the shelter of their homes and the care of their friends, and to warn off the stranger with the mournful cry, "Unclean, unclean!" The friendly hands of Jesus of Nazareth, that never refused to touch with healing the loathsome leper, were folded silently upon his breast, bearing the marks of the cruel nails. Those lips, that had answered his petition of relief with the comforting words: "I will; be thou clean," were silent now in death. Men never knew how much Christ was to the world, till his light was quenched in the darkness of the tomb. They heard the sufferers helplessly calling for Jesus until their voices were lost in death. (3SP 190.1)

The revenge which the priests thought would be so sweet had already become bitterness to them. They knew that they were meeting the severe censure of the people; they knew that the very persons whom they had influenced against Jesus were now horrified by their own shameful work. As they witnessed all these proofs of the divine influence of Jesus, they were more afraid of his dead body in the tomb than they had been of him when he was living and among them. The possibility of his coming forth from the sepulcher filled their guilty souls with indescribable terror. They felt that Jesus might at any time stand before them, the accused to become the accuser, the condemned to in turn condemn, the slain to demand justice in the death of his murderers. (3SP 190.2)

*****

Chapter 13
The Resurrection

Every preparation had been made at the sepulcher to prevent any surprise or fraud being perpetrated by the disciples. The night had worn slowly away, and the darkest hour before daybreak had come. The Roman guards were keeping their weary watch, the sentinels pacing to and fro before the sepulcher, while the remainder of the detachment of one hundred soldiers were reclining upon the ground in different positions, taking what rest they could. But angels were also guarding the sepulcher, one of whom could have stricken down the whole Roman army by the putting forth of his power. (3SP 191.1)

One of the most exalted order of angels is sent from Heaven; his countenance is like the lightning, and his garments white as snow. He parts the darkness from his track, and the whole heavens are lit with his resplendent glory. The sleeping soldiers start simultaneously to their feet, and gaze with awe and wonder at the open, lighted heavens, and the vision of brightness which approaches. The earth trembles and heaves; soldiers, officers, and sentinels all fall as dead men prostrate upon the earth. The evil angels, who have triumphantly claimed the body of Christ, flee in terror from the place. One of the mighty, commanding angels who has, with his company, been keeping watch over the tomb of his Master, joins the powerful angel who comes from Heaven; and together they advance directly to the sepulcher. (3SP 191.2)

The angelic commander laid hold of the great stone which had required many strong men to place it in position, rolled it away, and took his seat upon it, while his companion entered the sepulcher and unwound the wrappings from the face and head of Jesus. Then the mighty angel, with a voice that caused the earth to quake, was heard: Jesus, thou Son of God, thy Father calls thee! Then he who had earned the power to conquer death and the grave came forth, with the tread of a conqueror, from the sepulcher, amid the reeling of the earth, the flashing of lightning, and the roaring of thunder. An earthquake marked the hour when Christ laid down his life; and another earthquake signaled the moment when he took it up again in triumph. (3SP 192.1)

Jesus was the first-fruits of them that slept. When he came forth from the tomb he called a multitude from the dead, thus settling forever the long-disputed question of the resurrection. In raising this multitude of captives from the dead, he gives evidence that there will be a final resurrection of those who sleep in Jesus. The believers in Christ thus receive the very light they want in regard to the future life of the pious dead. (3SP 192.2)

Satan was bitterly incensed that his angels had fled from the presence of the heavenly angels, and that Christ had conquered death, and shown by this act what his future power was to be. All the triumph that Satan had experienced in witnessing his own power over men, which had urged them on to insult and murder the Son of God, fled before this exhibition of the divine power of Christ. He had dared to hope that Jesus would not take up his life again; but his courage failed him when the Saviour came forth, having paid the full ransom of man, and enabled him to overcome Satan in his own behalf in the name of Christ, the Conqueror. The arch-enemy now knew that he must eventually die, and that his kingdom would have an end. (3SP 193.1)

In this scene of the resurrection of the Son of God is given a lively image of the glory that will be revealed at the general resurrection of the just at the second appearing of Christ in the clouds of heaven. Then the dead that are in their graves shall hear his voice and come forth to life; and not only the earth, but the heavens themselves, shall be shaken. A few graves were opened at the resurrection of Christ; but at his second coming all the precious dead, from righteous Abel to the last saint that dies, shall awake to glorious, immortal life. (3SP 193.2)

If the soldiers at the sepulcher were so filled with terror at the appearance of one angel clothed with heavenly light and strength, that

Chapter 13 - The Resurrection (3SP 193.3)

they fell as dead men to the ground, how will his enemies stand before the Son of God, when he comes in power and great glory, accompanied by ten thousand times ten thousand, and thousands of thousands of angels from the courts of Heaven? Then the earth shall reel to and fro like a drunkard, and be removed as a cottage. The elements shall be in flames, and the heavens shall be rolled together as a scroll. (3SP 193.3)

At the death of Jesus the soldiers had beheld the earth wrapped in profound darkness at midday; but at the resurrection they saw the brightness of the angels illuminate the night, and heard the inhabitants of Heaven singing with great joy and triumph: Thou hast vanquished Satan and the powers of darkness! Thou hast swallowed up death in victory! "And I heard a loud voice saying in Heaven, Now is come salvation and strength, and the kingdom of our God, and the power of his Christ; for the accuser of our brethren is cast down, who accused them before our God day and night." (3SP 194.1)

The casting down of Satan as an accuser of the brethren in Heaven was accomplished by the great work of Christ in giving up his life. Notwithstanding Satan's persistent opposition, the plan of redemption was being carried out. Man was esteemed of sufficient value for Christ to sacrifice his life for him. Satan, knowing that the empire he had usurped would in the end be wrested from him, determined to spare no pains to destroy as many as possible of the creatures whom God had created in his image. He hated man because Christ had manifested for him such forgiving love and pity, and he now prepared to practice upon him every species of deception by which he might be lost; he pursued his course with more energy because of his own hopeless condition. (3SP 194.2)

Christ came to earth to vindicate the claims of his Father's law, and his death shows the immutability of that law. But Satan thrusts upon man the fallacy, that the law of God was abolished by the death of Christ, and he thus leads many professed Christians to transgress the Father's commandments, while they assume devotion to his Son. (3SP 195.1)

The Christian world is not sufficiently acquainted with the history of Satan, and the terrible power that he wields. Many look upon him as a mere imaginary being. Meanwhile he has crept into the popular mind; he sways the people–he assumes the character of an angel of light–he marshals his trained forces like a skilled general–he has gained profound knowledge of human nature, and can be logical, philosophical, or hypocritically religious. (3SP 195.2)

He now prepared to work upon the minds of the priests in regard to the event of the resurrection of Christ. He knew that, having already fallen into his trap, and committed the horrible crime of slaying the Son of God, they were entirely in his power, and their only course to escape the wrath of the people was to persist in denouncing Jesus as an impostor, and to accuse his disciples of stealing away his body that they might declare him to be risen from the dead. (3SP 195.3)

After the exceeding glory of the angelic messenger had faded from the heavens and from the sepulcher, the Roman guards ventured to raise their heads and to look about them. They saw that the great stone at the door of the sepulcher was removed, and they arose in consternation to find the body of Jesus gone and the tomb empty. They turned from the sepulcher, overwhelmed by what they had seen and heard, and made their way with all haste to the city, relating to those whom they met the marvelous scenes they had witnessed. Some of the disciples, who had passed a sleepless night, heard the wonderful story with mingled hope and fear. Meanwhile a messenger was dispatched to the priests and rulers, announcing to them: Christ whom ye crucified is risen from the dead! (3SP 195.4)

A servant was immediately sent with a private message summoning the Roman guard to the palace of the high priest. There they were closely questioned; they gave a full statement of what they had witnessed at the sepulcher: That an awful messenger had come from Heaven with face like the lightning for brightness, and with garments white as snow; that the earth shook and trembled, and they were stricken powerless; that the angel had laid hold of the immense stone at the door of the sepulcher, and had rolled it away as if it had been a pebble; that a form of great glory had emerged from the sepulcher; that a chorus of voices had made the heavens and earth vocal with songs of victory and joy; that when the light had faded out, and the music had ceased, they had recovered their strength, found the tomb empty, and the body of Jesus nowhere to be found. (3SP 196.1)

When the priests, scribes, and rulers heard this account, their faces were blanched to a deadly pallor. They could not utter a word. With horror they perceived that two-thirds of the prophecy concerning Messiah had now been fulfilled, and their hearts failed them with fear of what might be about to take place. They could not question the evidence of the witnesses before them. Jesus of Nazareth, the crucified one, had indeed risen from the dead. (3SP 196.2)

When they had recovered from their first shock at hearing this news, they began to consider what course they would best pursue, and Satan was present to suggest ways and means. They felt that they had placed themselves where they had no alternative but to brave it out, and deny Christ to the very last. They reasoned that if this report should be circulated among the people, they would not only be stripped of their honor and authority, but would probably lose their lives. Jesus had said that he would rise from the dead and ascend to Heaven; they determined to keep the people in ignorance of the fulfillment of his word. They thought this could be done if the Roman guard could be bought with money. (3SP 197.1)

They found upon trial that the guard could be induced by large bribes to deny their former report, and to testify that the disciples had stolen the body of Jesus in the night, while the sentinels slept. It was a crime punishable by death for a sentinel to sleep at his post; and, in order to secure the evidence they wished, the priests promised to insure the safety of the guard. The Roman soldiers sold their integrity to the false Jews for money. They came in before the priests burdened with a most startling message of truth, and went out with a burden of money, and with a lying report upon their tongues which had been framed for them by the priests. (3SP 197.2)

Meanwhile a messenger had been sent, bearing the news to Pilate. When he heard what had occurred, his soul was filled with terror. He shut himself within his home, not wishing to see any one; but the priests found their way into his presence, and urged him to make no investigation of the affirmed neglect of the sentinels, but to let the matter pass. Pilate at length consented to this, after having a private interview with the guard, and learning all the particulars from them. They dared not conceal anything from the governor for fear of losing their lives. Pilate did not prosecute the matter farther, but from that time there was no more peace or comfort for him. (3SP 198.1)

*****

Chapter 14
The Women at the Tomb

The spices with which the body of Jesus was to be anointed had been prepared on the day preceding the Sabbath. Early in the morning of the first day of the week, the Marys, with certain other women, went to the sepulcher to proceed with the work of embalming the body of the Saviour. As they neared the garden, they were surprised to see the heavens beautifully lighted up, and the earth trembling beneath their feet. They hastened to the sepulcher, and were astonished to find that the stone was rolled away from the door, and that the Roman guard were not there. They noticed a light shining about the tomb, and, looking in, saw that it was empty. (3SP 198.2)

Mary then hastened with all speed to the disciples, and informed them that Jesus was not in the sepulcher where they had laid him. While she was upon this errand, the other women, who waited for her at the sepulcher, made a more thorough examination of the interior, to satisfy themselves that their Lord was indeed gone. Suddenly they beheld a beautiful young man, clothed in shining garments, sitting by the sepulcher. It was the angel who had rolled away the stone, and who now assumed a character that would not terrify the women who had been the friends of Christ, and assisted him in his public ministry. But notwithstanding the veiling of the brightness of the angel, the women were greatly amazed and terrified at the glory of the Lord which encircled him. They turned to flee from the sepulcher, but the heavenly messenger addressed them with soothing and comforting words: "Fear not ye; for I know that ye seek Jesus, who was crucified. He is not here, for he is risen, as he said. Come, see the place where the Lord lay. And go quickly, and tell his disciples that he is risen from the dead; and behold, he goeth before you into Galilee; there shall ye see him; lo, I have told you." (3SP 199.1)

As the women responded to the invitation of the angel, and looked again into the sepulcher, they saw another angel of shining brightness, who addressed them with the inquiry: "Why seek ye the living among the dead? He is not here, but is risen; remember how he spake unto you when he was yet in Galilee, saying, The Son of man must be delivered into the hands of sinful men, and be crucified, and the third day rise again." These angels were well acquainted with the words of Jesus to his disciples, for they had been with him in the capacity of guardian angels, through all the scenes of his life, and had witnessed his trial and crucifixion. (3SP 199.2)

With combined wisdom and tenderness, the angels reminded the women of the words of Jesus, warning them beforehand of his crucifixion and resurrection. The women now fully comprehended the words of their Master, which at the time were veiled in mystery to them. They gathered fresh hope and courage. Jesus had declared that he would rise from the dead, and had rested his claims as the Son of God, the Redeemer of the world, upon his future resurrection from the dead. (3SP 200.1)

Mary, who had first discovered that the tomb was empty, hurried to Peter and John, and announced that the Lord had been taken out of the sepulcher, and she knew not where they had laid him. At these words the disciples both hastened to the sepulcher, and found it as Mary had said. The body of their Master was not there, and the linen clothes lay by themselves. Peter was perplexed; but John believed that Jesus had risen from the dead, as he had told them he should do. They did not understand the scripture of the Old Testament, which taught that Christ should rise from the dead; but the belief of John was based upon the words of Jesus himself while he was yet with them. (3SP 200.2)

The disciples left the sepulcher, and returned to their homes; but Mary could not bear to leave while all was uncertainty as to what had become of the body of her Lord. As she stood weeping, she stooped down to once more look into the sepulcher; and lo, there were two angels, clothed in garments of white. They were disguised by an appearance of humanity, and

Mary did not recognize them as celestial beings. One sat where the head of Jesus had rested, and the other where his feet had been. They addressed Mary with the words: "Woman, why weepest thou? She saith unto them, Because they have taken away my Lord, and I know not where they have laid him." In view of the open sepulcher, and the disappearance of her Master's body, Mary was not easily comforted. (3SP 200.3)

In her abandonment of grief she did not notice the heavenly appearance of those who addressed her. As she turned aside to weep, another voice inquired, "Woman, why weepest thou? Whom seekest thou?" Her eyes were so blinded by tears that she did not observe the person who spoke to her, but she immediately grasped the idea of obtaining from her interrogator some information concerning the whereabouts of her Master's body. She thought that the speaker might be the one who had charge of the garden, and she addressed him pleadingly: "Sir, if thou have borne him hence, tell me where thou hast laid him, and I will take him away." (3SP 201.1)

She felt that if she could only gain possession of the precious crucified body of her Saviour, it would be a great consolation to her grief. She thought that if this rich man's tomb was considered too honorable a place for her Lord, she would herself provide a place for him. Her great anxiety was to find him, that she might give him honorable burial. But now the voice of Jesus himself fell upon her astonished ears. He said to her, "Mary." Instantly her tears were brushed away; and he whom she supposed was the gardener stood revealed before her–it was Jesus! For a moment she forgot in her joy that he had been crucified; she stretched forth her hands to him, saying, "Rabboni!" Jesus then said, "Touch me not, for I am not yet ascended to my Father; but go to my brethren, and say unto them, I ascend unto my Father, and your Father; and to my God, and your God." (3SP 201.2)

Jesus refused to receive the homage of his people until he knew that his sacrifice had been accepted by the Father, and until he had received the assurance from God himself that his atonement for the sins of his people had been full and ample, that through his blood they might gain eternal life. Jesus immediately ascended to Heaven and presented himself before the throne of God, showing the marks of shame and cruelty upon his brow, his hands and feet. But he refused to receive the coronet of glory, and the royal robe, and he also refused the adoration of the angels as he had refused the homage of Mary, until the Father signified that his offering was accepted. (3SP 202.1)

He also had a request to prefer concerning his chosen ones upon earth. He wished to have the relation clearly defined that his redeemed should hereafter sustain to Heaven, and to his Father. His church must be justified and accepted before he could accept heavenly honor. He declared it to be his will that where he was, there his church should be; if he was to have glory, his people must share it with him. They who suffer with him on earth must finally reign with him in his kingdom. In the most explicit manner Christ pleaded for his church, identifying his interest with theirs, and advocating, with a love and constancy stronger than death, their rights and titles gained through him. (3SP 202.2)

God's answer to this appeal goes forth in the proclamation: "Let all the angels of God worship him." Every angelic commander obeys the royal mandate, and Worthy, worthy is the Lamb that was slain; and that lives again a triumphant conqueror! echoes and re-echoes through all Heaven. The innumerable company of angels prostrate themselves before the Redeemer. The request of Christ is granted; the church is justified through him, its representative and head. Here the Father ratifies the contract with his Son, that he will be reconciled to repentant and obedient men, and take them into divine favor through the merits of Christ. Christ guarantees that he will make a man "more precious than fine gold, even a man than the golden wedge of Ophir." All power in Heaven and on earth is now given to the Prince of life; yet he does not for a moment forget his poor disciples in a sinful world, but prepares to return to them, that he may impart to them his power and glory. Thus did the Redeemer of mankind, by the sacrifice of himself, connect earth with Heaven, and finite man with the infinite God. (3SP 203.1)

Jesus said to Mary, "Touch me not; for I am not yet ascended to my Father." When he closed his eyes in death upon the cross, the soul of Christ did not go at once to Heaven, as many believe, or how could his words be true–"I am not yet ascended to my Father"? The spirit of Jesus slept in the tomb with his body, and did not wing its way to Heaven, there to maintain a separate existence, and to look down upon the

Chapter 14 - The Women at the Tomb (3SP 203.2)

mourning disciples embalming the body from which it had taken flight. All that comprised the life and intelligence of Jesus remained with his body in the sepulcher; and when he came forth it was as a whole being; he did not have to summon his spirit from Heaven. He had power to lay down his life and to take it up again. (3SP 203.2)

The brightest morning that ever dawned upon a fallen world, was that in which the Saviour rose from the dead; but it was of no greater importance to man than the day upon which his trial and crucifixion took place. It was no marvel to the heavenly host that He who controlled the power of death, and had life in himself, should awaken from the sleep of the grave. But it was a marvel to them that their loved Commander should die for rebellious men. (3SP 204.1)

Christ rested in the tomb on the Sabbath day, and when holy beings of both Heaven and earth were astir on the morning of the first day of the week, he rose from the grave to renew his work of teaching his disciples. But this fact does not consecrate the first day of the week, and make it a Sabbath. Jesus, prior to his death, established a memorial of the breaking of his body and the spilling of his blood for the sins of the world, in the ordinance of the Lord's supper, saying "For as often as ye eat this bread, and drink this cup, ye do show the Lord's death till he come." And the repentant believer, who takes the steps required in conversion, commemorates in his baptism the death, burial, and resurrection of Christ. He goes down into the water in the likeness of Christ's death and burial, and he is raised out of the water in the likeness of his resurrection–not to take up the old life of sin, but to live a new life in Christ Jesus. (3SP 204.2)

The other women who had seen and been addressed by the angels, left the sepulcher with mingled feelings of fear and great joy. They hastened to the disciples, as the angels had directed, and related to them the things which they had seen and heard. Peter was expressly mentioned by the angel as one to whom the women were to communicate their news. This disciple had been the most despondent of all the little company of Christ's followers, because of his shameful denial of the Lord. Peter's remorse for his crime was well understood by the holy angels, and their tender compassion for the wayward and sorrowing is revealed in the solicitude they manifested for the unhappy disciple, and which evidenced to him that his repentance was accepted, and his sin forgiven. (3SP 205.1)

When the disciples heard the account which the women brought, they were astonished. They began to recall the words of their Lord which foretold his resurrection. Still, this event, which should have filled their hearts with joy, was a great perplexity to them. After their great disappointment in the death of Christ, their faith was not strong enough to accept the fact of the resurrection. Their hopes had been so blighted that they could not believe the statement of the women, but thought that they were the subjects of an illusion. Even when Mary Magdalene testified that she had seen and spoken with her Lord, they still refused to believe that he had risen. (3SP 205.2)

They were terribly depressed by the events that had crowded upon them. On the sixth day they had seen their Master die; upon the first day of the succeeding week they found themselves deprived of his body, and the stigma resting upon them of having stolen it away for the purpose of practicing a deception upon the people. They despaired of ever correcting the false impressions that had gained ground against them; and now they were newly perplexed by the reports of the believing women. In their trouble their hearts yearned for their beloved Master, who had always been ready to explain the mysteries that perplexed them and to smooth their difficulties. (3SP 205.3)

*****

Chapter 15
Jesus at Emmaus

On this same day Jesus met several of his disciples, and greeted them with "All hail," upon which they approached him and held him by the feet and worshiped him. He permitted this homage, for he had then ascended to his Father, and had received his approval, and the worship of the holy angels. Late in the afternoon of the same day, two of the disciples were on their way to Emmaus, eight miles from Jerusalem. They had come to the city to keep the passover, and the news of the morning in regard to the removal of the body of Jesus from the sepulcher had greatly perplexed them. This perplexity had been increased by the reports of the women concerning the heavenly messengers, and the appearance of Jesus himself. They were now returning to their home to meditate and pray, in hope of gaining some light in reference to these matters which so confused their understanding. (3SP 206.1)

These two disciples had not held a prominent position beside Jesus in his ministry, but they were earnest believers in him. Soon after they began their journey, they observed a stranger coming up behind them, who presently joined their company; but they were so busy with perplexing thoughts, which they were communicating to each other, that they scarcely noticed they were not alone. Those strong men were so burdened with grief that they wept as they traveled on. Christ's pitying heart of love saw here a sorrow which he could relieve. The disciples were reasoning with each other concerning the events of the past few days, and marveling how the fact of Jesus yielding himself up to a shameful death could be reconciled with his claims as the Son of God. (3SP 207.1)

One maintained that he could be no pretender, but had been himself deceived in regard to his mission and his future glory. They both feared that what his enemies had flung in his teeth was too true–"He saved others; himself he cannot save." Yet they wondered how he could be so mistaken in himself, when he had given them such repeated evidence that he could read the hearts of others. And the strange reports of the women threw them into still greater uncertainty. (3SP 207.2)

Long might these disciples have perplexed themselves over the mysteries of the past few days, if they had not received enlightenment from Jesus. He, disguised as a stranger, entered into conversation with them. "But their eyes were holden that they should not know him. And he said unto them, What manner of communications are these that ye have one to another, as ye walk, and are sad? And the one of them whose name was Cleopas, answering said unto him, Art thou only a stranger in Jerusalem, and hast not known the things which are come to pass there in these days? And he said unto them, What things? And they said unto him, Concerning Jesus of Nazareth, which was a prophet mighty in deed and word before God and all the people." (3SP 207.3)

They then recounted to him the facts of the trial and crucifixion of their Master, together with the testimony of the women in regard to the removal of his body, the vision of angels which they had seen, the news of the resurrection, and the report of those disciples who had gone to the sepulcher. "Then he said unto them, O fools, and slow of heart to believe all that the prophets have spoken; ought not Christ to have suffered these things, and to enter into his glory? And beginning at Moses and all the prophets, he expounded unto them in all the Scriptures the things concerning himself." (3SP 208.1)

The disciples were silent from amazement and delight. They did not venture to ask the stranger who he was. They listened to him intently, charmed by his intelligence, and drawn toward him by his gracious words and manner, as he opened the Scriptures to their understanding, showing them from prophecy how Christ must suffer, and after suffering enter into his glory. (3SP 208.2)

Jesus began with the first book written by Moses, and traced down through all the prophets

Chapter 15 - Jesus at Emmaus (3SP 208.3)

the inspired proof in regard to his life, his mission, his suffering, death, and resurrection. He did not deem it necessary to work a miracle to evidence that he was the risen Redeemer of the world; but he went back to the prophecies, and gave a full and clear explanation of them to settle the question of his identity, and the fact that all which had occurred to him was foretold by the inspired writers. Jesus ever carried the minds of his hearers back to the precious mine of truth found in the Old-Testament Scriptures. The esteem in which he held those sacred records is exemplified in the parable of the rich man and Lazarus, where he says, "If they hear not Moses and the prophets, neither will they be persuaded though one rose from the dead." The apostles also all testify to the importance of the Old-Testament Scriptures. Peter says: "For the prophecy came not in old time by the will of man; but holy men of God spake as they were moved by the Holy Ghost." Luke thus speaks of the prophets who predicted the coming of Christ: "Blessed be the Lord God of Israel; for he hath visited and redeemed his people; and hath raised up a horn of salvation for us in the house of his servant David, as he spake by the mouth of his holy prophets, which have been since the world began." (3SP 208.3)

It is the voice of Christ that speaks through the prophets and patriarchs, from the days of Adam even down to the closing scenes of time. This truth was not discerned by the Jews who rejected Jesus, and it is not discerned by many professing Christians today. A beautiful harmony runs through the Old and New Testaments; passages which may seem dark at a first reading, present clear interpretations when diligently studied, and compared with other scripture referring to the same subject. A careful search of the prophecies would have so enlightened the understanding of the Jews that they would have recognized Jesus as the predicted Messiah. But they had interpreted those predictions to meet their own perverted ideas and ambitious aspirations. (3SP 209.1)

The disciples had been confused by the interpretations and traditions of the priests, and hence their darkness and unbelief in regard to the trial, death, and resurrection of their Master. These misinterpreted prophecies were now made plain to the understanding of the two disciples, by Him who, through his Holy Spirit, inspired men to write them. Jesus showed his disciples that every specification of prophecy regarding Messiah had found an exact fulfillment in the life and death of their Master. He addressed them as a stranger, and as one who was astonished that they had not interpreted the Scriptures correctly, which would have relieved them from all their difficulties. (3SP 210.1)

Although Jesus had previously taught them in regard to the prophecies, yet they had been unable to entirely relinquish the idea of the temporal kingdom of Christ at his first coming. Their preconceived views led them to look upon his crucifixion as the final destruction of all their hopes. But when, in the midst of their discouragement, they were shown that the very things which had caused them to despair formed the climax of proof that their belief had been correct, their faith returned with increased strength. They now comprehended many things which their Master had said before his trial, and which they could not at that time understand. Everything was clear and plain to their minds. In the life and death of Jesus they saw the fulfillment of prophecy, and their hearts burned with love for their Saviour. (3SP 210.2)

Many professed Christians throw aside the Old Testament, and shut themselves up to the New. The cry now is, "Away with the law and the prophets, and give us the gospel of Christ." If the life of Christ and the teachings of the New-Testament Scriptures were all that was necessary to establish belief, why did not Jesus upon this occasion merely refer to the doctrines he had taught, the wisdom and purity of his character, and the miracles he had performed, as sufficient evidence of his Messiahship? (3SP 211.1)

The history of the life, death, and resurrection of Jesus, as that of the Son of God, cannot be fully demonstrated without the evidence contained in the Old Testament. Christ is revealed in the Old Testament as clearly as in the New. The one testifies of a Saviour to come, while the other testifies of a Saviour that has come in the manner predicted by the prophets. In order to appreciate the plan of redemption, the Scripture of the Old Testament must be thoroughly understood. It is the glorified light from the prophetic past that brings out the life of Christ and the teachings of the New Testament with clearness and beauty. The miracles of Jesus are a proof of his divinity; but the strongest proofs that he is the world's Redeemer are found in the prophecies of the Old Testament compared with the history of the New. Jesus said

Chapter 15 - Jesus at Emmaus (3SP 214.1)

to the Jews "Search the Scriptures; for in them ye think ye have eternal life, and they are they which testify of me." At that time there was no other scripture in existence save that of the Old Testament; so the injunction of the Saviour is plain. (3SP 211.2)

As the disciples walked on with Jesus, listening intently to his gracious words, nothing in his bearing suggested to them that they were listening to other than a casual pilgrim, returning from the feast, but one who thoroughly understood the prophecies. He walked as carefully as they over the rough stones, halting with them for a little rest after climbing some unusually steep place. Thus the two disciples made their way along the mountainous road in company with the divine Saviour, who could say, "All power is given unto me in Heaven and on earth." (3SP 212.1)

This mighty conqueror of death, who had reached to the very depths of human misery to rescue a lost world, assumed the humble task of walking with the two disciples to Emmaus, to teach and comfort them. Thus he ever identifies himself with his suffering and perplexed people. In our hardest and most trying paths, lo, Jesus is with us to smooth the way. He is the same Son of man, with the same sympathies and love which he had before he passed through the tomb and ascended to his Father. (3SP 212.2)

At length, as the sun was going down, the disciples with their companion arrived at their home. The way had never before seemed so short to them, nor had time ever passed so quickly. The stranger made no sign of halting; but the disciples could not endure the thought of parting so soon from one who had inspired their hearts with new hope and joy, and they urged him to remain with them over night. Jesus did not at once yield to their invitation, but seemed disposed to pursue his journey. Thereupon the disciples, in their affection for the stranger, importuned him earnestly to tarry with them, urging as a reason that "the day was far spent." Jesus yielded to their entreaties and entered their humble abode. (3SP 212.3)

The Saviour never forces his presence upon us. He seeks the company of those whom he knows need his care, and gives them an opportunity to urge his continuance with them. If they, with longing desire, entreat him to abide with them he will enter the humblest homes, and brighten the lowliest hearts. While waiting for the evening meal, Jesus continued to open the Scriptures to his hosts, bringing forward evidence of his divinity, and unfolding to them the plan of salvation. The simple fare was soon ready, and the three took their position at the table, Jesus taking his place at the head as was his custom. (3SP 213.1)

The duty of asking a blessing upon the food usually devolved upon the head of the family; but Jesus placed his hands upon the bread and blessed it. At the first word of his petition the disciples looked up in amazement. Surely none other than their Lord had ever done in this manner. His voice strikes upon their ear as the voice of their Master, and, behold, there are the wounds in his hands! It is indeed the well-known form of their beloved Master! For a moment they are spell-bound; then they arise to fall at his feet and worship him; but he suddenly disappears from their midst. (3SP 213.2)

Now they know that they have been walking and talking with the risen Redeemer. Their eyes had been clouded so that they had not before discerned him, although the truths he uttered had sunk deep in their discouraged hearts. He who had endured the conflict of the garden, the shame of the cross, and who had gained the victory over death and the tomb–He, before whom angels had fallen prostrate, worshiping with thanksgiving and praise, had sought the two lonely and desponding disciples, and been in their presence for hours, teaching and comforting them, yet they had not known him. (3SP 213.3)

Jesus did not first reveal himself in his true character to them, and then open the Scriptures to their minds; for he knew that they would be so overjoyed to see him again, risen from the dead, that their souls would be satisfied. They would not hunger for the sacred truths which he wished to indelibly impress upon their minds, that they might impart them to others, who should in their turn spread the precious knowledge, until thousands of people should receive the light given that day to the despairing disciples as they journeyed to Emmaus. (3SP 214.1)

He maintained his disguise till he had interpreted the Scriptures, and had led them to an intelligent faith in his life, his character, his mission to earth, and his death and resurrection. He wished the truth to take firm root in their minds, not because it was supported by his personal testimony, but because the typical law, and the prophets of the Old Testament, agreeing with the facts of his life and death, presented

Chapter 15 - Jesus at Emmaus (3SP 214.2)

unquestionable evidence of that truth. When the object of his labors with the two disciples was gained, he revealed himself to them that their joy might be full, and then vanished from their sight. (3SP 214.2)

When these disciples left Jerusalem, to return to their homes, they intended to take up their old employment again, and conceal their blighted hopes as best they could. But now their joy exceeded their former despair. "And they said one to another, Did not our heart burn within us, while he talked with us by the way, and while he opened to us the Scriptures?" (3SP 215.1)

They forgot their hunger and fatigue, and left the prepared repast, for they could not tarry in their homes and hold their newly found knowledge from the other disciples. They longed to impart their own joy to their companions, that they might rejoice together in a living Saviour risen from the dead. Late as it was, they set about retracing their way to Jerusalem; but how different were their feelings now from those which depressed them when they set out upon their way to Emmaus. Jesus was by their side, but they knew it not. He heard with gladness their expressions of joy and gratitude as they talked with each other by the way. (3SP 215.2)

They were too happy to notice the difficulties of the rough, uncertain road. There was no moon to light them, but their hearts were light with the joy of a new revelation. They picked their way over the rough stones, and the dangerous ledges, sometimes stumbling and falling in their haste. But not at all disconcerted by this, they pressed resolutely on. Occasionally they lost their path in the darkness, and were obliged to retrace their steps until they found the track, when they renewed their journey with fresh speed. They longed to deliver their precious message to their friends. Never before had human lips such tidings to proclaim; for the fact of Christ's resurrection was to be the great truth around which all the faith and hope of the church would center. (3SP 215.3)

*****

Chapter 16
In the Upper Chamber

When the disciples arrived at Jerusalem they entered the eastern gate, which was open on festal occasions. The houses were dark and silent, but they made their way through the narrow streets by the light of the rising moon. They knew that they would find their brethren in the memorable upper chamber where Jesus had spent the last night before his death. Here the disciples had passed the Sabbath in mourning for their Lord. And now they had no disposition to sleep, for exciting events were being related among them. Cautious hands unbarred the door to the repeated demand of the two travelers; they entered, and with them also entered Jesus, who had been their unseen companion all the way. (3SP 216.1)

They found the disciples assembled, and in a state of excitement. Hope and faith were struggling for ascendency in their minds. The report of Mary Magdalene, and that of the other women, had been heard by all; but some were too hopeless to believe their testimony. The evidence of Peter, concerning his interview with the risen Lord, was borne with great ardor and assurance, and had more weight with the brethren, and their faith began to revive. When the disciples from Emmaus entered with their joyful tidings, they were met by the exclamation from many voices: "The Lord is risen indeed, and hath appeared to Simon." (3SP 216.2)

The two from Emmaus told their story of how the Lord had opened their eyes, and revealed to them the straight chain of prophecy which reached from the days of the patriarchs to that time, and foreshadowed all that had transpired regarding their Saviour. The company heard this report in breathless silence. Some were inspired with new faith; others were incredulous. Suddenly Jesus himself was in their midst. His hands were raised in blessing, and he said unto them, "Peace be unto you." (3SP 217.1)

"But they were terrified and affrighted, and supposed that they had seen a spirit. And he said unto them, Why are ye troubled? and why do thoughts arise in your hearts? Behold my hands and my feet, that it is I myself; handle me, and see; for a spirit hath not flesh and bones, as ye see me have. And when he had thus spoken, he showed them his hands and his feet." (3SP 217.2)

There they beheld the feet and hands marred by the cruel nails; and they recognized his melodious voice, like none other they had ever heard. "And while they yet believed not for joy, and wondered, he said unto them, Have ye here any meat? And they gave him a piece of a broiled fish, and of an honeycomb. And he took it, and did eat before them." Faith and joy now took the place of doubt and unbelief, and they acknowledged their risen Saviour with feelings which no words could express. (3SP 217.3)

Jesus now expounded the Scriptures to the entire company, commencing with the first book of Moses, and dwelling particularly on the prophecy pointing to the time then present, and foretelling the sufferings of Christ and his resurrection. "And he said unto them, These are the words which I spake unto you, while I was yet with you, that all things must be fulfilled, which were written in the law of Moses, and in the prophets, and in the Psalm, concerning me. Then opened he their understanding, that they might understand the Scriptures. And said unto them, Thus it is written, and thus it behooved Christ to suffer, and to rise from the dead the third day; and that repentance and remission of sins should be preached in his name among all nations, beginning at Jerusalem. And ye are witnesses of these things." (3SP 218.1)

The disciples now began to realize the nature and extent of their commission. They were to proclaim to the world the wonderful truths which Christ had intrusted to them. The events of his life, his death, and resurrection, the harmony of prophecy with those events, the sacredness of the law of God, the mysteries of the plan of salvation, the power of Jesus for the remission of sins–to all these things were they witnesses, and it was their work to make them

Chapter 16 - In the Upper Chamber (3SP 218.2)

known to all men, beginning at Jerusalem. They were to proclaim a gospel of peace and salvation through repentance and the power of the Saviour. At the first advent of Jesus to the world, the angel announced: Peace on earth, and good will to men. After his earthly life was completed, he came forth from the dead, and, appearing for the first time to his assembled disciples, addressed them with the blessed words, "Peace be unto you." (3SP 218.2)

Jesus is ever ready to speak peace to souls that are troubled with doubts and fear. This precious Saviour waits for us to open the door of our heart to him, and say, Abide with us. He says, "Behold, I stand at the door, and knock; if any man hear my voice, and open the door, I will come in to him, and will sup with him, and he with me." Our life is a continual strife; we must war against principalities and powers, against spiritual wickedness, and foes that never sleep; we must resist temptations, and overcome as Christ overcame. When the peace of Jesus enters our heart we are calm and patient under the severest trials. (3SP 219.1)

The resurrection of Jesus was a sample of the final resurrection of all who sleep in him. The risen body of the Saviour, his deportment, the accents of his speech, were all familiar to his followers. In like manner will those who sleep in Jesus rise again. We shall know our friends even as the disciples knew Jesus. Though they may have been deformed, diseased, or disfigured in this mortal life, yet in their resurrected and glorified body their individual identity will be perfectly preserved, and we shall recognize, in the face radiant with the light shining from the face of Jesus, the lineaments of those we love. (3SP 219.2)

The death of Jesus had left Thomas in blank despair. His faith seemed to have gone out in utter darkness. He was not present in the upper chamber when Jesus appeared to his disciples. He had heard the reports of the others, and had received copious proof that Jesus had risen, but stolid gloom and stubborn unbelief closed his heart against all cheering testimony. As he heard the disciples repeat their account of the wonderful manifestation of the resurrected Saviour, it only served to plunge him in deeper despair; for if Jesus had really risen from the dead there could be no farther hope of his literal earthly kingdom. It also wounded his vanity to think that his Master would reveal himself to all his disciples but him; so he was determined not to believe, and for an entire week he brooded over his wretchedness, which seemed all the darker as contrasted with the reviving hope and faith of his brethren. (3SP 219.3)

During this time he frequently, when in company with his brethren, reiterated the words, "Except I shall see in his hands the print of the nails, and put my finger into the print of the nails, and thrust my hand into his side, I will not believe." He would not see through the eyes of his brethren, nor exercise faith which was dependent upon their testimony. He ardently loved his Lord, but jealousy and unbelief took possession of his mind and heart. (3SP 220.1)

The upper chamber was the home of a number of the disciples, and every evening they all assembled in this place. On a certain evening Thomas decided to meet with his brethren; for notwithstanding his unbelief, he cherished a faint hope, unacknowledged to himself, that the good news was true. While the disciples were partaking of their usual meal, and meanwhile canvassing the evidences of the truth of their faith which Christ had given them in the prophecies, "then came Jesus, the doors being shut, and stood in the midst, and said, Peace be unto you." (3SP 220.2)

He then reproved the unbelieving who had not received the testimony of those who had seen him, and, turning to Thomas, said, "Reach hither thy finger, and behold my hands; and reach hither thy hand, and thrust it into my side; and be not faithless, but believing." These words showed that he had read the thoughts and words of Thomas. The doubting disciple knew that none of his companions had seen Jesus for a week, and therefore could not have told the Master of his stubborn unbelief. He recognized the person before him as his Lord who had been crucified; he had no desire for farther proof; his heart leaped for joy as he realized that Jesus was indeed risen from the dead. He cast himself at the feet of his Master in deep affection and devotion, crying, "My Lord and my God." (3SP 221.1)

Jesus accepted his acknowledgment, but mildly rebuked him for his unbelief: "Thomas, because thou hast seen me, thou has believed; blessed are they that have not seen, and yet have believed." Jesus here showed Thomas that his faith would have been more acceptable to him if he had believed the evidence of his brethren, and had not refused to believe until he had seen Jesus with his own eyes. If the world should follow this example of Thomas, no one would believe unto salvation; for all who now receive Christ do so through the testimony of others. (3SP 221.2)

Many who have a weak and wavering faith, reason that if they had the evidence which Thomas had from his companions they would not doubt as he did. They do not realize that they have not only that evidence, but additional testimony piled up about them on every side. Many who, like Thomas, wait for all cause of doubt to be removed, may never realize their desire as he did, but gradually become entrenched in their unbelief, until they cannot perceive the weight of evidence in favor of Jesus, and, like the skeptical Jews, what little light they have will go out in the darkness which closes around their minds. To reject the plain and conclusive evidences of divine truth hardens the heart, and blinds the understanding. The precious light, being neglected, fades utterly from the mind that is unwilling to receive it. (3SP 221.3)

Jesus, in his treatment of Thomas, gave his followers a lesson regarding the manner in which they should treat those who have doubts upon religious truth, and who make those doubts prominent. He did not overwhelm Thomas with words of reproach, nor did he enter into a controversy with him; but, with marked condescension and tenderness, he revealed himself unto the doubting one. Thomas had taken a most unreasonable position, in dictating the only conditions of his faith; but Jesus, by his generous love and consideration, broke down all the barriers he had raised. Persistent controversy will seldom weaken unbelief, but rather put it upon self-defense, where it will find new support and excuse. Jesus, revealed in his love and mercy as the crucified Saviour, will wring from many once unwilling lips the acknowledgment of Thomas, "My Lord, and my God." (3SP 222.1)

Chapter 17
Jesus at Galilee

The captives brought up from the graves at the time of the resurrection of Jesus were his trophies as a conquering Prince. Thus he attested his victory over death and the grave; thus he gave a pledge and an earnest of the resurrection of all the righteous dead. Those who were called from their graves went into the city, and appeared unto many in their resurrected forms, and testified that Jesus had indeed risen from the dead, and that they had risen with him. The voice that cried, "It is finished," was heard among the dead. It pierced the walls of sepulchers, and summoned the sleepers to arise. Thus shall it be when God's voice shall be heard shaking the heavens and earth. That voice will penetrate the graves and unbar the tombs. A mighty earthquake will then cause the world to reel to and fro like a drunkard. Then Christ, the King of Glory, shall appear, attended by all the heavenly angels. The trumpet shall sound, and the Life-giver shall call forth the righteous dead to immortal life. (3SP 223.1)

It was well known to the priests and rulers that certain persons who were dead had risen at the resurrection of Jesus. Authentic reports were brought to them of different ones who had seen and conversed with these resurrected ones, and heard their testimony that Jesus, the Prince of life, whom the priests and rulers had slain, was risen from the dead. The false report that the disciples had robbed the sepulcher of the body of their Master was so diligently circulated that very many believed it. But the priests, in manufacturing their false report, overreached themselves, and all thinking persons, not blinded by bigotry, detected the falsehood. (3SP 223.2)

If the soldiers had been asleep, they could not know how the sepulcher became empty. If one sentinel had been awake, he would assuredly have wakened others. If they had really slept, as they affirmed they had, the consequence was well known to all. The penalty for such neglect of duty was death, and there could be no hope of pardon; so the offenders would not be likely to proclaim their fault. If the Jewish priests and rulers had discovered the sentinels asleep at their post, they would not have passed the matter over so lightly, but would have demanded a thorough investigation of the matter, and the full penalty of the law upon the unfaithful soldiers. (3SP 224.1)

Had they had the least faith in the truthfulness of their statements, they would have called the disciples to account, and visited upon them the most unrelenting punishment. That they did not do this was a thorough proof of the innocence of the disciples, and of the fact that the priests were driven to the dire necessity of fabricating and circulating a lie to meet the evidence accumulating against them, and establishing the truth of the resurrection of Jesus, and his claims as the divine Son of God. The oft-repeated appearance of Jesus to his disciples, and the persons of the dead who were resurrected with him, also did much to plant the truth in the minds of those who were willing to believe. (3SP 224.2)

This fabrication of the Jews has a parallel in our time; the proud persecutors of righteousness expend their time, influence, and money to silence or controvert the evidence of truth; and the most inconsistent measures are taken to accomplish this object. And there are not wanting persons of intelligence who will greedily swallow the most ridiculous falsehoods because they accord with the sentiments of their hearts. This reveals the sad fact that God has given them up to blindness of mind, and hardness of heart. There are innocent persons, who may be deceived for a time because of the confidence they place in their deceivers; but if they are teachable, and really desire a knowledge of the truth, they will have opportunity to perceive it. Doubts and perplexities will vanish; they will discover the inconsistencies of their false guides; for error itself bears a constrained testimony for the truth. (3SP 224.3)

The priests and rulers were in continual dread lest, in walking the streets, or within the privacy of their own homes, they should meet

Chapter 17 - Jesus at Galilee (3SP 227.3)

face to face with the resurrected Christ. They felt that there was no safety for them; bolts and bars seemed but poor protection against the risen Son of God. (3SP 225.1)

Before his death Jesus had, in the upper chamber, told his disciples that after he was risen he would go before them into Galilee; and on the morning of the resurrection the angel at the sepulcher had said unto the women, "Go your way; tell his disciples, and Peter, that he goeth before you into Galilee; there shall ye see him, as he said unto you." The disciples were detained at Jerusalem during the passover week, for their absence would have been interpreted as disaffection and heresy. During that time they assembled together at evening in the upper chamber, where some of them had their home; here Jesus twice revealed himself to them, and bade them tarry for a time at Jerusalem. (3SP 225.2)

As soon as the passover was finished, the brethren left Jerusalem, and went to Galilee as they had been directed. Seven of the disciples were in company; they were clad in the humble garb of fishermen; they were poor in worldly goods, but rich in the knowledge and practice of the truth, which gave them, in the sight of Heaven, the highest rank as teachers. They had not been students in the school of the prophets, but for three years they had taken lessons from the greatest educator the world has ever known. Under his tuition they had become elevated, intelligent, and refined, fit mediums through which the souls of men might be led to a knowledge of the truth. (3SP 226.1)

Much of the time of the Saviour's ministry was spent on the shores of Galilee, and there many of his most wonderful miracles were performed. As the disciples gathered together in a place where they were not likely to be disturbed, their minds were full of Jesus and his mighty works. On this sea, when their hearts were filled with terror, and the fierce storm was hurrying them on to destruction, Jesus had walked upon the crested billows to their rescue. Here the wildest storm was hushed by his voice, which said to the raging deep, "Peace, be still." Within sight was the beach, where, by a mighty miracle, he had fed above ten thousand persons from a few small loaves and fishes. Not far distant was Capernaum, the scene of his most wonderful manifestations, in healing the sick and in raising the dead. As the disciples looked again upon Galilee, their minds were full of the words and deeds of their Saviour. (3SP 226.2)

The evening was pleasant, and Peter, who retained much of his old love for boats and fishing, proposed that they should go out upon the sea and cast their nets. This proposition met with the approval of all, for they were poor and in need of food and clothing, which they would be able to procure with the proceeds of a successful night's fishing. So they went out upon the sea in their boat, to pursue their old employment. But they toiled through the entire night with no success. Through the long, weary hours they talked of their absent Lord, and recalled the scenes and events of thrilling interest which had been enacted in that vicinity, and of which they had been witnesses. They speculated upon what their own future would be, and grew sad at the prospect before them. (3SP 227.1)

All the while a lone watcher upon the shore followed them with his eye, while he himself was unseen. At length the morning dawned. The boat was but a little distance from the shore, and the disciples saw a stranger standing upon the beach, who accosted them with the question, "Children, have ye any meat?" Not recognizing Jesus, they answered, "No." "And he said unto them, Cast the net on the right side of the ship, and ye shall find. They cast therefore, and now they were not able to draw it for the multitude of fishes." (3SP 227.2)

The disciples were filled with wonder at the result of their trial; but John now discerned who the stranger was, and exclaimed to Peter, "It is the Lord." Joy now took the place of disappointment. Peter immediately girt about him his fisher's coat, and, throwing himself into the water, was soon standing by the side of his Lord. The other disciples came in their boat, dragging the net with fishes. "As soon then as they were come to land, they saw a fire of coals there, and fish laid thereon, and bread." (3SP 227.3)

They were too much amazed to question whence came the fire and the repast. "Jesus saith unto them, Bring of the fish which ye have now caught." Peter, obeying the command, rushed for the net which he had so unceremoniously dropped, and helped his brethren drag it to the shore. After the work was all done, and the preparation made, Jesus bade the disciples come and dine. He broke the bread and the fish, and divided it among them, and in so doing he was known and acknowledged of all the seven. The miracle of feeding the five thousand upon the mountain-side was now brought distinctly to

Chapter 17 - Jesus at Galilee (3SP 228.1)

their minds; but a mysterious awe was upon them, and they kept silent as they looked upon their resurrected Saviour. (3SP 228.1)

They remembered that at the commencement of his ministry a similar scene had been enacted to that which had just taken place. Jesus had then bade them launch out into the deep, and let down their nets for a draught, and the net had broken because of the amount of fishes taken. Then he had bade them leave their nets and follow him, and he would make them fishers of men. This last miracle that Jesus had just wrought was for the purpose of making the former miracle more impressive; that the disciples might perceive that, notwithstanding they were to be deprived of the personal companionship of their Master, and of the means of sustenance by the pursuit of their favorite employment, yet a resurrected Saviour had a care over them, and would provide for them while they were doing his work. Jesus also had a purpose in bidding them cast their net upon the right side of the ship. On that side stood Christ upon the shore. If they labored in connection with him–his divine power uniting with their human effort–they would not fail of success. (3SP 228.2)

The repetition of the miraculous draught of fishes was a renewal of Christ's commission to his disciples. It showed them that the death of their Master did not remove their obligation to do the work which he had assigned them. To Peter, who had acted on many occasions as representative of the twelve, a special lesson was given. The part which he had acted on the night of his Lord's betrayal was so shameful and inconsistent with his former assertions of loyalty and devotion, that it was necessary for him to give evidence to all the disciples that he sincerely repented of his sin before he could resume his apostolic work. The Saviour designed to place him where he could regain the entire confidence of his brethren, lest, in the time of emergency, their distrust because of his former failure might cripple his usefulness. (3SP 229.1)

The disciples expected that Peter would no longer be allowed to occupy the prominent position in the work which he had hitherto held, and he himself had lost his customary self-confidence. But Jesus, while dining by the sea-side, singled out Peter, saying, "Simon, son of Jonas, lovest thou me more than these?" referring to his brethren. Peter had once said, "Though all men shall be offended because of thee, yet will I never be offended," and had expressed himself ready to go to prison and to death with his Master. But now he puts a true estimate upon himself in the presence of the disciples: "Yea, Lord, thou knowest that I love thee." In this response of Peter there is no vehement assurance that his affection is greater than that of his companions; he does not even express his own opinion of his devotion to his Saviour, but appeals to that Saviour, who can read all the motives of the human heart, to himself judge as to his sincerity,–"Thou knowest that I love thee." (3SP 229.2)

The reply of Jesus was positively favorable to the repentant disciple, and placed him in a position of trust. It was, "Feed my lambs." Again Jesus applied the test to Peter, repeating his former words: "Simon, son of Jonas, lovest thou me?" This time he did not ask the disciple whether he loved him better than did his brethren. The second response of Peter was like the first, free from all extravagant assurance: "Yea, Lord, thou knowest that I love thee." Jesus said unto him, "Feed my sheep." Once more the Saviour put the trying question: "Simon, son of Jonas, lovest thou me?" Peter was grieved, for he thought the repetition of this question indicated that Jesus did not believe his statement. He knew that his Lord had cause to doubt him, and with an aching heart he answered, "Lord, thou knowest all things; thou knowest that I love thee." Jesus said to him, "Feed my sheep." (3SP 230.1)

Three times had Peter openly denied his Lord, and three times did Jesus draw from him the assurance of his love and loyalty, by pressing home that pointed question, like a barbed arrow, to his wounded heart. Jesus, before the assembled disciples, brought out the depth of Peter's penitence, and showed how thoroughly humbled was the once boasting disciple. He was now intrusted with the important commission of caring for the flock of Christ. Though every other qualification might be unexceptionable, yet without the love of Christ he could not be a faithful shepherd over the Christian flock. Knowledge, eloquence, benevolence, gratitude, and zeal are all aids in the good work, but without an inflowing of the love of Jesus in the heart, the work of the Christian minister is a failure. (3SP 230.2)

Peter was naturally forward and impulsive, and Satan had taken advantage of these characteristics to lead him astray. When Jesus

Chapter 17 - Jesus at Galilee (3SP 233.1)

had opened before his disciples the fact that he must go to Jerusalem to suffer and die at the hands of the chief priests and scribes, Peter had presumptuously contradicted his Master, saying, "Be it far from thee, Lord; this shall not be unto thee." He could not conceive it possible that the Son of God should be put to death. Satan suggested to his mind that if Jesus was the Son of God he could not die. Just prior to the fall of Peter, Jesus had said to him, "Satan hath desired to have you, that he may sift you as wheat; but I have prayed for thee, that thy faith fail not; and when thou art converted, strengthen thy brethren." That period had now come, and the transformation wrought in Peter was evident. The close, testing questions of the Lord had not provoked one forward, self-sufficient reply; and because of his humiliation and repentance he was better prepared than ever before to fill the office of shepherd to the flock. (3SP 231.1)

The lesson which he had received from the chief Shepherd, in the treatment of his case, was a most important one to Peter, and also to the other disciples. It taught them to deal with the transgressor with patience, sympathy, and forgiving love. During the time in which Peter denied his Lord, the love which Jesus bore him never faltered. Just such love should the under-shepherd feel for the sheep and lambs committed to his care. Remembering his own weakness and failure, Peter was to deal with his flock as tenderly as Christ had dealt with him. (3SP 232.1)

Jesus walked alone with Peter, for there was something which he wished to communicate to him only. In that memorable upper chamber, previous to his death, Jesus had said to his disciple, "Whither I go thou canst not follow me now; but thou shalt follow me afterwards;" Peter had replied to this: "Lord, why cannot I follow thee now? I will lay down my life for thy sake." Jesus now, in sympathy for him, and that he might be strengthened for the final test of his faith in Christ, opened before him his future. He told him that after living a life of usefulness, when age was telling upon his strength, he should indeed follow his Lord. Said Jesus, "When thou wast young, thou girdedst thyself and walkedst whither thou wouldest; but when thou shalt be old, thou shalt stretch forth thy hands, and another shall gird thee, and carry thee whither thou wouldest not. This spake he, signifying by what death he should glorify God." (3SP 232.2)

Jesus here explicitly stated to Peter the fact and manner of his death; he even referred to the stretching forth of his hands upon the cross; and after he had thus spoken he repeated his former injunction: "Follow me." The disciple was not disconcerted by the revelation of his Master. He felt willing to suffer any death for his Lord. Peter saw that John was following, and a desire came over him to know his future, and he "saith to Jesus, Lord, and what shall this man do? Jesus saith unto him, If I will that he tarry till I come, what is that to thee? follow thou me." Peter should have considered that his Lord would reveal to him all that it was best for him to know, without inquiry on his part. It is the duty of every one to follow Christ, without undue anxiety as to the duty assigned to others. In saying of John, "If I will that he tarry till I come," Jesus gave no assurance that this disciple should live until the second coming of Christ; he merely asserted his own supreme power, and that even if he should will this to be so, it would in no way affect the work of Peter. The future of both John and Peter was in the hands of their Lord, and obedience in following him was the duty required of each. (3SP 232.3)

John lived to be very aged; he witnessed the fulfillment of the words of Christ in regard to the desolation of Jerusalem. He saw the stately temple of the Jews in ruins, and not one stone left upon another that was not thrown down. Peter was now an entirely converted man; but the honor and authority received from Christ did not give him supremacy over his brethren. He was venerated, and had much influence in the church because of the favor of God in forgiving him his apostasy, and intrusting to him the feeding of his flock, and because he ever remained one of the closest followers of Christ in his daily life. (3SP 233.1)

Chapter 18
Meeting of the Brethren

Then the eleven disciples went away into Galilee, into a mountain where Jesus had appointed them. And when they saw him, they worshiped him; but some doubted." There were others besides the eleven who assembled on the mountain-side. After he had revealed himself to them, certain followers of Jesus were only partially convinced of his identity with the crucified One. But none of the eleven had any doubt upon the subject. They had listened to his words, revealing the straight chain of prophecy in regard to himself. He had eaten with them, and shown them his wounded side and his pierced hands and feet, and they had handled him, so there was no room for unbelief in their minds. (3SP 234.1)

This meeting at Galilee had been appointed by the Saviour; the angel from Heaven had announced it to several of the disciples; and Jesus himself had given them special directions in regard to it, saying, "After I am risen again, I will go before you into Galilee." The place upon the mountain-side was selected by Jesus, because of its accommodation for a large company. This meeting was of the utmost importance to the church, which was soon to be left to carry on the work without the personal presence of the Saviour. Jesus here designed to manifest himself to all the brethren that should assemble, in order that all their doubt and unbelief might be swept away. (3SP 234.2)

The appointment of Jesus was repeated to those who believed on him, while they were yet lingering at Jerusalem, attending the festal occasions which followed the passover. The tidings reached many lonely ones who were mourning the death of their Lord; and they made their way to the place of meeting by circuitous routes, coming in from every direction, that they might not excite the suspicion of the jealous Jews. With the most intense interest they assembled together. Those who had been favored with a sight of the resurrected Saviour recounted to the doubting ones the messages of the angels, and their interviews with their Master. They reasoned from scripture, as Jesus had done with them, showing how every specification of prophecy relating to the first advent of Christ had been fulfilled in the life, death, and resurrection of Jesus. (3SP 234.3)

Thus the favored disciples passed from group to group, encouraging and strengthening the faith of their brethren. Many of those assembled heard these communications with amazement. A new train of thought was started in their minds regarding the crucified One. If what they had just heard was true, then Jesus was more than a prophet. No one could triumph over death, and burst the fetters of the tomb, but Messiah. Their ideas of Messiah and his mission had been so confused by the false teachings of the priests that it was necessary for them to unlearn what had been taught them, in order to be able to accept the truth, that Christ, through ignominy, suffering, and death, should finally take his throne. (3SP 235.1)

With mingled anxiety, fear, and hope, they waited to see if Jesus would indeed appear to fulfill his appointment. Thomas recounted to an eager, listening crowd his former unbelief, and his refusal to believe unless he saw the wounded hands, feet, and side of his Lord, and put his finger in the prints of the nails. He told them how his doubts were swept away forever by the sight of his Saviour, bearing the cruel marks of the crucifixion, and that he wished for no farther evidence. (3SP 235.2)

While the people were watching and waiting, suddenly Jesus stood in their midst. No one could tell from whence or how he came. The disciples recognized him at once, and hastened to pay him homage. Many who were present had never before seen him, but when they looked upon his divine countenance, and then upon his wounded hands and feet, pierced by the nails of the crucifixion, they knew it was the Saviour, and worshiped him. (3SP 236.1)

But there were some who still doubted; they could not believe the joyous truth. "And Jesus came and spake unto them, saying, All power is given unto me in Heaven and in earth." This assurance of Jesus exceeded all their expectations. They knew of his power, while he was one among them, over disease of every type, and over Satan and his angels; but they could not at first grasp the grand reality that all power in Heaven and on earth had been given to Him who had walked their streets, and sat at their tables, and taught in their midst. (3SP 236.2)

Jesus sought to draw their minds away from himself personally, to the importance of his position as the heir of all things, an equal with God himself; that through suffering and conflict he had gained his great inheritance, the kingdoms of Heaven and of earth. He wished them to understand at once how ample was his authority, and, as one above all powers and principalities, he issued the great commission to his chosen disciples:– (3SP 236.3)

"Go ye, therefore, and teach all nations, baptizing them in the name of the Father, and of the Son, and of the Holy Ghost; teaching them to observe all things whatsoever I have commanded you; and lo, I am with you alway, even unto the end of the world. Amen." (3SP 237.1)

A wide door was thus thrown open before his amazed listeners, who had heretofore been taught the most rigid seclusion from all save their own nation. A new and fuller interpretation of the prophecies dawned upon their minds; they labored to comprehend the work that was assigned them. The world regarded Jesus as an impostor; only a few hundreds ranked under his banner, and the faith of these had been fearfully shaken by the fact of his death, and they had not been able to settle upon any definite plan of action. Now Christ had revealed himself to them in his resurrected form, and had given them a mission so extensive that, with their limited views, they could scarcely comprehend it. It was difficult for them to realize that the faith which had bound them to the side of Jesus should not only be the religion of the Jews, but of all nations. (3SP 237.2)

Superstition, tradition, bigotry, and idolatry ruled the world. The Jews alone claimed to have a certain knowledge of God, and they were so exclusive, both socially and religiously, that they were despised by every other people. The high wall of separation which they had raised made the Jews a little world to themselves, and they called all other classes heathen and dogs. But Jesus committed to his disciples the scheme of making known their religion to all nations, tongues, and people. It was the most sublime enterprise ever intrusted to man–to preach a crucified and risen Saviour, and a full and free salvation to all men, both rich and poor, learned and ignorant–to teach that Christ came to the world to pardon the repentant, and to offer them a love high as heaven, broad as the world, and enduring as eternity. (3SP 237.3)

They were to teach the observance of all things whatsoever Jesus had commanded them, and were to baptize in the name of the Father, the Son, and the Holy Ghost. Jesus was about to be removed from his disciples; but he assured them that although he should ascend to his Father, his Spirit and influence would be with them always, and with their successors even unto the end of the world. Christ could not have left his followers a more precious legacy than the assurance that his presence would be with them through all the dark and trying hours of life. When Satan seems ready to destroy the church of God, and bring his people to confusion, they should remember that One has promised to be with them who has said, "All power is given unto me in Heaven and on earth." (3SP 238.1)

Persecution and reproach have ever been the lot of the true followers of Christ. The world hated the Master, and it has ever hated his servants; but the Holy Spirit, the Comforter which Christ sent unto his disciples, cheers and strengthens them to do his work with fidelity during his personal absence. The Comforter, the Spirit of truth, was to abide with them forever, and Christ assured them that the union existing between himself and the Father, now also embraced them. (3SP 238.2)

The understanding of the disciples, which had been clouded by misinterpretation of the prophecies, was now fully opened by Jesus, who shed a clear light upon those scriptures referring to himself. He showed them the true character of his kingdom; and they now began to see that it was not the mission of Christ to establish a temporal power, but that his kingdom of divine grace was to be manifested in the hearts of his people, and that only through his humiliation, suffering, and death, could the kingdom of his glory finally be established. (3SP 239.1)

The power of death was held by the devil; but Jesus had removed its stinging despair, by meeting the enemy upon his own territory and there conquering him. Henceforth death would be robbed of its terror for the Christian, since

Chapter 18 - Meeting of the Brethren (3SP 239.2)

Christ himself had felt its pangs, and risen from the grave to sit at the right hand of the Father in Heaven, having all power in Heaven and on earth. The conflict between Christ and Satan was determined when the Lord arose from the dead, shaking the prison-house of his enemy to its foundations, and robbing him of his spoils by bringing up a company of the sleeping dead, as a fresh trophy of the victory achieved by the second Adam. This resurrection was a sample, and an assurance, of the final resurrection of the righteous dead at Christ's second coming. (3SP 239.2)

Jerusalem had been the scene of Christ's amazing condescension for the human race. There had he suffered, been rejected, and condemned. The land of Judea, of which Jerusalem was the metropolis, was his birthplace. There, clad in the garb of humanity, he had walked with men, and few had discerned how near Heaven came to earth when Jesus dwelt among them. It was, therefore, very appropriate that the work of the disciples should begin at Jerusalem. While all minds were agitated by the thrilling scenes of the past few weeks, it was a most fitting opportunity for the message to be borne to that city. (3SP 239.3)

As the instruction of Jesus to the apostles was drawing to a close, and as the hour of his separation from them approached, he directed their minds more definitely to the work of the Spirit of God in fitting them for their mission. Through the medium of a familiar intercourse, he illuminated their minds to understand the sublime truths which they were to reveal to the world. But their work was not to be entered upon till they should know of a surety, by the baptism of the Holy Ghost, that they were connected with Heaven. They were promised new courage and joy from the heavenly illumination they should then experience, and which would enable them to comprehend the depth and breadth and fullness of God's love. (3SP 240.1)

After being fitted for their mission by the descent of the Holy Ghost, the disciples were to proclaim pardon for sin, and salvation through repentance, and the merits of a crucified and risen Saviour, and to reveal the principles of the kingdom of Christ, beginning at Jerusalem, and from thence extending their labors throughout Judea, and into Samaria, and finally to the uttermost parts of the earth. Here is a lesson to all who have a message of truth to give to the world: Their own hearts must first be imbued with the Spirit of God, and their labors should commence at home; their families should have the benefit of their influence; and the transforming power of the Spirit of God should be demonstrated in their own homes by a well-disciplined family. Then the circle should widen; the whole neighborhood should perceive the interest felt for their salvation, and the light of truth should be faithfully presented to them; for their salvation is of as much importance as that of persons at a distance. From the immediate neighborhood, and adjoining cities and towns, the circle of the labors of God's servants should widen, till the message of truth is given to the uttermost parts of the earth. (3SP 240.2)

This was the order which Christ instituted for the labors of his disciples; but it is frequently reversed by the evangelical workers of this time. They neglect the inner circle; it is not felt to be a necessity that the quickening influence of the Spirit of God should first operate upon their own hearts, and sanctify and ennoble their lives. The simplest duties, lying directly in their path, are neglected for some wider and more distant field, where their labors are frequently expended in vain. Whereas in a field easier of access they would have labored with success, and encountered fewer trials, gaining influence and new courage as the way opened and broadened before them. (3SP 241.1)

The apostles might have entreated the Lord that, in view of the unappreciated efforts which had been put forth in Jerusalem, and the insult and cruel death to which Christ had been subjected, they might be permitted to seek some more promising field, where they would find hearts more ready to hear and receive their message. But no such plea was made. Jesus was the sole director of the work. The very ground where the greatest of all teachers had scattered the seeds of truth, was to be thoroughly cultivated by the apostles until those seeds should spring up and yield an abundant harvest. In their labors the disciples were to endure the hatred, oppression, and jealousy of the Jews; but this had been experienced by their Master before them, and they were not to fly from it. (3SP 241.2)

Before his death, Jesus had said to his disciples, while comforting them in view of his approaching humiliation and death, "Peace I leave with you; my peace I give unto you." Now, after the conflict and the victory, after triumphing over death, and receiving his reward, in a more emphatic manner he bestowed upon them that peace which passeth all understanding. He qualified them to enter upon the work which he had commenced. As he had been sent by his Father, so he sent forth the disciples. He breathed upon them, and said, "Receive ye the Holy Ghost." (3SP 242.1)

The apostles were not sent forth to be witnesses for Christ until they had received that spiritual endowment necessary to fit them for the execution of their great commission. All professions of Christianity are but lifeless expressions of faith until Jesus imbues the believer with his spiritual life, which is the Holy Ghost. The evangelist is not prepared to teach the truth, and to be the representative of Christ, till he has received this heavenly gift. (3SP 242.2)

Men in responsible positions, who are proclaiming the truth of God in the name of Jesus without the spiritual energy given by the quickening power of God, are doing an unreal work, and cannot be certain whether success or defeat will attend their labors. Many forget that religion and duty are not dreary sentimentalisms, but earnest action. It is not the great services and lofty aspirations which receive the approval of God, but the love and consecration through which the service is performed, be it great or little. Storms of opposition and rebuffs are God's providences to drive us under the shelter of his wing. When the cloud envelops us, his voice is heard: "Peace I leave with you, my peace I give unto you; not as the world giveth, give I unto you." (3SP 242.3)

The act of Christ in breathing upon his disciples the Holy Ghost, and in imparting his peace to them, was as a few drops before the plentiful shower to be given on the day of Pentecost. Jesus impressed this fact upon his disciples, that as they should proceed in the work intrusted to them, they would the more fully comprehend the nature of that work, and the manner in which the kingdom of Christ was to be set up on earth. They were appointed to be witnesses for the Saviour; they were to testify what they had seen and heard of his resurrection; they were to repeat the gracious words which proceeded from his lips. They were acquainted with his holy character; he was as an angel standing in the sun, yet casting no shadow. It was the sacred work of the apostles to present the spotless character of Christ to men, as the standard for their lives. The disciples had been so intimately associated with this Pattern of holiness that they were in some degree assimilated to him in character, and were specially fitted to make known to the world his precepts and example. (3SP 243.1)

The more that the minister of Christ associates with his Master, through contemplation of his life and character, the more closely will he resemble him, and the better qualified will he be to teach his truths. Every feature in the life of the great Example should be studied with care, and close converse should be held with him through the prayer of living faith. Thus will the defective human character be transformed into the image of his glorious character. Thus will the teacher of the truth be prepared to lead souls to Christ. (3SP 244.1)

Jesus, in giving the disciples their first commission, had said, "I will give unto thee the keys of the kingdom of Heaven, and whatsoever thou [referring to responsible men who should represent his church] shalt bind upon earth shall be bound in Heaven, and whatsoever thou shalt loose on earth shall be loosed in Heaven." In renewing the commission of those to whom he had imparted the Holy Ghost, he said, "Whosoever sins ye remit, they are remitted unto them; and whosoever sins ye retain, they are retained." These words conveyed to the disciples a sense of the sacredness of their work, and its tremendous results. Imbued with the Spirit of God, they were to go forth preaching the merits of a sin-pardoning Saviour; and they had the assurance that all Heaven was interested in their labors, and that what they did on earth, in the spirit and power of Christ, should be ratified in Heaven. (3SP 244.2)

Jesus did not, by this assurance, give the apostles or their successors power to forgive sins, as his representatives. The Roman Catholic Church directs its people to confess the secrets of their lives to the priest, and from him, acting in the place of Christ, to receive absolution from their sins. The Saviour taught that his is the only name given under Heaven whereby men shall be saved. Jesus, however, delegated to his church upon earth, in her organized capacity, the power to censure and to remove censure according to the rules prescribed by inspiration; but these acts were only to be done by men of good repute, who were consecrated by the great Head of the church, and who showed by their lives that they were earnestly seeking to follow the guidance of the Spirit of God. (3SP 244.3)

Chapter 18 - Meeting of the Brethren (3SP 245.1)

No man was to exercise an arbitrary power over another man's conscience. Christ gave no ecclesiastical right to forgive sin, nor to sell indulgences, that men may sin without incurring the displeasure of God, nor did he give his servants liberty to accept a gift or bribe for cloaking sin, that it may escape merited censure. Jesus charged his disciples to preach the remission of sin in his name among all nations; but they themselves were not empowered to remove one stain of sin from the children of Adam. Nor were they to execute judgment against the guilty; the wrath of an offended God was to be proclaimed against the sinner; but the power which the Roman Church assumes to visit that wrath upon the offender is not established by any direction of Christ; he himself will execute the sentence pronounced against the impenitent. Whoever would attract the people to himself as one in whom is invested power to forgive sins, incurs the wrath of God, for he turns souls away from the heavenly Pardoner to a weak and erring mortal. (3SP 245.1)

Jesus showed his disciples that only as they should partake of his Spirit, and be assimilated to his merciful character, would they be endowed with spiritual discernment and miraculous power. All their strength and wisdom must come from him. When dealing with obstinately offending members, the holy men of the church were to follow the directions laid down by Christ; this, the only course of safety for the church, has been traced step by step by the apostles with the pen of inspiration. (3SP 246.1)

When the church takes up the case of an offender, the prayer of faith will bring Christ into the midst as an all-wise counselor. Men are in danger of being controlled by prejudice or the reports and opinions of others. Their own unsanctified judgment may balance their decisions. Therefore, where important decisions are to be made in reference to individuals in the church, the judgment of one man, however wise and experienced he may be, is not to be regarded as sufficient to act upon. (3SP 246.2)

Jesus has said, "Where two or three are gathered together in my name, there am I in the midst." With Christ to preside over the council of the church, how cautiously should each man speak and act. Prayer should be offered for the erring, and every means be used to restore him to the favor of God and the church; but if the voice of the church is disregarded, and his individual will is set up above it, then the offender must be promptly dealt with, and the decision of the brethren, made with prayer and faith, and according to the wisdom given them of God, is ratified by Heaven. (3SP 246.3)

The repentance of the sinner is to be accepted by the church with grateful hearts. The church is empowered to absolve sins only in the sense of assuring the repenting sinner of the forgiving mercy of the Saviour, and in leading him out from the darkness of unbelief and guilt, to the light of faith and righteousness. It may place his trembling hand in the loving hand of Jesus. Such a remission is ratified by Heaven. The directions of the apostles in regard to condemnation or acquittal in case of church trials are to remain valid till the end of time. And the promise of Christ's presence in answer to prayer should comfort and encourage his church today as much as it comforted and encouraged the apostles whom Christ directly addressed. Those who despise the authority of the church despise the authority of Christ himself. (3SP 247.1)

Notwithstanding the refusal of Heaven's best gift by Jerusalem, the work of the apostles was to commence there. The first overtures of mercy were to be made to the murderers of the Son of God. There were also many there who had secretly believed on Jesus, and many who had been deceived by the priests and rulers, but were ready to accept him, if it could be proven that he was indeed the Christ. The apostles, as eyewitnesses, were to testify of Jesus and his resurrection. They were to open to the people the prophecies relating to him, and to show how perfectly they had been fulfilled. They were to bring before the people the most convincing evidence of the truths which they taught, and they were to proclaim the joyful tidings of salvation to the world. (3SP 247.2)

As all minds were interested in the history and mission of Jesus, because of the events which had just transpired at Jerusalem, this was a time when the preaching of his gospel would make the most decided impression upon the public mind. At the commencement of their work the disciples were to receive a marvelous power. Their testimony of Christ was to be confirmed by signs and wonders, and the performance of miracles by the apostles, and those who received their message. Said Jesus, "They shall cast out devils; they shall speak with new tongues; they shall take up serpents, [as in the case of Paul] and if they drink any deadly thing, it shall not hurt them; they shall lay hands on the sick, and they shall recover." (3SP 247.3)

At that time, poisoning was practiced to quite an extent. Unscrupulous men did not hesitate to remove by this means those who stood in the way of their ambition. Jesus knew that his apostles would be subject to this danger, if not specially protected from it. He knew that there would be many who would be so deluded as to think it would be doing God service to put these witnesses to death by any means. He therefore guarded them against this insidious evil. Thus the Lord assured his servants that they were not to labor in their own strength, but in the strength of the Holy Ghost. Though the disciples received their commission to preach the gospel to all nations, they did not at the time comprehend the vast extent, and wonderful character of the work that was before them–a work that was to descend to their successors, and to be carried on to the end of time. (3SP 248.1)

Chapter 19
Ascension of Christ

After the meeting of Jesus with the brethren, at Galilee, the disciples returned to Jerusalem; and while the eleven were gathered together in the city Jesus met with them, and again led their minds out into the prophecies concerning himself. He deeply impressed upon their understanding the necessity of thoroughly studying the ancient prophecies regarding Messiah, and of comparing them with the facts of his life, death, and resurrection, in order to establish their fulfillment in himself. They were to diligently trace link after link of sacred truth revealed by the prophets, in types and figures representing the Lamb slain from the foundation of the world. He lifted the vail from their understanding, concerning the typical system of the Jews, and they now saw clearly the meaning of the forms and symbols which were virtually abolished by the death of Christ. (3SP 249.1)

The Saviour of the world, as a divine Conqueror, was about to ascend to his Father's throne. He selected the Mount of Olives as the scene of this last display of his glory. Accompanied by the eleven, he made his way to the mountain. The disciples were not aware that this was to be their last season with their Master. He employed the time in sacred converse with them, reiterating his former instructions. As they passed through the gates of Jerusalem, many wondering eyes looked upon the little company, led by one whom a few weeks before the priests and rulers had condemned and crucified. (3SP 249.2)

They crossed the Kedron, and approached Gethsemane. Here Jesus paused, that his disciples might call to mind the lessons he had given them while on his way to the garden on the night of his great agony. He looked again upon the vine which he had then used as a symbol to represent the union of his church with himself and his Father; and he refreshed the memory of his followers by repeating the impressive truths which he had then illustrated to them. Reminders of the unrequited love of Jesus were all around him; even the disciples walking by his side, who were so dear to his heart, had, in the hour of his humiliation, when he most needed their sympathy and comfort, reproached and forsaken him. (3SP 250.1)

Christ had sojourned in the world for thirty-three years; he had endured its scorn, insult, and mockery; he had been rejected and crucified. Now, when about to ascend to his throne of glory–as he reviews the ingratitude of the people he came to save–will he not withdraw his sympathy and love from them? Will not his affections be centered on that world where he is appreciated, and where sinless angels adore him, and wait to do his bidding? No; his promise to those loved ones whom he leaves on earth is "Lo, I am with you alway, even unto the end of the world." Before his conflict, he had prayed the Father that they might not be taken out of the world, but should be kept from the evil which is in the world. (3SP 250.2)

At length the little company reach the Mount of Olives. This place had been peculiarly hallowed by the presence of Jesus while he bore the nature of man. It was consecrated by his prayers and tears. When he had ridden into Jerusalem, just prior to his trial, the steeps of Olivet had echoed the joyous shouts of the triumphant multitude. On its sloping descent was Bethany, where he had often found repose at the house of Lazarus. At the foot of the mount was the garden of Gethsemane, where he had agonized alone, and moistened the sod with his blood. (3SP 250.3)

Jesus led the way across the summit, to the vicinity of Bethany. He then paused, and they all gathered about him. Beams of light seemed to radiate from his countenance, as he looked with deep love upon his disciples. He upbraided them not for their faults and failures; but words of unutterable tenderness were the last which fell upon their ears from the lips of their Lord. With hands outstretched in blessing them, and as if in assurance of his protecting care, he slowly ascended from among them, drawn heavenward by a power stronger than any earthly attraction. As he passed upward, the awe-struck disciples looked with straining eyes for the last glimpse of their ascending Lord. A cloud of glory received him out of their sight, and at the same moment there floated down to their charmed senses the sweetest and most joyous music from the angel choir. (3SP 251.1)

While their gaze was still riveted upward, voices addressed them which sounded like the music which had just charmed them. They turned, and saw two beings in the form of men; yet their heavenly character was immediately discerned by the disciples, whom they addressed in comforting accents, saying, "Ye men of Galilee, why stand ye gazing up into heaven? this same Jesus, which is taken up from you into Heaven, shall so come in like manner as ye have seen him go into Heaven." These angels were of the company that had been waiting in a shining cloud to escort Jesus to his throne; and in sympathy and love for those whom the Saviour had left, they came to remove all uncertainty from their minds, and to give them the assurance that he would come to earth again. (3SP 251.2)

All Heaven was waiting to welcome the Saviour to the celestial courts. As he ascended he led the way, and the multitude of captives whom he had raised from the dead at the time when he came forth from the tomb, followed him. The heavenly host, with songs of joy and triumph, escorted him upward. At the portals of the city of God an innumerable company of angels awaited his coming. As they approached the gates of the city, the angels who were escorting the Majesty of Heaven, in triumphant tones addressed the company at the portals: "Lift up your heads, O ye gates, and be ye lifted up, ye everlasting doors, and the King of Glory shall come in!" (3SP 252.1)

The waiting angels at the gates of the city inquire in rapturous strains, "Who is this King of Glory?" The escorting angels joyously reply in songs of triumph, "The Lord, strong and mighty! The Lord, mighty in battle! Lift up your heads, O ye gates, even lift them up, ye everlasting doors, and the King of Glory shall come in!" Again the waiting angels ask, "Who is this King of Glory?" and the escorting angels respond in melodious strains, "The Lord of hosts! He is the King of Glory!" Then the portals of the city of God are widely opened, and the heavenly train pass in amid a burst of angelic music. All the heavenly host surround their majestic Commander as he takes his position upon the throne of the Father. (3SP 252.2)

With the deepest adoration and joy, the hosts of angels bow before him, while the glad shout rings through the courts of Heaven: "Worthy is the Lamb that was slain to receive power, and riches, and wisdom, and strength, and honor, and glory, and blessing!" Songs of triumph mingle with music from angelic harps, till Heaven seems to overflow with delightful harmony, and inconceivable joy and praise. The Son of God has triumphed over the prince of darkness, and conquered death and the grave. Heaven rings with voices in lofty strains proclaiming: "Blessing, and honor, and glory, and power be unto Him that sitteth upon the throne, and unto the Lamb forever and ever!" (3SP 253.1)

He is seated by the side of his Father on his throne. The Saviour presents the captives he has rescued from the bonds of death, at the price of his own life. His hands place immortal crowns upon their brows; for they are the representatives, and samples, of those who shall be redeemed, by the blood of Christ, from all nations, tongues, and people, and come forth from the dead, when he shall call the just from their graves at his second coming. Then shall they see the marks of Calvary in the glorified body of the Son of God. Their greatest joy will be found in the presence of Him who sitteth on the throne; and the enraptured saints will exclaim, My Beloved is mine, and I am his! He is the chief among ten thousand, and altogether lovely! (3SP 253.2)

The disciples returned to Jerusalem, not mourning, but full of joy. When last they looked upon their Lord, his countenance shone with heavenly brightness, and he smiled lovingly upon them. Those hands that had so often been stretched forth in the act of blessing the sick and the afflicted, and in rebuking demons–those hands which had been bruised by the cruel nails, were mercifully extended, as though in the disciples they embraced the whole world, and called down a blessing upon all the followers of Christ. Beams of light seemed to emanate from those dear hands and to fall upon the watching, waiting ones. (3SP 253.3)

The most precious fact to the disciples in the ascension of Jesus was that he went from them into Heaven in the tangible form of their divine Teacher. The very same Jesus, who had walked, and talked, and prayed with them; who

Chapter 19 - Ascension of Christ (3SP 254.1)

had broken bread with them; who had been with them in their boats on the lake; who had sought retirement with them in the groves; and who had that very day toiled with them up the steep ascent of Olivet,–had ascended to Heaven in the form of humanity. And the heavenly messengers had assured them that the very same Jesus whom they had seen go up into Heaven, should come again in like manner as he had ascended. This assurance has ever been, and will be till the close of time, the hope and joy of all true lovers of Christ. (3SP 254.1)

The disciples not only saw the Lord ascend, but they had the testimony of the angels that he had gone to occupy his Father's throne in Heaven. The last remembrance that the disciples were to have of their Lord was as the sympathizing Friend, the glorified Redeemer. Moses veiled his face to hide the glory of the law which was reflected upon it, and the glory of Christ's ascension was veiled from human sight. The brightness of the heavenly escort, and the opening of the glorious gates of God to welcome him, were not to be discerned by mortal eyes. (3SP 254.2)

Had the track of Christ to Heaven been revealed to the disciples in all its inexpressible glory, they could not have endured the sight. Had they beheld the myriads of angels, and heard the bursts of triumph from the battlements of Heaven, as the everlasting doors were lifted up, the contrast between that glory and their own lives in a world of trial, would have been so great that they would hardly have been able to again take up the burden of their earthly lives, prepared to execute with courage and faithfulness the commission given them by the Saviour. Even the Comforter, the Holy Ghost which was sent to them, would not have been properly appreciated, nor would it have strengthened their hearts sufficiently to bear reproach, contumely, imprisonment, and death if need be. (3SP 255.1)

Their senses were not to become so infatuated with the glories of Heaven that they would lose sight of the character of Christ on earth, which they were to copy in themselves. They were to keep distinctly before their minds the beauty and majesty of his life, the perfect harmony of all his attributes, and the mysterious union of the divine and human in his nature. It was better that the earthly acquaintance of the disciples with their Saviour should end in the solemn, quiet, and sublime manner in which it did. His visible ascent from the world was in harmony with the meekness and quiet of his life. (3SP 255.2)

The disciples returned to Jerusalem rejoicing, not that they were deprived of their Master and Teacher, for this was to them a cause for personal mourning rather than joy. But Jesus had assured them that he would send the Comforter, as an equivalent for his visible presence. He had said, "If ye loved me, ye would rejoice, because I said, I go unto the Father." They rejoiced because Jesus had wrought out salvation for man; he had answered the claims of the law, and had become a perfect offering for man; he had ascended to Heaven to carry forward the work of atonement begun on earth. He was the Advocate of man, his Intercessor with the Father. (3SP 256.1)

Jesus, who was born in Bethlehem; who worked with his earthly father at the carpenter's trade; who sat in weariness by Jacob's well; who slept in weariness in Peter's fishing-boat; who hungered and thirsted; who took little children in his arms and blessed them; who was rejected, scourged, and crucified,–ascended in the form of a man to Heaven, and took his place at the right hand of God. Having felt our infirmities, our sorrows, and temptations, he is amply fitted to plead for man as his representative. Jesus, when upon earth, was the most perfect type of man; and it is the Christian's joy and comfort that this patient, loving Saviour is to be his King and Judge; for "the Father judgeth no man, but hath committed all judgment unto the Son." (3SP 256.2)

We are not inclined to associate kingly glory and judicial authority with the self-denial, patience, love, and forgiveness shown in the life of Christ; yet these attributes qualified the Saviour for his exalted position. The qualities of character which he developed on earth constitute his exaltation in glory. His triumphs were gained by love, not by force. In coming to Christ the sinner consents to be elevated to the noblest ideal of man. (3SP 256.3)

"Do ye not know that the saints shall judge the world?" The attributes which exalted Christ, if obtained by his followers, will place the scepter in their hands, and they shall be kings and priests with God. Christ pledged himself to keep the law which Adam transgressed, and to magnify that law and make it honorable by demonstrating that it was not arbitrary, and could be kept inviolate by man. Christ showed by his life that the law of

Chapter 19 - Ascension of Christ (3SP 259.3)

God is faultless, and that man, by disobeying it, brings upon himself the evils which its restrictions seek to avert from him. (3SP 257.1)

When the disciples returned to Jerusalem alone, people looked at them, expecting to see in their faces expressions of sorrow, confusion, and defeat; but they saw there gladness and triumph. They did not wail over disappointed hopes, but were continually in the temple, praising and blessing God. The priests and rulers were at a loss to understand this mystery. After the discouraging events connected with the trial, condemnation, and ignominious death of their Master, the disciples were supposed to be defeated and ashamed; but they now came forth with buoyant spirits, and countenances beaming with a joy not born of earth. (3SP 257.2)

They told the wonderful story of Christ's glorious resurrection, and ascension to Heaven, and many believed their testimony. The disciples had no longer a vague distrust of the future; they knew that Jesus was in Heaven; that his sympathies were unchanged; that he was identifying himself with suffering humanity, receiving the prayers of his people; that he was pleading with God the merits of his own precious blood, showing his wounded hands and feet, as a remembrance of the price he had paid for his redeemed. They knew that he would come again escorted by the heavenly host, and they looked upon this event, not as a dreaded calamity, but as an occasion for great joy and longing anticipation. They knew that he would stand again upon the Mount of Olives, while the Hebrew hallelujahs should mingle with Gentile hosannas, and myriads of voices should unite in the glad acclamation of "Crown him Lord of all!" They knew that he had ascended to Heaven to prepare mansions for his obedient children, and that he would return and take them unto himself. (3SP 257.3)

With joy the disciples related to their brethren the news of their Lord's ascension. They now felt that they had a Friend at the throne of God, and were eager to prefer their requests to the Father in the name of Jesus. They gathered together in solemn awe and bowed in prayer, repeating to each other the assurance of the Saviour, "Whatsoever ye shall ask the Father in my name he will give it you. Hitherto have ye asked nothing in my name; ask, and ye shall receive, that your joy may be full." During the ten days following the ascension, they, with one accord, devoted the time to prayer and praise, waiting for the descent of the Holy Ghost. They extended the hand of faith higher and higher, with the mighty argument, "It is Christ that died, yea rather, that is risen again, who is even at the right hand of God, who also maketh intercession for us." (3SP 258.1)

"Great is the mystery of godliness: God was manifest in the flesh, justified in the Spirit, seen of angels, preached unto the Gentiles, believed on in the world, received up into glory." The Saviour came into the world, outwardly the son of David, not manifesting the full significance of his character. His spirit was subject to that discipline and experience through which humanity must in some measure pass. His divinity was veiled beneath humanity. He hid within himself those all-powerful attributes which belonged to him as one equal with God. At times his divine character flashed forth with such wonderful power that all who were capable of discerning spiritual things pronounced him the Son of God. (3SP 259.1)

Christ exiled himself to the world that he might bring heavenly light within the reach of humanity. The Jews did not comprehend the twofold character of Christ; and as he did not assume temporal, kingly power, and establish his reign on David's throne, bringing into subjection every foreign authority, the Jewish dignitaries refused to accept him. They could not connect man's suffering, grief, and poverty with their idea of the Messiah. Yet this was the only Saviour the Word of God through his prophets had ever predicted. (3SP 259.2)

The Jews utterly failed to understand the spiritual connection which identified Christ with both the human and the divine, and gave fallen man a presentation of what he should strive to become. Christ was God in the flesh. As the son of David, he stood forth a perfect type of true manhood, bold in doing his duty, and of the strictest integrity, yet full of love, compassion, and tender sympathy. In his miracles he revealed himself as Lord. When he was asked by Philip to show him the Father, he answered, "Have I been so long time with you, and yet hast thou not known me, Philip? He that hath seen me, hath seen the Father." (3SP 259.3)

The Jews were continually seeking for and expecting a Divinity among them that would be revealed in outward show, and by one flash of overmastering will would change the current of all minds, force from them an acknowledgment of his superiority, elevate himself, and gratify the ambition of his people. This being the case, when Christ was treated with contempt, there was a powerful temptation before him to reveal his heavenly character, and to compel his persecutors to admit that he was Lord above kings and potentates, priests and temple. But it was his difficult task to maintain the level of humanity. (3SP 260.1)

In the intercessory prayer of Jesus with his Father, he claimed that he had fulfilled the conditions which made it obligatory upon the Father to fulfill his part of the contract made in Heaven, with regard to fallen man. He prayed: "I have finished the work which thou gavest me to do. [That is, he had wrought out a righteous character on earth as an example for men to follow.] And now, O Father, glorify thou me with thine own self, with the glory which I had with thee before the world was." In this prayer he farther goes on to state what is comprehended by the work which he has accomplished, and which has given him all those who believe on his name. He values this recompense so highly that he forgets the anguish it has cost him to redeem fallen man. He declares himself glorified in those who believe on him. The church, in his name, is to carry to glorious perfection the work which he has commenced; and when that church shall be finally ransomed in the Paradise of God, he will look upon the travail of his soul and be satisfied. Through all eternity the ransomed host will be his chief glory. (3SP 260.2)

Jesus, the Majesty of Heaven, humbled himself, and became obedient unto death, even the death of the cross; "wherefore God also hath highly exalted him, and given him a name which is above every name." This mighty Saviour has promised to come again, and to take his church to the mansions he has prepared for them. While he is in Heaven carrying on the work of intercession and atonement commenced on earth, his life and character are to be exemplified by his church upon earth. He has promised that, "He that believeth on me, the works that I do shall he do also; and greater works than these shall he do, because I go unto my Father." And again, "Hitherto have ye asked nothing in my name." "Whatsoever ye shall ask the Father in my name, he will give it you." (3SP 261.1)

He who considered it not robbery to be equal with God, once trod the earth, bearing our suffering and sorrowing nature, and tempted in all points like as we are; and now he appears in the presence of God as our great High Priest, ready to accept the repentance, and to answer the prayers of his people, and, through the merits of his own righteousness, to present them to the Father. He raises his wounded hands to God, and claims their blood-bought pardon. I have graven them on the palms of my hands, he pleads. Those memorial wounds of my humiliation and anguish secure to my church the best gifts of Omnipotence. (3SP 261.2)

What a source of joy to the disciples, to know that they had such a Friend in Heaven to plead in their behalf! Through the visible ascension of Christ all their views and contemplation of Heaven are changed. Their minds had formerly dwelt upon it as a region of unlimited space, tenanted by spirits without substance. Now Heaven was connected with the thought of Jesus, whom they had loved and reverenced above all others, with whom they had conversed and journeyed, whom they had handled, even in his resurrected body, who had spoken hope and comfort to their hearts, and who, while the words were upon his lips, had been taken up before their eyes, the tones of his voice coming back to them as the cloudy chariot of angels received him: "Lo, I am with you alway, even unto the end of the world." (3SP 262.1)

Heaven could no longer appear to them as an indefinite, incomprehensible space, filled with intangible spirits. They now looked upon it as their future home, where mansions were being prepared for them by their loving Redeemer. Prayer was clothed with a new interest, since it was a communion with their Saviour. With new and thrilling emotions and a firm confidence that their prayer would be answered, they gathered in the upper chamber to offer their petitions, and to claim the promise of the Saviour, who had said, "Ask, and ye shall receive, that your joy may be full." They prayed in the name of Jesus. (3SP 262.2)

They had a gospel to preach–Christ in human form, a man of sorrows; Christ in humiliation, taken by wicked hands and crucified; Christ resurrected, and ascended to Heaven, into the presence of God, to be man's Advocate; Christ to come again with power and great glory in the clouds of heaven, and to receive the obedient and loyal to himself. (3SP 263.1)

The apostles went forth with courage and hope, to do their Master's work with fidelity. They knew that the most acceptable way of waiting for Christ was to work for him. It was theirs to direct others to the coming Lord, and to teach them to wait patiently for his appearing. This work was given to every disciple of Christ. (3SP 263.2)

*****

Chapter 20
The Pentecost

When Jesus opened the understanding of the disciples to the meaning of the prophecies concerning himself, he assured them that all power was given him in Heaven and on earth, and bade them go preach the gospel to every creature. The disciples, with a sudden revival of their old hope that Jesus would take his place upon the throne of David at Jerusalem, inquired, "Wilt thou at this time restore again the kingdom to Israel?" The Saviour threw an uncertainty over their minds in regard to the subject by replying that it was not for them "to know the times or the seasons, which the Father hath put in his own power." (3SP 263.3)

The disciples began to hope that the wonderful descent of the Holy Ghost would influence the Jewish people to accept Jesus. The Saviour forbore to farther explain, for he knew that when the Holy Spirit should come upon them in full measure their minds would be illuminated and they would fully understand the work before them, and take it up just where he had left it. (3SP 264.1)

The disciples assembled in the upper chamber, uniting in supplications with the believing women, with Mary the mother of Jesus, and with his brethren. These brethren, who had been unbelieving, were now fully established in their faith by the scenes attending the crucifixion, and by the resurrection and ascension of the Lord. The number assembled was about one hundred and twenty. While they were awaiting the descent of the Holy Ghost, they supplied the office left vacant by Judas. Two men were selected, who, in the careful judgment of the believers, were best qualified for the place. But the disciples, distrusting their ability to decide the question farther, referred it to One that knew all hearts. They sought the Lord in prayer to ascertain which of the two men was more suitable for the important position of trust, as an apostle of Christ. The Spirit of God selected Matthias for the office. (3SP 264.2)

Both men who had been selected were considered to be persons of stern integrity, and in every way worthy of the vacant position; but notwithstanding the disciples were intimately acquainted with them, they felt that their own judgment was imperfect, and trusted the selection only to the Lord, whose eyes could read the hidden secrets of the heart. There is a lesson for our time in this occurrence. Many who are apparently well qualified to labor for God, are urged into the ministry, without a proper consideration of their case, and at length become a grievous burden to the church instead of burden-bearers. If the church of the present time would act as cautiously and wisely as did the apostles in filling the vacancy among them, much perplexity and serious injury might be saved the cause of God. The work has often suffered much by putting persons forward to do that which they were not capable of doing. (3SP 264.3)

After filling the vacancy in the apostolic number, the disciples gave their time to meditation and prayer, being often in the temple, testifying of Christ, and praising God. The Pentecost was a feast celebrated seven weeks after the passover. Upon these occasions the Jews were required to repair to the temple and to present the first-fruits of all the harvest, thus acknowledging their dependence on the great Giver of all good, and their obligation to render back to God, in gifts and offerings to sustain his cause, that which he had intrusted to them. On this day of divine appointment, the Lord graciously poured out his Spirit on the little company of believers, who were the first-fruits of the Christian church. (3SP 265.1)

"And when the day of Pentecost was fully come, they were all with one accord in one place. And suddenly there came a sound from heaven as of a rushing mighty wind, and it filled all the house where they were sitting. And there appeared unto them cloven tongues like as of fire, and it sat upon each of them. And they were all filled with the Holy Ghost, and began to speak with other tongues, as the Spirit gave them utterance." The Holy Ghost assuming the form of tongues of fire divided at the tips, and resting upon those assembled, was an emblem of the gift which was bestowed upon them of speaking with fluency several different languages, with which they had formerly been unacquainted. And the appearance of fire signified the fervent zeal with which they would labor, and the power which would attend their words. (3SP 265.2)

Under this heavenly illumination, the scriptures which Christ had explained to them, stood forth in their minds with the vivid luster and loveliness of clear and powerful truth. The vail which had prevented them from seeing the end of that which was abolished was now removed, and the object of Christ's mission and the nature of his kingdom were comprehended with perfect clearness. (3SP 266.1)

The Jews had been scattered to almost every nation, and spoke various languages. They had come long distances to Jerusalem, and had temporarily taken up their abode there, to remain through the religious festivals then in progress, and to observe their requirements. When assembled, they were of every known tongue. This diversity of languages was a great obstacle to the labors of God's servants in publishing the doctrine of Christ to the uttermost parts of the earth. That God should supply the deficiency of the apostles in a miraculous manner was to the people the most perfect confirmation of the testimony of these witnesses for Christ. The Holy Spirit had done for them that which they could not have accomplished for themselves in a lifetime; they could now spread the truth of the gospel abroad, speaking with accuracy the language of those for whom they were laboring. This miraculous gift was the highest evidence they could present to the world that their commission bore the signet of Heaven. (3SP 266.2)

"And there were dwelling at Jerusalem Jews, devout men, out of every nation under heaven. Now when this was noised abroad, the multitude came together, and were confounded, because that every man heard them speak in his own language. And they were all amazed, and marveled, saying one to another, Behold, are not all these which speak Galileans? And how hear we every man in our own tongue, wherein we were born? Parthians, and Medes, and Elamites, and the dwellers in Mesopotamia, and in Judea, and Cappadocia, in Pontus, and Asia, Phrygia, and Pamphylia, in Egypt, and in the parts of Libya about Cyrene, and strangers of Rome, Jews and proselytes, Cretes and Arabians, we do hear them speak in our tongues the wonderful works of God. And they were all amazed, and were in doubt, saying one to another, What meaneth this? Others mocking said, These men are full of new wine." (3SP 267.1)

The priests and rulers were greatly enraged at this wonderful manifestation, which was reported throughout all Jerusalem and the vicinity; but they dared not give way to their malice, for fear of exposing themselves to the hatred of the people. They had put the Master to death, but here were his servants, unlearned men of Galilee, tracing out the wonderful fulfillment of prophecy, and teaching the doctrine of Jesus in all the languages then spoken. They spoke with power of the wonderful works of the Saviour, and unfolded to their hearers the plan of salvation in the mercy and sacrifice of the Son of God. Their words convicted and converted thousands who listened. The traditions and superstitions inculcated by the priests were swept away from their minds, and they accepted the pure teachings of the Word of God. (3SP 267.2)

The priests and rulers, determined to account for the miraculous power of the disciples in some natural way, declared that they were simply drunken from partaking largely of the new wine prepared for the feast. Some of the most ignorant seized this suggestion as the truth; but the more intelligent knew that it was false; and those speaking the different languages testified to the accuracy with which they were used by the disciples. And Peter, in answer to the vile accusation of the priests, addressed the assembly in these words:– (3SP 268.1)

"Ye men of Judea, and all ye that dwell at Jerusalem, be this known unto you, and hearken to my words; for these are not drunken, as ye suppose, seeing it is but the third hour of the day. But this is that which was spoken by the prophet Joel: And it shall come to pass in the last days, saith God, I will pour out of my Spirit upon all flesh; and your sons and your daughters shall prophesy, and your young men shall see visions, and your old men shall dream dreams." (3SP 268.2)

The effect of Peter's words was very marked; and many who had ridiculed the religion of Jesus were now convinced of its truth. It was certainly unreasonable to suppose that more than one hundred persons should become intoxicated at that unseasonable hour of the day, and on the

Chapter 20 - The Pentecost (3SP 268.3)

occasion of a solemn religious festival. This wonderful demonstration was before the customary meal at which wine was taken. Peter showed them that this manifestation was the direct fulfillment of the prophecy of Joel, wherein he foretold that such power would come upon men of God to fit them for a special work. (3SP 268.3)

Peter traced back the lineage of Christ in a direct line to the honorable house of David. He did not use any of the teachings of Jesus to prove his true position, because he knew their prejudices were so great that it would be of no effect. But he referred them to David, whom the Jews regarded as a venerable patriarch of their nation. Said Peter:- (3SP 269.1)

"For David speaketh concerning him, I foresaw the Lord always before my face; for he is on my right hand, that I should not be moved. Therefore did my heart rejoice, and my tongue was glad; moreover also my flesh shall rest in hope; because thou wilt not leave my soul in hell, neither wilt thou suffer thine Holy One to see corruption. Thou hast made known to me the ways of life; thou shalt make me full of joy with thy countenance. Men and brethren, let me freely speak unto you of the patriarch David, that he is both dead and buried, and his sepulcher is with us unto this day. Therefore being a prophet, and knowing that God had sworn with an oath to him, that of the fruit of his loins, according to the flesh, he would raise up Christ to sit on his throne; he, seeing this before, spake of the resurrection of Christ, that his soul was not left in hell, neither his flesh did see corruption. This Jesus hath God raised up, whereof we all are witnesses. Therefore being by the right hand of God exalted, and having received of the Father the promise of the Holy Ghost, he hath shed forth this, which ye now see and hear. For David is not ascended into the heavens; but he saith himself, The Lord said unto my Lord, Sit thou on my right hand, until I make thy foes thy footstool. Therefore let all the house of Israel know assuredly, that God hath made that same Jesus, who ye have crucified, both Lord and Christ." (3SP 269.2)

Peter here shows that David could not have spoken in reference to himself, but definitely of Jesus Christ. David died a natural death like other men; his sepulcher, with the honored dust it contained, had been preserved with great care until that time. David, as king of Israel, and also as a prophet, had been specially honored by God.

In prophetic vision he was shown the future life and ministry of Christ. He saw his rejection, his trial, crucifixion, burial, resurrection, and ascension. (3SP 270.1)

David testified that the soul of Christ was not to be left in hell (the grave), nor was his flesh to see corruption. Peter shows the fulfillment of this prophecy in Jesus of Nazareth. God had actually raised him up from the tomb before his body saw corruption. He was now the exalted One in the Heaven of heavens. (3SP 270.2)

The surprising demonstrations on the occasion of the Feast of Pentecost could only be accounted for in this way: The promise which Christ had given the disciples of the descent of the Holy Ghost from the Father was in this manner fulfilled. "He hath shed forth this which ye now see and hear." Peter assures them that David's prophecy could not refer to himself, for he had not ascended into the heavens; he was resting in his sepulcher. If the soul of David had gone to Heaven, Peter could not have been so positive in his assurances to his brethren. He testified to the sleep of the dead in their graves till the resurrection. (3SP 270.3)

In the words of David referred to by Peter-"The Lord said unto my Lord, Sit thou at my right hand, until I make thine enemies thy footstool," the Father is called Lord, who said unto Christ, who is also Lord, and equal with the Father, "Sit thou on my right hand." "Therefore," said Peter, "let all the house of Israel know assuredly, that God hath made that same Jesus, whom ye have crucified, both Lord and Christ." (3SP 271.1)

David called the Messiah, in his divine character, Lord, although, after the flesh, he was the son of David by direct descent. David, by prophetic foresight, saw Christ enter into the heavens, and take his position at the right hand of God. The demonstration witnessed by the Jews at the Pentecost was an exhibition of the power of that very Jesus whom the priests and rulers had contemptuously rejected and crucified. According to his promise he had sent the Holy Spirit from Heaven to his followers, as a token that he had, as priest and king, received all authority in Heaven and on earth, and was the Anointed One over his people. (3SP 271.2)

On that memorable occasion, large numbers who had heretofore ridiculed the idea of so unpretending a person as Jesus being the Son of God, became thoroughly convinced of the truth, and acknowledged him as their Saviour. Three thousand souls were added to the church. The apostles spoke by the power of the Holy Ghost; and their words could not be controverted, for they were confirmed by mighty miracles, wrought by them through the outpouring of the Spirit of God. The disciples were themselves astonished at the results of this visitation, and the quick and abundant harvest of souls. All the people were filled with amazement. Those who did not yield their prejudice and bigotry were so overawed that they dared not by voice or violence attempt to stay the mighty work, and, for the time being, their opposition ceased. (3SP 271.3)

This testimony in regard to the establishment of the Christian church is given us, not only as an important portion of sacred history, but also as a lesson. All who profess the name of Christ should be waiting, watching, and praying with one heart. All differences should be put away, and unity and tender love one for another pervade the whole. Then our prayers may go up together to our Heavenly Father with strong, earnest faith. Then we may wait with patience and hope the fulfillment of the promise. (3SP 272.1)

The answer may come with sudden velocity and overpowering might; or it may be delayed for days and weeks, and our faith receive a trial. But God knows how and when to answer our prayer. It is our part of the work to put ourselves in connection with the divine channel. God is responsible for his part of the work. He is faithful who hath promised. The great and important matter with us is to be of one heart and mind, putting aside all envy and malice, and, as humble supplicants, to watch and wait. Jesus, our Representative and Head, is ready to do for us what he did for the praying, watching ones on the day of Pentecost. (3SP 272.2)

Jesus is as willing to impart courage and grace to his followers today as he was to the disciples of the early church. None should rashly invite an opportunity to battle with the principalities and powers of darkness. When God bids them engage in the conflict it will be time enough; he will then give the weak and hesitating boldness and utterance beyond their hope or expectation. (3SP 273.1)

The same scorn and hatred that was manifested against Christ may be seen now to exist against those whom he has evidently chosen to be his co-workers. Those whose spirits rise up against the doctrines of truth make hard work for the servants of Christ. But God will make their wrath to praise him; they accomplish his purpose by stirring up minds to investigate the truth. God may allow men to follow their own wicked inclinations for a time, in opposing him; but when he sees it is for his glory, and the good of his people, he will arrest the scorners, expose their presumptive course, and give triumph to his truth. (3SP 273.2)

The arguments of the apostles alone, although clear and convincing, would not have removed the prejudice of the Jews which had withstood so much evidence. But the Holy Ghost sent those arguments home with divine power to their hearts. They were as sharp arrows of the Almighty, convicting them of their terrible guilt in rejecting and crucifying the Lord of glory. "Now when they heard this, they were pricked in their heart, and said unto Peter and to the rest of the apostles, Men and brethren, what shall we do? Then Peter said unto them, Repent, and be baptized every one of you in the name of Jesus Christ for the remission of sins, and ye shall receive the gift of the Holy Ghost." (3SP 273.3)

The disciples and apostles of Christ had a deep sense of their own inefficiency, and with humiliation and prayer they joined their weakness to his strength, their ignorance to his wisdom, their unworthiness to his righteousness, their poverty to his inexhaustible wealth. Thus strengthened and equipped they hesitated not in the service of their Master. (3SP 274.1)

Peter urged home upon the convicted people the fact that they had rejected Christ because they had been deceived by the priests and rulers; and if they continued to look to them for counsel, and waited for those leaders to acknowledge Christ before they dared to do so, they would never accept him. Those powerful men, although they made a profession of sanctity, were ambitious, and zealous for riches and earthly glory. They would never come to Christ to receive light. Jesus had foretold a terrible retribution to come upon that people for their obstinate unbelief, notwithstanding the most powerful evidences given them that Jesus was the Son of God. (3SP 274.2)

"Then they that gladly received his word were baptized; and the same day there were added unto them about three thousand souls. And they continued steadfastly in the apostles' doctrine and fellowship, and in breaking of bread, and in prayers. And fear came upon every

Chapter 20 - The Pentecost (3SP 274.3)

soul; and many wonders and signs were done by the apostles." (3SP 274.3)

From this time forth the language of the disciples was pure, simple, and accurate in word and accent, whether they spoke their native tongue or a foreign language. These humble men, who had never learned in the school of the prophets, presented truths so elevated and pure as to astonish those who heard them. They could not go personally to the uttermost parts of the earth; but there were men at the feast from every quarter of the world, and the truths received by them were carried to their various homes, and published among their people, winning souls to Christ. (3SP 275.1)

*****

Chapter 21
The Cripple Healed

A short time after the descent of the Holy Spirit, and immediately after a season of fervent prayer, Peter and John, going up to the temple to worship, saw a distressed and poverty-stricken cripple, forty years of age, who had known no other life than one of pain and infirmity. This unfortunate man had long desired to go to Jesus and be healed; but he was almost helpless, and was removed far from the scene of the great Physician's labors. Finally his earnest pleadings induced some kind persons to bear him to the gate of the temple. But upon arriving there he discovered that the Healer, upon whom his hopes were centered, had been put to a cruel death. (3SP 275.2)

His disappointment excited the pity of those who knew how long he had eagerly hoped and expected to be healed by Jesus, and they daily brought him to the temple, that the passers-by might be moved to give him a trifle to relieve his present wants. As Peter and John passed, he begged charity from them. The disciples regarded him with compassion. "And Peter, fastening his eyes upon him with John, said, Look on us." "Silver and gold have I none; but such as I have give I thee. In the name of Jesus Christ of Nazareth rise up and walk." (3SP 275.3)

The poor man's countenance had fallen when Peter declared his own poverty, but grew bright with hope and faith as the disciple continued. "And he took him by the right hand, and lifted him up; and immediately his feet and ankle bones received strength. And he leaping up stood, and walked, and entered with them into the temple, walking, and leaping, and praising God. And all the people saw him walking and praising God. And they knew that it was he which sat for alms at the Beautiful gate of the temple; and they were filled with wonder and amazement at that which had happened unto him." (3SP 276.1)

The Jews were astonished that the disciples could perform miracles similar to those of Jesus. He, they supposed, was dead, and they had expected all such wonderful manifestations to cease with him. Yet here was this man who had been a helpless cripple for forty years, now rejoicing in the full use of his limbs, free from pain, and happy in believing upon Jesus. (3SP 276.2)

The apostles saw the amazement of the people, and questioned them why they should be astonished at the miracle which they had witnessed, and regard them with awe as though it were through their own power they had done this thing. Peter assured them it was done through the merits of Jesus of Nazareth, whom they had rejected and crucified, but whom God had raised from the dead the third day. "And his name through faith in his name hath made this man strong, whom ye see and know; yea, the faith which is by him hath given him this perfect soundness in the presence of you all. And now brethren, I wot that through ignorance ye did it, as did also your rulers. But those things which God before had showed by the mouth of all his prophets, that Christ should suffer, he hath so fulfilled." (3SP 276.3)

The manner of Jesus in working his miracles was very different from that of his apostles. His language was that of one who possessed power in himself. "Be thou clean." "Peace, be still." Neither did he hesitate to accept the honor offered him on these occasions, nor seek to divert the minds of the people from himself, as though his miracles were not wrought by his own power, for his own glory. But the apostles wrought miracles only in the name of Jesus, and refused to receive the least honor to themselves. They claimed to be only instruments of that Jesus whom the Jews had crucified, but whom God had raised and elevated to his right hand. He was to receive all the honor and praise. (3SP 277.1)

After the performance of this miracle, the people flocked together in the temple, and Peter addressed them in one part of the temple, while John spoke to them in another part. The apostles, having spoken plainly of the great crime of the

Chapter 21 - The Cripple Healed (3SP 277.2)

Jews, in rejecting and putting to death the Prince of Life, were careful not to drive them to madness or despair. Peter was willing to lessen the atrocity of their guilt as much as possible, by presuming that they did the deed ignorantly. He declared to them that the Holy Ghost was calling for them to repent of their sins and to be converted; that there was no hope for them except through the mercy of that Christ whom they had crucified; through faith in him only could their sins be canceled by his blood. (3SP 277.2)

This preaching the resurrection of Christ, and that through his death and resurrection he would finally bring up all the dead from their graves, deeply stirred the Sadducees. They felt that their favorite doctrine was in danger, and their reputation at stake. Some of the officials of the temple, and the captain of the temple, were Sadducees. The captain, with the help of a number of Sadducees, arrested the two apostles, and put them in prison, as it was too late for their cases to be examined that night. (3SP 278.1)

These opponents of Christ and of the doctrines of the apostles, could but believe, although they refused to acknowledge, that Jesus had risen from the dead and remained on the earth for forty days afterward; the evidence was too convincing for them to doubt it. Yet, nevertheless, their hearts did not soften, nor their consciences smite them for the terrible deed they had committed in putting him to death. When the power from Heaven came upon the apostles in so remarkable a manner, fear held them from violence, but their bitterness and malice were unchanged. Five thousand had already embraced the new doctrine taught by the apostles, and both Pharisees and Sadducees decided among themselves that if those teachers were suffered to go unchecked, their own influence would be in greater danger than when Jesus was upon earth. If one or two discourses from the disciples could accomplish such marvelous results, the world would soon believe on Christ if they were left free, and the influence of priests and potentates would be lost. (3SP 278.2)

The following day Annas and Caiaphas, with the other dignitaries of the temple, met together for the trial of the prisoners, who were then brought before them. In that very room, and before those very men, Peter had shamefully denied his Lord. All this came distinctly before the mind of the disciple, as he now appeared for his own trial. He had now an opportunity of redeeming his former wicked cowardice. (3SP 279.1)

The company present remembered the part Peter had acted at the trial of his Master, and they flattered themselves that he could be intimidated by the threat of imprisonment and death. But the Peter who denied Christ in the hour of his greatest need, was the impulsive, self-confident disciple, differing widely from the Peter who was before the Sanhedrim for examination that day. He had been converted; he was distrustful of self, and no longer a proud boaster. He was filled with the Holy Spirit, and through its power he had become firm as a rock, courageous, yet modest, in magnifying Christ. He was ready to remove the stain of his apostasy by honoring the name he had once disowned. (3SP 279.2)

Hitherto the priests had avoided having the crucifixion or resurrection of Jesus mentioned; but now, in fulfillment of their purpose, they were forced to inquire of the accused by what power they had accomplished the remarkable cure of the impotent man. Then Peter, filled with the Holy Ghost, addressed the priests and elders respectfully, and declared: "Be it known unto you all, and to all the people of Israel, that by the name of Jesus Christ of Nazareth, whom ye crucified, whom God raised from the dead, even by him doth this man stand here before you whole. This is the stone which was set at naught of you builders, which is become the head of the corner. Neither is there salvation in any other; for there is none other name under heaven given among men, whereby we may be saved." (3SP 279.3)

The seal of Christ was on the words of Peter, and his countenance was illuminated by the Holy Spirit. Close beside him, as a convincing witness, stood the man who had been so miraculously cured. The appearance of this man, who but a few hours before was a helpless cripple, now restored to soundness of body, and being enlightened concerning Jesus of Nazareth, added a weight of testimony to the words of Peter. Priests, rulers, and people were silent. The rulers had no power to refute his statement. They had been obliged to hear that which they most desired not to hear: the fact of the resurrection of Jesus Christ, and his power in Heaven to perform miracles through the medium of his apostles on earth. (3SP 280.1)

The crowning miracle of raising Lazarus

Chapter 21 - The Cripple Healed (3SP 283.1)

from the dead had sealed the determination of the priests to rid the world of Jesus and his wonderful works, which were fast destroying their own influence with the people. But here was a convincing proof that the death of Jesus had not put a stop to the working of miracles in his name, nor to the promulgation of the doctrine he had taught. Already the news of the miracle, and the preaching of the apostles, had filled all Jerusalem with excitement. (3SP 280.2)

The defense of Peter, in which he boldly avowed from whence his strength was obtained, appalled them. He had referred to the stone set at naught by the builders,–meaning the authorities of the church, who should have perceived the value of Him whom they rejected,–but which had nevertheless become the head of the corner. In those words he directly referred to Christ, who was the foundation-stone of the church. (3SP 281.1)

The people were amazed at the boldness of the disciples. They supposed, because they were ignorant fishermen, they would be overcome with embarrassment when confronted by the priests, scribes, and elders. But they took knowledge that they had been with Jesus. The apostles spoke as he had spoken, with a convincing power that silenced their adversaries. In order to conceal their perplexity, the priests and rulers ordered the apostles to be taken away, that they might counsel among themselves. (3SP 281.2)

They all agreed that it would be useless to deny that the man had been healed through power given the apostles in the name of the crucified Jesus. They would gladly have covered up the miracle by falsehoods; but the work was done in the full light of day, and before a crowd of people, and had already come to the knowledge of thousands. They felt that the work must be immediately stopped, or Jesus would gain many believers, their own disgrace would follow, and they would be held guilty of the murder of the Son of God. (3SP 281.3)

But notwithstanding their disposition to destroy the disciples, they dared not do worse than threaten them with the severest punishment if they continued to teach or work in the name of Jesus. Thereupon Peter and John boldly declared that their work had been given them of God, and they could not but speak the things which they had seen and heard. The priests would gladly have punished these noble men for their unswerving fidelity to their sacred calling, but they feared the people, "for all men glorified God for that which was done." So, with repeated threats and injunctions, the apostles were set at liberty. (3SP 281.4)

While Peter and John were prisoners, the other disciples, knowing the malignity of the Jews, had prayed for them unceasingly, fearing that the cruelty exercised upon Christ would be repeated upon their brethren. As soon as the apostles were released they sought their anxious brethren and reported to them the result of the examination. Great was the joy of the believers, and they again betook themselves to prayer, that greater strength might be imparted to them in their work of the ministry, which they saw would meet the same determined opposition which Christ encountered when upon earth. The disciples had no desire to glorify themselves, but sought to exalt Jesus, and to rescue souls through his saving message. (3SP 282.1)

While their united prayers were ascending in faith to Heaven, the answer came. The place where they were assembled was shaken, and they were filled with the Holy Ghost. They went forth to their work, speaking the Word of God with convincing power, and there were daily large additions to the church. Great numbers had collected at Jerusalem to observe the sacred feast. The exciting scenes of the crucifixion and resurrection had called out a much larger number than usual. When the truth taught by the apostles was brought suddenly and with convincing power before them, thousands were converted in a day. (3SP 282.2)

These early believers were most of them immediately cut off from family and friends by the zealous bigotry of the Jews. Many of the converts were thrown out of business, and exiled from their homes because they followed the convictions of their consciences, and espoused the cause of Christ. It was necessary to provide this large number, congregated at Jerusalem, with homes and sustenance. Those having money and possessions cheerfully sacrificed them to the existing emergency. Their means were laid at the feet of the apostles, who made distribution to every man according as he had need; and there were none among them who lacked. (3SP 283.1)

One example of noble benevolence is particularly mentioned in the Scriptures: "And Joses, who by the apostles was surnamed Barnabas (which is, being interpreted, the son of consolation), a Levite, and of the country of Cyprus, having land, sold it, and brought the

Chapter 21 - The Cripple Healed (3SP 283.2)

money, and laid it at the apostles' feet." This was the effect of the pouring out of the Spirit of God upon the believers. It made them of one heart and soul. They had one common interest–the success of the mission intrusted to them. Their love for their brethren, and the cause which they had espoused, was far greater than their love for money and possessions. They acted out their faith, and by their works testified that they accounted the souls of men of far greater value than any earthly heritage. (3SP 283.2)

When selfish love of the world enters the heart, spirituality dies. The very best antidote for love of the world is the outpouring of the Spirit of God. When the love of Christ takes full possession of the heart, we shall strive to follow the example of Him who for our sakes became poor, that through his poverty we might be made rich. When it becomes apparent that the Spirit of truth weakens the affections of its disciples from the world, and renders them self-sacrificing and benevolent, in order to save their fellow-men, the advocates of the truth will have a powerful influence upon their hearers. (3SP 284.1)

As a contrast to the example which has been cited, another case has been recorded by the inspired pen which leaves a dark stain upon the first church: "But a certain man named Ananias, with Sapphira his wife, sold a possession, and kept back part of the price, his wife also being privy to it, and brought a certain part, and laid it at the apostles' feet." This couple had noted the fact that those who had parted with their possessions to supply the wants of their poorer brethren were held in high esteem among the believers. They therefore, upon consulting together, decided to sell their property, and affect to give all the proceeds into the general fund, but really to retain a large share for themselves. They thus designed to receive their living, which they intended to estimate much higher than it really was, from the common stock, and to secure the high esteem of their brethren. (3SP 284.2)

But a holy God hates hypocrisy and falsehood. The apostles were impressed by a sense of the true state of the case, and when Ananias presented himself with his offering, representing it as the entire proceeds of the sale of his property, Peter said to him, "Ananias, why hath Satan filled thine heart to lie to the Holy Ghost, and to keep back part of the price of the land? While it remained, was it not thine own? and after it was sold, was it not in thine own power? Why hast thou conceived this thing in thine heart? Thou hast not lied unto men, but unto God. And Ananias, hearing these words, fell down, and gave up the ghost; and great fear came on all them that heard these things." (3SP 284.3)

Peter asked, "Was it not thine own?" thus showing that no undue influence had been brought to bear upon Ananias and Sapphira to compel them to sacrifice their possessions to the general good. They had acted from choice. But in pretending to be wrought upon by the Holy Ghost, and attempting to deceive the apostles, they had lied to the Almighty. (3SP 285.1)

"And it was about the space of three hours after, when his wife, not knowing what was done, came in. And Peter answered unto her, Tell me whether ye sold the land for so much? And she said, Yea, for so much. Then Peter said unto her, How is it that ye have agreed together to tempt the Spirit of the Lord? Behold, the feet of them which have buried thy husband are at the door, and shall carry thee out. Then fell she down straightway at his feet, and yielded up the ghost; and the young men came in, and found her dead, and, carrying her forth, buried her by her husband. And great fear came upon all the church, and upon as many as heard these things." (3SP 285.2)

This signal manifestation of the wrath of God upon the dissemblers was a check which Infinite Wisdom knew was needed. The church would have been disgraced, if, in the rapid increase of professed Christians, there were persons professing to serve God, but worshiping mammon. There are many Ananiases and Sapphiras in our day, whom Satan tempts to dissemble, because of their love of money. By various plans and excuses they withhold from the treasury of God the means intrusted to them for the advancement of the cause of God. Should the punishment of Ananias and Sapphira be visited upon this class, there would be many dead bodies in our churches requiring burial. (3SP 285.3)

This marked judgment upon two avaricious hypocrites, whose sin had been detected by the evidence of the Spirit of God to the apostles, excited the reverential awe of all the new converts. From that time there was greater caution manifested by them, and a more thorough self-examination, testing the motives of their actions. In any great religious movement there is always a class who are carried away by the current of feeling, but who soon reveal

Chapter 21 - The Cripple Healed (3SP 289.1)

selfishness and vain-glory. Such persons can never be an honor to the cause they advocate. (3SP 286.1)

The discernment of the apostles in detecting hidden sin added to the confidence of their brethren in them and the message which they preached. The apostles continued their work of mercy, in healing the afflicted and in proclaiming a crucified and risen Saviour, with great power. Numbers were continually added to the church by baptism, but none dared join them who were not united heart and mind with the believers in Christ. Multitudes flocked to Jerusalem, bringing their sick, and those who were vexed by unclean spirits. Many sufferers were laid in the streets as Peter and John passed by, that their shadows might fall upon and heal them. The power of the risen Saviour had indeed fallen upon the apostles, and they worked signs and miracles that daily increased the number of believers. (3SP 286.2)

These things greatly perplexed the priests and rulers, especially those among them who were Sadducees. They saw that if the apostles were allowed to preach a resurrected Saviour, and to do miracles in his name, their doctrine that there was no resurrection of the dead would be rejected by all, and their sect would soon become extinct. The Pharisees saw that the tendency of their preaching would be to undermine the Jewish ceremonies, and make the sacrificial offerings of none effect. Their former efforts to suppress these preachers had been in vain; but they now felt determined to put down the excitement. (3SP 287.1)

The apostles were accordingly arrested and imprisoned, and the Sanhedrim was called to try their case. A large number of learned men, in addition to the council, were summoned, and they counseled together what should be done with these disturbers of the peace. "But the angel of the Lord by night opened the prison doors, and brought them forth, and said, Go, stand and speak in the temple to the people all the words of this life. And when they heard that, they entered into the temple early in the morning, and taught." (3SP 287.2)

When the apostles appeared among the believers, and recounted how the angel had led them directly through the band of soldiers guarding the prison, and bade them resume the work which had been interrupted by the priests and rulers, the brethren were filled with joy and amazement. (3SP 287.3)

The priests and rulers in council decided to fix upon them the charge of insurrection, and accuse them of murdering Ananias and Sapphira, and of conspiring to deprive the priests of their authority and put them to death. They trusted that the mob would then be excited to take the matter in hand, and to deal by the apostles as they had dealt by Jesus. They were aware that many who did not accept the doctrine of Christ were weary of the arbitrary rule of the Jewish authorities, and were anxious for some decided change. If these persons became interested in and embraced the belief of the apostles, acknowledging Jesus as the Messiah, they feared the anger of the entire people would be raised against the priests, who would be made to answer for the murder of Christ. They decided to take strong measures to prevent this. They finally sent for the supposed prisoners to be brought before them. Great was their amazement when the report was brought back that the prison doors were found securely bolted, and the guard stationed before them, but that the prisoners were nowhere to be found. (3SP 288.1)

Soon the report was brought: "Behold, the men whom ye put in prison are standing in the temple, and teaching the people." Although the apostles were miraculously delivered from prison, they were not saved from examination and punishment. Christ had said when he was with them, "Take heed to yourselves, for they shall deliver you up to councils." God had given them a token of his care, and an assurance of his presence, by sending the angel to them; it was now their part to suffer for the sake of that Jesus whom they preached. The people were so wrought upon by what they had seen and heard that the priests and rulers knew it would be impossible to excite them against the apostles. (3SP 288.2)

"Then went the captain with the officers, and brought them without violence; for they feared the people, lest they should have been stoned. And when they had brought them, they set them before the council; and the high priest asked them, saying, Did not we straitly command you that ye should not teach in this name? and, behold, ye have filled Jerusalem with your doctrine, and intend to bring this man's blood upon us." They were not as willing to bear the blame of slaying Jesus as when they swelled the cry with the debased mob: "His blood be on us and on our children!" (3SP 289.1)

Peter, with the other apostles, took up the

Chapter 21 - The Cripple Healed (3SP 289.2)

same line of defense he had followed at his former trial: "Then Peter and the other apostles answered and said, We ought to obey God rather than men." It was the angel sent by God who delivered them from prison, and who commanded them to teach in the temple. In following his directions they were obeying the divine command, which they must continue to do at any cost to themselves. Peter continued: "The God of our fathers raised up Jesus, whom ye slew and hanged on a tree. Him hath God exalted with his right hand to be a Prince and a Saviour, for to give repentance to Israel, and forgiveness of sins. And we are his witnesses of these things; and so is also the Holy Ghost, whom God hath given to them that obey him." (3SP 289.2)

The spirit of inspiration was upon the apostles, and the accused became the accusers, charging the murder of Christ upon the priests and rulers who composed the council. The Jews were so enraged at this that they decided, without any further trial, and without authority from the Roman officers, to take the law into their own hands, and put the prisoners to death. Already guilty of the blood of Christ, they were now eager to imbrue their hands in the blood of his apostles. But there was one man of learning and high position whose clear intellect saw that this violent step would lead to terrible consequences. God raised up a man of their own council to stay the violence of the priests and rulers. (3SP 290.1)

Gamaliel, the learned Pharisee and doctor, a man of great reputation, was a person of extreme caution, who, before speaking in behalf of the prisoners, requested them to be removed. He then spoke with great deliberation and calmness: "Ye men of Israel, take heed to yourselves what ye intend to do as touching these men. For before these days rose up Theudas, boasting himself to be somebody; to whom a number of men, about four hundred, joined themselves; who was slain; and all, as many as obeyed him, were scattered, and brought to naught. After this man rose up Judas of Galilee in the days of the taxing, and drew away much people after him; he also perished; and all, even as many as obeyed him, were dispersed. And now I say unto you, Refrain from these men, and let them alone; for if this counsel or this work be of men, it will come to naught. But if it be of God, ye cannot overthrow it; lest haply ye be found even to fight against God." (3SP 290.2)

The priests could not but see the reasonableness of his views; they were obliged to agree with him, and very reluctantly released the prisoners, after beating them with rods, and charging them again and again to preach no more in the name of Jesus, or their lives would pay the penalty of their boldness. "And they departed from the presence of the council, rejoicing that they were counted worthy to suffer shame for his name. And daily in the temple, and in every house, they ceased not to teach and preach Jesus Christ." Well might the persecutors of the apostles be troubled when they saw their inability to overthrow these witnesses for Christ, who had faith and courage to turn their shame into glory, and their pain into joy for the sake of their Master, who had borne humiliation and agony before them. Thus these brave disciples continued to teach in public, and secretly in private houses, by the request of the occupants who dared not openly confess their faith, for fear of the Jews. (3SP 291.1)

*****

Chapter 22
The Seven Deacons

"And in those days, when the number of the disciples was multiplied, there arose a murmuring of the Grecians against the Hebrews, because their widows were neglected in the daily ministration." These Grecians were residents of other countries, where the Greek language was spoken. By far the larger number of converts were Jews who spoke Hebrew; but these had lived in the Roman Empire, and spoke only Greek. Murmurings began to rise among them that the Grecian widows were not so liberally supplied as the needy among the Hebrews. Any partiality of this kind would have been grievous to God; and prompt measures were taken to restore peace and harmony to the believers. (3SP 291.2)

The Holy Spirit suggested a method whereby the apostles might be relieved from the task of apportioning to the poor, and similar burdens, so that they could be left free to preach Christ. "Then the twelve called the multitude of the disciples unto them, and said, It is not reason that we should leave the word of God, and serve tables. Wherefore, brethren, look ye out among you seven men of honest report, full of the Holy Ghost and wisdom, whom we may appoint over this business. But we will give ourselves continually to prayer, and to the ministry of the word." (3SP 292.1)

The church accordingly selected seven men full of faith and the wisdom of the Spirit of God, to attend to the business pertaining to the cause. Stephen was chosen first; he was a Jew by birth and religion, but spoke the Greek language, and was conversant with the customs and manners of the Greeks. He was therefore considered the most proper person to stand at the head, and have supervision of the disbursement of the funds appropriated to the widows, orphans, and the worthy poor. This selection met the minds of all, and the dissatisfaction and murmuring were quieted. (3SP 292.2)

The seven chosen men were solemnly set apart for their duties by prayer and the laying on of hands. Those who were thus ordained, were not thereby excluded from teaching the faith. On the contrary, it is recorded that "Stephen, full of faith and power, did great wonders and miracles among the people." They were fully qualified to instruct in the truth. They were also men of calm judgment and discretion, well calculated to deal with difficult cases of trial, of murmuring or jealousy. (3SP 292.3)

This choosing of men to transact the business of the church, so that the apostles could be left free for their special work of teaching the truth, was greatly blessed of God. The church advanced in numbers and strength. "And the word of God increased; and the number of the disciples multiplied in Jerusalem greatly; and a great company of the priests were obedient to the faith." (3SP 293.1)

It is necessary that the same order and system should be maintained in the church now as in the days of the apostles. The prosperity of the cause depends very largely upon its various departments being conducted by men of ability, who are qualified for their positions. Those who are chosen of God to be leaders in the cause of God, having the general oversight of the spiritual interest of the church, should be relieved, as far as possible, from cares and perplexities of a temporal nature. Those whom God has called to minister in word and doctrine should have time for meditation, prayer, and study of the Scriptures. Their clear spiritual discernment is dimmed by entering into the lesser details of business, and dealing with the various temperaments of those who meet together in church capacity. It is proper for all matters of a temporal nature to come before the proper officers, and be by them adjusted. But if they are of so difficult a character as to baffle their wisdom, they should be carried into the council of those who have the oversight of the entire church. (3SP 293.2)

Stephen was very active in the cause of God, and declared his faith boldly. "Then there arose

Chapter 22 - The Seven Deacons (3SP 294.1)

certain of the synagogue, which is called the synagogue of the Libertines, and Cyrenians, and Alexandrians, and of them of Cilicia and of Asia, disputing with Stephen. And they were not able to resist the wisdom and the spirit by which he spake." These students of the great Rabbis had felt confident that in a public discussion they could obtain a complete victory over Stephen, because of his supposed ignorance. But he not only spoke with the power of the Holy Ghost, but it was plain to all the vast assembly that he was also a student of the prophecies, and learned in all matters of the law. He ably defended the truths he advocated, and utterly defeated his opponents. (3SP 294.1)

The priests and rulers who witnessed the wonderful manifestation of the power that attended the ministration of Stephen, were filled with bitter hatred. Instead of yielding to the weight of evidence he presented, they determined to silence his voice by putting him to death. They had on several occasions bribed the Roman authorities to pass over without comment instances where the Jews had taken the law into their own hands, and tried, condemned, and executed prisoners according to their national custom. The enemies of Stephen did not doubt that they could pursue such a course without danger to themselves. They determined to risk the consequences at all events, and they therefore seized Stephen and brought him before the Sanhedrim council for trial. (3SP 294.2)

Learned Jews from the surrounding countries were summoned for the purpose of refuting the arguments of the accused. Saul, who had distinguished himself as a zealous opponent of the doctrine of Christ, and a persecutor of all who believed on him, was also present. This learned man took a leading part against Stephen. He brought the weight of eloquence and the logic of the Rabbis to bear upon the case, and convince the people that Stephen was preaching delusive and dangerous doctrines. (3SP 295.1)

But Saul met in Stephen one as highly educated as himself, and one who had a full understanding of the purpose of God in the spreading of the gospel to other nations. He believed in the God of Abraham, Isaac, and Jacob, and was fully established in regard to the privileges of the Jews; but his faith was broad, and he knew the time had come when the true believers should worship not alone in temples made with hands; but, throughout the world, men might worship God in Spirit and in truth. The vail had dropped from the eyes of Stephen, and he discerned to the end of that which was abolished by the death of Christ. (3SP 295.2)

The priests and rulers prevailed nothing against his clear, calm wisdom, though they were vehement in their opposition. They determined to make an example of Stephen, and, while they thus satisfied their revengeful hatred, prevent others, through fear, from adopting his belief. Charges were preferred against him in a most imposing manner. False witnesses were hired to testify that they had heard him speak blasphemous words against the temple and the law. Said they, "For we have heard him say, that this Jesus of Nazareth shall destroy this place, and shall change the customs which Moses delivered us." (3SP 295.3)

As Stephen stood face to face with his judges, to answer to the crime of blasphemy, a holy radiance shone upon his countenance. "And all that sat in the council, looking steadfastly on him, saw his face as it had been the face of an angel." Those who exalted Moses might have seen in the face of the prisoner the same holy light which radiated the face of that ancient prophet. The shekinah was a spectacle which they would never again witness in the temple whose glory had departed forever. Many who beheld the lighted countenance of Stephen trembled and veiled their faces; but stubborn unbelief and prejudice never faltered. (3SP 296.1)

Stephen was questioned as to the truth of the charges against him, and took up his defense in a clear, thrilling voice that rang through the council hall. He proceeded to rehearse the history of the chosen people of God, in words that held the assembly spell-bound. He showed a thorough knowledge of the Jewish economy, and the spiritual interpretation of it now made manifest through Christ. He began with Abraham, and traced down through history from generation to generation, going through all the national records of Israel to Solomon, taking up the most impressive points to vindicate his cause. (3SP 296.2)

He showed that God commended the faith of Abraham, which claimed the land of promise, though he owned no foot of land. He dwelt especially upon Moses, who received the law by the dispensation of angels. He repeated the words of Moses which foretold of Christ: "A prophet shall the Lord your God raise up unto you of your brethren, like unto me; him shall ye hear." He presented distinctly before them that the sin of Israel was in not heeding the voice of the angel, who was Christ himself. Said he, "This is he that was in the church in the wilderness with the angel which spake to him in the mount Sina, and with our fathers, who received the lively oracles to give unto us." (3SP 296.3)

He made plain his own loyalty to God and to the Jewish faith, while he showed that the law in which they trusted for salvation had not been able to preserve Israel from idolatry. He connected Jesus Christ with all the Jewish history. He referred to the building of the temple by Solomon, and to the words of both Solomon and Isaiah: "Howbeit the Most High dwelleth not in temples made with hands." "Heaven is my throne, and earth is my footstool. What house will ye build me? saith the Lord; or what is the place of my rest? Hath not my hand made all these things? The place of God's highest worship was in Heaven. (3SP 297.1)

When Stephen had reached this point there was a tumult among the people. The prisoner read his fate in the countenances before him. He perceived the resistance that met his words, which were spoken at the dictation of the Holy Ghost. He knew that he was giving his last testimony. Few who read this address of Stephen properly appreciate it. The occasion, the time and place should be borne in mind to make his words convey their full significance. (3SP 297.2)

When he connected Jesus Christ with the prophecies, and spoke of the temple as he did, the priest, affecting to be horror-stricken, rent his robe. This act was to Stephen a signal that his voice would soon be silenced forever. Although he was just in the midst of his sermon, he abruptly concluded it by suddenly breaking away from the chain of history, and, turning upon his infuriated judges, said, "Ye stiff-necked and uncircumcised in heart and ears, ye do always resist the Holy Ghost; as your fathers did, so do ye. Which of the prophets have not your fathers persecuted? and they have slain them which showed before of the coming of the Just One; of whom ye have been now the betrayers and murderers; who have received the law by the disposition of angels, and have not kept it." (3SP 298.1)

At this the priests and rulers were beside themselves with anger. They were more like wild beasts of prey than like human beings. They rushed upon Stephen, gnashing their teeth. But he was not intimidated; he had expected this. His face was calm, and shone with an angelic light.

The infuriated priests and the excited mob had no terrors for him. "But he, being full of the Holy Ghost, looked up steadfastly into Heaven, and saw the glory of God, and Jesus standing on the right hand of God, and said, Behold, I see the heavens opened, and the Son of man standing on the right hand of God." (3SP 298.2)

The scene about him faded from his vision; the gates of Heaven were ajar, and Stephen, looking in, saw the glory of the courts of God, and Christ, as if just risen from his throne, standing ready to sustain his servant, who was about to suffer martyrdom for his name. When Stephen proclaimed the glorious scene opened before him, it was more than his persecutors could endure. They stopped their ears, that they might not hear his words, and uttering loud cries ran furiously upon him with one accord. "And they stoned Stephen, calling upon God, and saying, Lord Jesus, receive my spirit. And he kneeled down, and cried with a loud voice, Lord, lay not this sin to their charge. And when he had said this he fell asleep." (3SP 298.3)

Amid the agonies of this most cruel death, the faithful martyr, like his divine Master, prayed for his murderers. The witnesses who had accused Stephen were required to cast the first stones. These persons laid down their clothes at the feet of Saul, who had taken an active part in the disputation, and had consented to the prisoner's death. (3SP 299.1)

The martyrdom of Stephen made a deep impression upon all who witnessed it. It was a sore trial to the church, but resulted in the conversion of Saul. The faith, constancy, and glorification of the martyr could not be effaced from his memory. The signet of God upon his face, his words, that reached to the very soul of all who heard them, except those who were hardened by resisting the light, remained in the memory of the beholders, and testified to the truth of that which he had proclaimed. (3SP 299.2)

There had been no legal sentence passed upon Stephen; but the Roman authorities were bribed by large sums of money to make no investigation of the case. Saul seemed to be imbued with a frenzied zeal at the scene of Stephen's trial and death. He seemed to be angered at his own secret convictions that Stephen was honored of God, at the very period when he was dishonored of men. He continued to persecute the church of God, hunting them down, seizing them in their houses, and

Chapter 22 - The Seven Deacons (3SP 299.3)

delivering them up to the priests and rulers for imprisonment and death. His zeal in carrying forward the persecution was a terror to the Christians in Jerusalem. The Roman authorities made no special effort to stay the cruel work, and secretly aided the Jews, in order to conciliate them, and to secure their favor. (3SP 299.3)

The learned Saul was a mighty instrument in the hands of Satan to carry out his rebellion against the Son of God; but a mightier than Satan had selected Saul to take the place of the martyred Stephen, and to labor and suffer for his name. Saul was a man of much esteem among the Jews, for both his learning and his zeal in persecuting the believers. He was not a member of the Sanhedrim council until after the death of Stephen, when he was elected to that body in consideration of the part he had acted on that occasion. (3SP 300.1)

After the death of Stephen the disciples were restrained in their active ministry, and many of the believers who had temporarily resided in Jerusalem now retired to their distant homes because of the violent persecution against them. But the apostles dared not leave Jerusalem till the Spirit of God indicated it to be their duty to do so; for Christ had bidden them to first work in that field. Although the priests and rulers bitterly persecuted the new converts, they did not venture for a time to arrest the apostles, being overawed by the dying testimony of Stephen, and realizing that their course with him had injured their own cause in the minds of the people. (3SP 300.2)

Christ had commanded his disciples to go and teach all nations; but the previous teachings which they had received from the Jews made it difficult for them to fully comprehend the words of their Master, and therefore they were slow to act upon them. They called themselves the children of Abraham, and regarded themselves as the heirs of divine promise. It was not until several years after the Lord's ascension that their minds were sufficiently expanded to clearly understand the intent of Christ's words, that they were to labor for the conversion of the Gentiles as well as that of the Jews. (3SP 300.3)

Their minds were particularly called out to this part of the work by the Gentiles themselves, many of whom embraced the doctrine of Christ. Closely following the death of Stephen, and the consequent scattering of the believers throughout Palestine, Samaria was greatly stirred. The Samaritans received the believers kindly, and manifested a willingness to hear concerning Jesus, who, in his first public labors, had preached to them with great power. Anything in regard to Christ was heard by them with intense interest. Here the disciples began to more fully understand that the gospel was not in any wise to be confined to the Jews; for conversions occurred among all classes, without any definite, special effort on the part of the Christian teachers. Many converts to Christ among the Gentiles demonstrated to the Jewish believers that they were not the only ones embraced in the message of Christ. (3SP 301.1)

The animosity existing between the Jews and Samaritans decreased, and it could no longer be said that they had no dealing with each other. Philip left Jerusalem, and preached a risen Redeemer in Samaria. Many believed, and received Christian baptism. Philip's preaching was marked with so great success, and so many were gathered into the fold of Christ, that he finally sent to Jerusalem for help. In answer to this petition, the church sent Peter and John to his assistance, who labored in Samaria with wonderful results. They now perceived the meaning of Christ, when he said, "Ye shall be witnesses unto me, both in Jerusalem, and in all Judea, and in Samaria, and unto the uttermost part of the earth." (3SP 301.2)

Among the converts in Samaria was one Simon, who, by the power of Satan through sorcerers, had gained great fame among the people. "To whom they all gave heed, from the least to the greatest, saying, This man is the great power of God. And to him they had regard, because that of long time he had bewitched them with sorceries." But when he saw a greater power manifested by the apostles in healing the sick and in converting souls to the truth, he thought that by uniting with the believers in Christ he might do wonders equal to those accomplished by the apostles. He hoped thus to add greatly to his fame and wealth, for he made merchandise of his sorceries and Satanic arts, pretending to impart their secrets to others. (3SP 302.1)

His darkened mind could not distinguish between the power of the Holy Ghost and that of Satan. He went to Peter and offered him money if he would give him power to heal the sick, and impart to men the Holy Ghost, by laying his hands upon them. Peter was filled with horror at such a proposal, and severely rebuked the presumption of Simon. Said he, "Thy money perish with thee, because thou hast thought that

Chapter 22 - The Seven Deacons (3SP 305.1)

the gift of God may be purchased with money. Thou hast neither part nor lot in this matter; for thy heart is not right in the sight of God. Repent therefore of this thy wickedness, and pray God, if perhaps the thought of thine heart may be forgiven thee. For I perceive that thou art in the gall of bitterness, and in the bond of iniquity." (3SP 302.2)

The magician trembled with fear as his sin was presented before him in this vivid manner. He began to perceive his own wicked audacity, and entreated Peter to pray that the wrath of God might not come upon him for his presumptuous sin. Peter had, with startling force, shown Simon that he was yet untouched by the grace of God; for if his mind had been thus enlightened, he would have known that the sacred power of the Holy Spirit could not be bought or sold for money. Christ, at the infinite price of himself, had obtained for his people the power of the Holy Spirit, to be given only to his chosen instruments, whose lives must be free from selfishness and sin. (3SP 303.1)

The Lord now sent his angel to Philip, directing him to cross the desert and go to Gaza. "And he arose and went. And, behold, a man of Ethiopia, an eunuch of great authority under Candace, queen of the Ethiopians, who had the charge of all her treasure, and had come to Jerusalem for to worship, was returning, and sitting in his chariot, read Esaias the prophet." The eunuch, in his blindness, had been groping for light. He believed the Scriptures, but could not fully understand them. He therefore went a journey to Jerusalem to the temple. Hungering and thirsting for knowledge, he laid his perplexities before the priests and scribes; but he was still more mystified than before by their interpretations of scripture. He prayed fervently for light and knowledge, and God heard his prayer, and sent his angel to Philip, bidding him go to Gaza for the purpose of preaching Christ to a single soul that hungered and thirsted for the truth. (3SP 303.2)

The eunuch had heard at Jerusalem various conflicting reports in regard to Jesus of Nazareth. His mind was troubled upon the subject. He had a copy of the Scriptures with him, and was diligently studying the prophecies in reference to the Messiah, when Philip met him. They were strangers; but the mind of Philip was impressed that this was the man who needed his help. Philip, walking by the side of the chariot, inquired of the eunuch if he understood the prophecies he was reading. He answered that he needed instruction, and invited Philip to take a seat beside him. (3SP 304.1)

The scripture he was studying was *Isaiah 53:7*. Philip understood the desire of his heart, and preached unto him Jesus Christ revealed in prophecy, and his mission to the earth to save sinners. He showed him the steps necessary to take in conversion–repentance toward God because of transgression of the Father's law, faith in Christ as the Saviour of men, and baptism in the likeness of his death. The eunuch's heart was all ready to receive the light and truth, and he accepted with gladness the gospel preached by Philip. (3SP 304.2)

"And as they went on their way, they came unto a certain water; and the eunuch said, See, here is water; what doth hinder me to be baptized? And Philip said, If thou believest with all thine heart, thou mayest. And he answered and said, I believe that Jesus Christ is the Son of God." The answer of the eunuch was prompt and decided. He commanded the chariot to be stopped, "and they went down both into the water, both Philip and the eunuch; and he baptized him. And when they were come up out of the water, the Spirit of the Lord caught away Philip, that the eunuch saw him no more; and he went on his way rejoicing." (3SP 304.3)

In this instance we have an illustration of the care of God for his children. He called Philip from his successful ministry in Samaria, to cross the desert and go to Gaza to labor for a single inquiring soul. The promptness with which the eunuch accepted the gospel and acted upon its belief should be a lesson to us. God designs that we should be prompt in accepting and confessing Christ, prompt in obeying him, and in answering the call of duty. The eunuch was a man of good repute, and occupied a high and responsible position. Through his conversion the gospel was carried to Ethiopia, and many there accepted Christ, and came out from the darkness of heathenism into the clear light of Christianity. (3SP 305.1)

*****

Chapter 23
Conversion of Saul

The mind of Saul was greatly stirred by the triumphant death of Stephen. He was shaken in his prejudice; but the opinions and arguments of the priests and rulers finally convinced him that Stephen was a blasphemer; that Jesus Christ whom he preached was an impostor, and that those ministering in holy offices must be right. Being a man of decided mind, and strong purpose, he became very bitter in his opposition to Christianity, after having once entirely settled in his mind that the views of the priests and scribes were right. His zeal led him to voluntarily engage in persecuting the believers. He caused holy men to be dragged before the councils, and to be imprisoned or condemned to death without evidence of any offense, save their faith in Jesus. Of a similar character, though in a different direction, was the zeal of James and John, when they would have called down fire from heaven to consume those who slighted and scorned their Master. (3SP 305.2)

Saul was about to journey to Damascus upon his own business; but he was determined to accomplish a double purpose, by searching out, as he went, all the believers in Christ. For this purpose he obtained letters from the high priest to read in the synagogues, which authorized him to seize all those who were suspected of being believers in Jesus, and to send by messengers to Jerusalem, there to be tried and punished. He set out upon his way, full of strength and vigor of manhood, and the fire of a mistaken zeal. (3SP 306.1)

As the weary travelers neared Damascus, the eyes of Saul rested with pleasure upon the fertile land, the beautiful gardens, the fruitful orchards, and the cool streams that ran murmuring amid the fresh, green shrubbery. It was very refreshing to look upon such a scene after a long, wearisome journey over a desolate waste. While Saul, with his companions, was gazing and admiring, suddenly a light above the brightness of the sun shone round about him, "and he fell to the earth, and heard a voice saying unto him, Saul, Saul, why persecutest thou me? And he said, Who art thou, Lord? And the Lord said, I am Jesus whom thou persecutest; it is hard for thee to kick against the pricks." (3SP 306.2)

The scene was one of the greatest confusion. The companions of Saul were stricken with terror, and almost blinded by the intensity of the light. They heard the voice, but saw no one, and to them all was unintelligible and mysterious. But Saul, lying prostrate upon the ground, understood the words that were spoken, and saw clearly before him the Son of God. One look upon that glorious Being, imprinted his image forever upon the soul of the stricken Jew. The words struck home to his heart with appalling force. A flood of light poured in upon the darkened chambers of his mind, revealing his ignorance and error. He saw that, while imagining himself to be zealously serving God in persecuting the followers of Christ, he had in reality been doing the work of Satan. (3SP 307.1)

He saw his folly in resting his faith upon the assurances of the priests and rulers, whose sacred office had given them great influence over his mind, and caused him to believe that the story of the resurrection was an artful fabrication of the disciples of Jesus. Now that Christ was revealed to Saul, the sermon of Stephen was brought forcibly to his mind. Those words which the priests had pronounced blasphemy, now appeared to him as truth and verity. In that time of wonderful illumination, his mind acted with remarkable rapidity. He traced down through prophetic history, and saw that the rejection of Jesus by the Jews, his crucifixion, resurrection, and ascension had been foretold by the prophets, and proved him to be the promised Messiah. He remembered the words of Stephen: "I see the heavens opened, and the Son of man standing on the right hand of God;" and he knew that the dying saint had looked upon the kingdom of Glory. (3SP 307.2)

What a revelation was all this to the persecutor of the believers. Clear, but terrible light had broken in upon his soul. Christ was revealed to him as having come to earth in fulfillment of his mission, being rejected, abused, condemned, and crucified by those whom he came to save, and as having risen from the dead, and ascended into the heavens. In that terrible moment he remembered that the holy Stephen had been sacrificed by his consent; and that through his instrumentality many worthy saints had met their death by cruel persecution. (3SP 308.1)

"And he, trembling and astonished, said, Lord, what wilt thou have me to do? And the Lord said unto him, Arise and go into the city, and it shall be told thee what thou must do." No doubt entered the mind of Saul that this was the veritable Jesus of Nazareth who spoke to him, and that he was indeed the long-looked-for Messiah, the Consolation and Redeemer of Israel. And now this Jesus, who had, while teaching upon earth, spoken in parables to his hearers, using familiar objects to illustrate his meaning, likened the work of Saul, in persecuting the followers of Christ, to kicking against the pricks. Those forcible words illustrated the fact that it would be impossible for any man to stay the onward progress of the truth of Christ. It would march on to triumph and victory, while every effort to stay it would result in injury to the opposer. The persecutor, in the end, would suffer a thousand-fold more than those whom he had persecuted. Sooner or later his own mind and heart would condemn him; he would find that he had, indeed, been kicking against the pricks. (3SP 308.2)

The Saviour had spoken to Saul through Stephen, whose clear reasoning from the Scriptures could not be controverted. The learned Jew had seen the face of the martyr reflecting the light of Christ's glory, and looking like the face of an angel. He had witnessed his forbearance toward his enemies, and his forgiveness of them. He had further witnessed the fortitude and cheerful resignation of other believers in Jesus while tormented and afflicted, some of whom had yielded up their lives with rejoicing for their faith's sake. (3SP 309.1)

All this testimony had appealed loudly to Saul, and thrust conviction upon his mind; but his education and prejudices, his respect for priests and rulers, and his pride of popularity, braced him to rebel against the voice of conscience, and the grace of God. He had struggled entire nights against conviction, and had always ended the matter by avowing his belief that Jesus was not the Messiah, that he was an impostor, and his followers were deluded fanatics. (3SP 309.2)

Now Christ had spoken to Saul with his own voice: "Saul, Saul, why persecutest thou me?" And the question, "Who art thou, Lord?" was answered by the same voice, "I am Jesus, whom thou persecutest." Here Christ identifies himself with his suffering people. Saul, in persecuting the followers of Jesus, had struck directly against the Lord of Heaven. Jesus declares that in afflicting his brethren upon earth, Saul had struck against their Head and Representative in Heaven. In falsely accusing and testifying against them, he had falsely accused and testified against the Saviour of the world. Here it is plainly seen that Christ suffers in the person of his saints. (3SP 309.3)

When the effulgent glory was withdrawn, and Saul arose from the earth, he found himself totally deprived of sight. The brightness of Christ's glory had been too intense for his mortal sight, and when it was removed the blackness of night settled upon his vision. He believed that his blindness was the punishment of God for his cruel persecution of the followers of Jesus. He groped about in terrible darkness, and his companions, in fear and amazement, led him by the hand into Damascus. (3SP 310.1)

How different from what he had anticipated was his entrance into that city! In proud satisfaction he had neared Damascus, expecting on his arrival to be greeted with ostentation and applause because of the honor conferred upon him by the high priest, and the great zeal and penetration he had manifested in searching out the believers, to carry them as captives to Jerusalem, there to be condemned, and punished without mercy. He had determined that his journey should be crowned with success; and his courageous and persevering spirit quailed at no difficulties nor dangers in the pursuance of his object. He had determined that no Christian should escape his vigilance; he would inquire of men, women, and children concerning their faith, and that of those with whom they were connected; he would enter houses, with power to seize their inmates, and to send them as prisoners to Jerusalem. (3SP 310.2)

But how changed was the scene from that which he had anticipated! Instead of wielding power, and receiving honor, he was himself virtually a prisoner, being deprived of sight, and dependent upon the guidance of his companions.

Chapter 23 - Conversion of Saul (3SP 311.1)

Helpless, and tortured by remorse, he felt himself to be under sentence of death, and knew not what farther disposition the Lord would make of him. (3SP 311.1)

He was taken to the house of the disciple Judas, and there he remained, solitary and alone, studying upon the strange revelation, that had broken up all his plans, and changed the entire current of his life. He passed three days in perfect blindness, occupying that terrible time with reflection, repentance, and earnest prayer, neither eating nor drinking during that entire period. With bitterness he remembered Stephen, and the evidence he had given of being sustained in his martyrdom, by a power higher than that of earth. He thought with horror of his own guilt in being carried away by the malice and prejudice of the priests and rulers, closing his eyes and ears against the most striking evidence, and relentlessly leading the van in the persecution of the believers in Christ. (3SP 311.2)

He was in lonely seclusion; he had no communication with the church, for they had been warned of the purpose of his journey to Damascus by the believers in Jerusalem; and they believed that he was acting a part the better to carry out his design of persecuting them. He had no desire to appeal to the unconverted Jews; for he knew they would not listen to or heed his statements. He seemed to be utterly shut out from human sympathy; and he reflected, and prayed with a thoroughly broken and repentant spirit. (3SP 311.3)

Those three days were like three years to the blind and conscience-smitten Jew. He was no novice in the Scriptures, and in his darkness and solitude he recalled the passages which referred to the Messiah, and traced down the prophecies, with a memory sharpened by the conviction that had taken possession of his mind. He became astonished at his former blindness of understanding, and at the blindness of the Jews in general, in rejecting Jesus as the promised Messiah. All now seemed plain to him, and he knew that it was prejudice and unbelief which had clouded his perceptions, and prevented him from discerning in Jesus of Nazareth the Messiah of prophecy. (3SP 312.1)

This wonderful conversion of Saul demonstrates in a startling manner the miraculous power of Christ in convicting the mind and heart of man. Saul had verily believed that to have faith in Jesus was virtually to repudiate the law of God, and the service of sacrificial offerings. He had believed that Jesus had himself disregarded the law, and had taught his disciples that it was now of no effect. He believed it to be his duty to strive with his utmost power to exterminate the alarming doctrine that Jesus was the Prince of life; and with conscientious zeal he had become a persevering persecutor of the church of Christ. (3SP 312.2)

But Jesus, whose name of all others he most hated and despised, had revealed himself to Saul, for the purpose of arresting him in his mad career, and of making, from this most unpromising subject, an instrument by which to bear the gospel to the Gentiles. Saul was overwhelmed by this revelation, and perceived that in opposing Jesus of Nazareth, he had arrayed himself against the Redeemer of the world. Overcome by a sense of his guilt he cried out, "Lord, what wilt thou have me to do?" Jesus did not then and there inform him of the work he had assigned him, but sent him for instruction to the very disciples whom he had so bitterly persecuted. (3SP 312.3)

The marvelous light that illuminated the darkness of Saul was the work of the Lord; but there was also a work that was to be done for him by the disciples of Christ. The answer to Saul's question is, "Arise, and go into the city, and it shall be told thee what thou must do." Jesus sends the inquiring Jew to his church, to obtain from them a knowledge of his duty. Christ performed the work of revelation and conviction; and now the penitent was in a condition to learn of those whom God had ordained to teach his truth. Thus Jesus gave sanction to the authority of his organized church, and placed Saul in connection with his representatives on earth. The light of heavenly illumination deprived Saul of sight; but Jesus, the great Healer, did not at once restore it. All blessings flow from Christ, but he had now established a church as his representative on earth, and to it belonged the work of directing the repentant sinner in the way of life. The very men whom Saul had purposed to destroy were to be his instructors in the religion he had despised and persecuted. (3SP 313.1)

The faith of Saul was severely tested during the three days of fasting and prayer at the house of Judas, in Damascus. He was totally blind, and in utter darkness of mind as to what was required of him. He had been directed to go to Damascus, where it would be told him what he was to do. In his uncertainty and distress he cried earnestly to God. "And there was a certain disciple at Damascus, named Ananias; and to him said the Lord in a vision, Ananias. And he said, Behold, I am here, Lord. And the Lord said unto him, Arise, and go into the street which is called Straight, and inquire in the house of Judas for one called Saul, of Tarsus; for, behold, he prayeth, and hath seen in a vision a man named Ananias coming in, and putting his hand on him, that he might receive his sight." (3SP 314.1)

Ananias could hardly credit the words of the angel messenger, for Saul's bitter persecution of the saints at Jerusalem had spread far and near. He presumed to expostulate; said he, "Lord, I have heard by many of this man, how much evil he hath done to thy saints at Jerusalem. And here he hath authority from the chief priests to bind all that call on thy name." But the command to Ananias was imperative: "Go thy way, for he is a chosen vessel unto me, to bear my name before the Gentiles, and kings, and the children of Israel." (3SP 314.2)

The disciple, obedient to the direction of the angel, sought out the man who had but recently breathed out threatenings against all who believed on the name of Jesus. He addressed him: "Brother Saul, the Lord, even Jesus, that appeared unto thee in the way as thou camest, hath sent me, that thou mightest receive thy sight and be filled with the Holy Ghost; and immediately there fell from his eyes as it had been scales, and he received sight forthwith, and arose and was baptized." (3SP 314.3)

Christ here gives an example of his manner of working for the salvation of men. He might have done all this work directly for Saul; but this was not in accordance with his plan. His blessings were to come through the agencies which he had ordained. Saul had something to do in the line of confession to those whose destruction he had meditated; and God had a responsible work for the men to do whom he had authorized to act in his stead. (3SP 315.1)

Saul becomes a learner of the disciples. In the light of the law he sees himself a sinner. He sees that Jesus, whom in his ignorance he had considered an impostor, is the author and foundation of the religion of God's people from the days of Adam, and the finisher of the faith now so clear to his enlightened vision; the vindicator of the truth, and the fulfiller of the prophecies. He had regarded Jesus as making of none effect the law of God; but when his spiritual vision was touched by the finger of God, he learned that Christ was the originator of the entire Jewish system of sacrifices; that he came into the world for the express purpose of vindicating his Father's law; and that in his death the typical law had met its antitype. By the light of the moral law, which he had believed himself to be zealously keeping, Saul saw himself a sinner of sinners. He repented, that is, died to sin, became obedient to the law of God, had faith in Jesus Christ as his Saviour, was baptized, and preached Jesus as earnestly and zealously as he had once denounced him. (3SP 315.2)

The Redeemer of the world does not sanction experience and exercise in religious matters independent of his organized and acknowledged church. Many have an idea that they are responsible to Christ alone for their light and experience, independent of his recognized followers on earth. But in the history of the conversion of Saul, important principles are given us, which we should ever bear in mind. He was brought directly into the presence of Christ. He was one whom Christ intended for a most important work, one who was to be "a chosen vessel" unto him; yet he does not personally impart to him the lessons of truth. He arrests his course and convicts him; but when asked by him, "What wilt thou have me to do?" the Saviour places him in connection with his church, and lets them direct him what to do. (3SP 316.1)

Jesus is the Friend of sinners; his heart is touched by their woe; he has all power, both in Heaven and upon earth; but he respects the means which he has ordained for the enlightenment and salvation of men; he directs sinners to the church, which he has made a channel of light to the world. (3SP 316.2)

Saul was a learned teacher in Israel; but, while in the midst of his blind error and prejudice, Christ reveals himself to him, and then places him in communication with his church, which is the light of the world. In this case Ananias represents Christ, and also represents Christ's ministers upon earth, who are appointed to act in his stead. In Christ's stead, Ananias touches the eyes of Saul that they may receive sight. In Christ's stead, he places his hands upon him, and, praying in Christ's name, Saul receives the Holy Ghost. All is done in the name and by the authority of Christ; but the church is the channel of communication. (3SP 316.3)

*****

Chapter 24
Paul Commences His Ministry

Paul was baptized by Ananias in the river of Damascus. He was then strengthened by food, and immediately began to preach Jesus to the believers in the city, the very ones whom he had set out from Jerusalem with the purpose of destroying. He also taught in the synagogues that Jesus who had been put to death was indeed the Son of God. His arguments from prophecy were so conclusive, and his efforts were so attended by the power of God, that the opposing Jews were confounded and unable to answer him. Paul's Rabbinical and Pharisaic education was now to be used to good account in preaching the gospel, and in sustaining the cause he had once used every effort to destroy. (3SP 317.1)

The Jews were thoroughly surprised and confounded by the conversion of Paul. They were aware of his position at Jerusalem, and knew what was his principal errand to Damascus, and that he was armed with a commission from the high priest that authorized him to take the believers in Jesus, and to send them as prisoners to Jerusalem; yet now they beheld him preaching the gospel of Jesus, strengthening those who were already its disciples, and continually making new converts to the faith he had once so zealously opposed. Paul demonstrated to all who heard him that his change of faith was not from impulse nor fanaticism, but was brought about by overwhelming evidence. (3SP 317.2)

As he labored in the synagogues his faith grew stronger; his zeal in maintaining that Jesus was the Son of God increased, in the face of the fierce opposition of the Jews. He could not remain long in Damascus, for after the Jews had recovered from their surprise at his wonderful conversion, and subsequent labors, they turned resolutely from the overwhelming evidence thus brought to bear in favor of the doctrine of Christ. Their astonishment at the conversion of Paul was changed into an intense hatred of him like unto that which they had manifested against Jesus. (3SP 318.1)

Paul's life was in peril, and he received a commission from God to leave Damascus for a time. He went into Arabia; and there, in comparative solitude, he had ample opportunity for communion with God, and for contemplation. He wished to be alone with God, to search his own heart, to deepen his repentance, and to prepare himself by prayer and study to engage in a work which appeared to him too great and too important for him to undertake. He was an apostle, not chosen of men, but chosen of God, and his work was plainly stated to be among the Gentiles. (3SP 318.2)

While in Arabia he did not communicate with the apostles; he sought God earnestly with all his heart, determining not to rest till he knew for a certainty that his repentance was accepted, and his great sin pardoned. He would not give up the conflict until he had the assurance that Jesus would be with him in his coming ministry. He was ever to carry about with him in the body the marks of Christ's glory, in his eyes, which had been blinded by the heavenly light, and he desired also to bear with him constantly the assurance of Christ's sustaining grace. Paul came in close connection with Heaven, and Jesus communed with him, and established him in his faith, bestowing upon him his wisdom and grace. (3SP 318.3)

Paul now returned to Damascus, and preached boldly in the name of Jesus. The Jews could not withstand the wisdom of his arguments, and they therefore counseled together to silence his voice by force–the only argument left to a sinking cause. They decided to assassinate him. The apostle was made acquainted with their purpose. The gates of the city were vigilantly guarded, day and night, to cut off his escape. The anxiety of the disciples drew them to God in prayer; there was little sleeping among them, as they were busy in devising ways and means for the escape of the chosen apostle. Finally they conceived a plan by which he was let down from a window, and lowered over the wall in a basket at night. In this humiliating manner

Chapter 24 - Paul Commences His Ministry (3SP 322.1)

Paul made his escape from Damascus. (3SP 319.1)

He now proceeded to Jerusalem, wishing to become acquainted with the apostles there, and especially with Peter. He was very anxious to meet the Galilean fishermen who had lived, and prayed, and conversed with Christ upon earth. It was with a yearning heart that he desired to meet the chief of apostles. As Paul entered Jerusalem, he regarded with changed views the city and temple. He now knew that the retributive judgment of God was hanging over them. (3SP 319.2)

The grief and anger of the Jews because of the conversion of Paul knew no bounds. But he was firm as a rock, and flattered himself that when he related his wonderful experience to his friends, they would change their faith as he had done, and believe on Jesus. He had been strictly conscientious in his opposition of Christ and his followers, and when he was arrested and convicted of his sin, he immediately forsook his evil ways, and professed the faith of Jesus. He now fully believed that when his friends and former associates heard the circumstances of his marvelous conversion, and saw how changed he was from the proud Pharisee who persecuted and delivered unto death those who believed in Jesus as the Son of God, they would also become convicted of their error, and join the ranks of the believers. (3SP 320.1)

He attempted to join himself to his brethren, the disciples; but great was his grief and disappointment when he found that they would not receive him as one of their number. They remembered his former persecutions, and suspected him of acting a part to deceive and destroy them. True, they had heard of his wonderful conversion, but as he had immediately retired into Arabia, and they had heard nothing definite of him farther, they had not credited the rumor of his great change. (3SP 320.2)

Barnabas, who had liberally contributed his money to sustain the cause of Christ, and to relieve the necessities of the poor, had been acquainted with Paul when he opposed the believers. He now came forward and renewed that acquaintance, heard the testimony of Paul in regard to his miraculous conversion, and his experience from that time. He fully believed and received Paul, took him by the hand and led him into the presence of the apostles. He related his experience which he had just heard–that Jesus had personally appeared to Paul while on his way to Damascus; that he had talked with him; that Paul had recovered his sight in answer to the prayers of Ananias, and had afterward maintained that Jesus was the Son of God in the synagogues of the city. (3SP 320.3)

The apostles no longer hesitated; they could not withstand God. Peter and James, who at that time were the only apostles in Jerusalem, gave the right hand of fellowship to the once fierce persecutor of their faith; and he was now as much beloved and respected as he had formerly been feared and avoided. Here the two grand characters of the new faith met–Peter, one of the chosen companions of Christ while he was upon earth, and Paul, a Pharisee, who, since the ascension of Jesus, had met him face to face, and had talked with him, and had also seen him in vision, and the nature of his work in Heaven. (3SP 321.1)

This first interview was of great consequence to both these apostles, but it was of short duration, for Paul was eager to get about his Master's business. Soon the voice which had so earnestly disputed with Stephen was heard in the same synagogue fearlessly proclaiming that Jesus was the Son of God–advocating the same cause that Stephen had died to vindicate. He related his own wonderful experience, and with a heart filled with yearning for his brethren and former associates, presented the evidences from prophecy, as Stephen had done, that Jesus, who had been crucified, was the Son of God. (3SP 321.2)

But Paul had miscalculated the spirit of his Jewish brethren. The same fury that had burst forth upon Stephen was visited upon himself. He saw that he must separate from his brethren, and sorrow filled his heart. He would willingly have yielded up his life, if by that means they might have been brought to a knowledge of the truth. The Jews began to lay plans to take his life, and the disciples urged him to leave Jerusalem; but he lingered, unwilling to leave the place, and anxious to labor a little longer for his Jewish brethren. He had taken so active a part in the martyrdom of Stephen that he was deeply anxious to wipe out the stain by boldly vindicating the truth which had cost Stephen his life. It looked to him like cowardice to flee from Jerusalem. (3SP 322.1)

While Paul, braving all the consequences of such a step, was praying earnestly to God in the temple, the Saviour appeared to him in vision, saying, "Make haste, and get thee quickly out of

Chapter 24 - Paul Commences His Ministry (3SP 322.2)

Jerusalem; for they will not receive thy testimony concerning me." Paul even then hesitated to leave Jerusalem without convincing the obstinate Jews of the truth of his faith; he thought that, even if his life should be sacrificed for the truth, it would not more than settle the fearful account which he held against himself for the death of Stephen. He answered, "Lord, they know that I imprisoned and beat in every synagogue them that believed on thee. And when the blood of thy martyr Stephen was shed, I also was standing by, and consenting unto his death, and kept the raiment of them that slew him." But the reply was more decided than before: "Depart; for I will send thee far hence unto the Gentiles." (3SP 322.2)

When the brethren learned of the vision of Paul, and the care which God had over him, their anxiety on his behalf was increased; for they realized that he was indeed a chosen vessel of the Lord, to bear the truth to the Gentiles. They hastened his secret escape from Jerusalem, for fear of his assassination by the Jews. The departure of Paul suspended for a time the violent opposition of the Jews, and the church had a period of rest, in which many were added to the number of believers. (3SP 323.1)

*****

Chapter 25
The Ministry of Peter

Peter, in pursuance of his work, visited the saints at Lydda. There he healed Aeneas, who had been confined to his bed for eight years with the palsy. "And Peter said unto him, Aeneas, Jesus Christ maketh thee whole; arise, and make thy bed. And he arose immediately. And all that dwelt at Lydda and Saron saw him, and turned to the Lord." (3SP 323.2)

Joppa was near Lydda, and at that time Tabitha–called Dorcas by interpretation–lay there dead. She had been a worthy disciple of Jesus Christ, and her life had been characterized by deeds of charity and kindness to the poor and sorrowful, and by zeal in the cause of truth. Her death was a great loss; the infant church could not well spare her noble efforts. When the believers heard of the marvelous cures which Peter had performed in Lydda, they greatly desired him to come to Joppa. Messengers were sent to him to solicit his presence there. (3SP 323.3)

"Then Peter arose and went with them. When he was come, they brought him into the upper chamber; and all the widows stood by him weeping, and showing the coats and garments which Dorcas made while she was with them." Peter had the weeping and wailing friends sent from the room. He then kneeled down, and prayed fervently to God to restore life and health to the pulseless body of Dorcas; "and turning him to the body said, Tabitha, arise. And she opened her eyes; and when she saw Peter, she sat up. And he gave her his hand, and lifted her up; and when he had called the saints and widows, he presented her alive." This great work of raising the dead to life was the means of converting many in Joppa to the faith of Jesus. (3SP 324.1)

"There was a certain man in Caesarea called Cornelius, a centurion of the band called the Italian band, a devout man, and one that feared God with all his house, which gave much alms to the people, and prayed to God always." Though Cornelius was a Roman, he had become acquainted with the true God, and had renounced idolatry. He was obedient to the will of God, and worshiped him with a true heart. He had not connected himself with the Jews, but was acquainted with, and obedient to, the moral law. He had not been circumcised, nor did he take part in the sacrificial offerings; he was therefore accounted by the Jews as unclean. He, however, sustained the Jewish cause by liberal donations, and was known far and near for his deeds of charity and benevolence. His righteous life made him of good repute, among both Jews and Gentiles. (3SP 324.2)

Cornelius had not an understanding faith in Christ, although he believed the prophecies, and was looking for Messiah to come. Through his love and obedience to God, he was brought nigh unto him, and was prepared to receive the Saviour when he should be revealed to him. Condemnation comes by rejecting the light given. The centurion was a man of noble family, and held a position of high trust and honor; but these circumstances had not tended to subvert the noble attributes of his character. True goodness and greatness united to make him a man of moral worth. His influence was beneficial to all with whom he was brought in contact. (3SP 325.1)

He believed in the one God, the Creator of Heaven and earth. He revered him, acknowledged his authority, and sought counsel of him in all the business of his life. He was faithful in his home duties as well as in his official responsibilities, and had erected the altar of God in his family. He dared not venture to carry out his plans, and bear the burden of his weighty responsibilities, without the help of God; therefore he prayed much and earnestly for that help. Faith marked all his works, and God regarded him for the purity of his actions, and his liberalities, and came near to him in word and Spirit. (3SP 325.2)

While Cornelius was praying, God sent a celestial messenger to him, who addressed him by name. The centurion was afraid, yet knew that

Chapter 25 - The Ministry of Peter (3SP 325.3)

the angel was sent of God to instruct him, and said, "What is it, Lord? And he said unto him, Thy prayers and thine alms are come up for a memorial before God. And now send men to Joppa, and call for one Simon, whose surname is Peter. He lodgeth with one Simon, a tanner, whose house is by the sea side. He shall tell thee what thou oughtest to do." (3SP 325.3)

Here again God showed his regard for the gospel ministry, and for his organized church. His angel was not the one to tell the story of the cross to Cornelius. A man, subject as himself to human frailties and temptations, was to instruct him concerning the crucified, risen and ascended Saviour. The heavenly messenger was sent for the express purpose of putting Cornelius in connection with the minister of God, who would teach him how he and his house could be saved. (3SP 326.1)

Cornelius was gladly obedient to the message, and sent messengers at once to seek out Peter, according to the directions of the angel. The explicitness of these directions, in which was even named the occupation of the man with whom Peter was then making his home, evidences that Heaven is well acquainted with the history and business of men in every grade of life. God is cognizant of the daily employment of the humble laborer, as well as of that of the king upon his throne. And the avarice, cruelty, secret crimes, and selfishness of men are known to him, as well as their good deeds, charity, liberality, and kindness. Nothing is hidden from God. (3SP 326.2)

Immediately after this interview with Cornelius, the angel went to Peter, who, very weary and hungry from journeying, was praying upon the housetop. While praying he was shown a vision, "and saw heaven opened, and a certain vessel descending unto him, as it had been a great sheet knit at the four corners, and let down to the earth; wherein were all manner of four-footed beasts of the earth, and wild beasts, and creeping things, and fowls of the air. And there came a voice to him, Rise, Peter; kill, and eat. But Peter said, Not so, Lord; for I have never eaten anything that is common or unclean. And the voice spake unto him again the second time, What God hath cleansed, that call not thou common. This was done thrice; and the vessel was received up again into heaven." (3SP 326.3)

Here we may perceive the workings of God's plan to set the machinery in motion, whereby his will may be done on earth as it is done in Heaven. Peter had not yet preached the gospel to the Gentiles. Many of them had been interested listeners to the truths which he taught; but the middle wall of partition, which the death of Christ had broken down, still existed in the minds of the apostles, and excluded the Gentiles from the privileges of the gospel. The Greek Jews had received the labors of the apostles, and many of them had responded to those efforts by embracing the faith of Jesus; but the conversion of Cornelius was to be the first one of importance among the Gentiles. (3SP 327.1)

By the vision of the sheet and its contents, let down from heaven, Peter was to be divested of his settled prejudices against the Gentiles; to understand that, through Christ, heathen nations were made partakers of the blessings and privileges of the Jews, and were to be thus benefited equally with them. Some have urged that this vision was to signify that God had removed his prohibition from the use of the flesh of animals which he had formerly pronounced unclean; and that therefore swines' flesh was fit for food. This is a very narrow, and altogether erroneous interpretation, and is plainly contradicted in the scriptural account of the vision and its consequences. (3SP 327.2)

The vision of all manner of live beasts, which the sheet contained, and of which Peter was commanded to kill and eat, being assured that what God had cleansed should not be called common or unclean by him, was simply an illustration presenting to his mind the true position of the Gentiles; that by the death of Christ they were made fellow-heirs with the Israel of God. It conveyed to Peter both reproof and instruction. His labors had heretofore been confined entirely to the Jews; and he had looked upon the Gentiles as an unclean race, and excluded from the promises of God. His mind was now being led to comprehend the world-wide extent of the plan of God. (3SP 328.1)

Even while he pondered over the vision, it was explained to him. "Now while Peter doubted in himself what this vision which he had seen should mean, behold, the men which were sent from Cornelius had made inquiry for Simon's house, and stood before the gate, and called, and asked whether Simon, which was surnamed Peter, were lodged there. While Peter thought on the vision, the Spirit said unto him, Behold, three men seek thee. Arise therefore, and get thee down, and go with them, doubting nothing; for I have sent them." (3SP 328.2)

It was a trying command to Peter; but he dared not act according to his own feelings, and therefore went down from his chamber, and received the messengers sent to him from Cornelius. They communicated their singular errand to the apostle, and, according to the direction he had just received from God, he at once agreed to accompany them on the morrow. He courteously entertained them that night, and in the morning set out with them for Caesarea, accompanied by six of his brethren, who were to be witnesses of all he should say or do while visiting the Gentiles; for he knew that he should be called to account for so direct an opposition to the Jewish faith and teachings. (3SP 328.3)

It was nearly two days before the journey was ended and Cornelius had the glad privilege of opening his doors to a gospel minister, who, according to the assurance of God, should teach him and his house how they might be saved. While the messengers were upon their errand, the centurion had gathered together as many of his relatives as were accessible, that they, as well as he, might be instructed in the truth. When Peter arrived, a large company were gathered, eagerly waiting to listen to his words. (3SP 329.1)

As Peter entered the house of the Gentile, Cornelius did not salute him as an ordinary visitor, but as one honored of Heaven, and sent to him by God. It is an Eastern custom to bow before a prince or other high dignitary, and for children to bow before their parents who are honored with positions of trust. But Cornelius, overwhelmed with reverence for the apostle who had been delegated by God, fell at his feet and worshiped him. Peter shrank with horror from this act of the centurion, and lifted him to his feet, saying, "Stand up; I myself also am a man." He then commenced to converse with him familiarly, in order to remove the sense of awe and extreme reverence with which the centurion regarded him. (3SP 329.2)

Had Peter been invested with the authority and position accorded to him by the Roman Catholic Church, he would have encouraged, rather than have checked, the veneration of Cornelius. The so-called successors of Peter require kings and emperors to bow at their feet; but Peter himself claimed to be only an erring and fallible man. (3SP 330.1)

Peter spoke with Cornelius and those assembled in his house, concerning the custom of the Jews; that it was considered unlawful for them to mingle socially with Gentiles, and involved ceremonial defilement. It was not prohibited by the law of God, but the tradition of men had made it a binding custom. Said he, "Ye know how that it is an unlawful thing for a man that is a Jew to keep company, or come unto one of another nation; but God hath showed me that I should not call any man common or unclean. Therefore came I unto you without gainsaying, as soon as I was sent for; I ask therefore for what intent ye have sent for me." (3SP 330.2)

Cornelius thereupon related his experience, and the words of the angel that had appeared to him in vision. In conclusion he said, "Immediately therefore I sent to thee; and thou hast well done that thou art come. Now therefore are we all here present before God, to hear all things that are commanded thee of God. Then Peter opened his mouth, and said, Of a truth I perceive that God is no respecter of persons; but in every nation he that feareth him, and worketh righteousness, is accepted with him." Although God had favored the Jews above all other nations, yet if they rejected light, and did not live up to their profession, they were no more exalted in his esteem than other nations. Those among the Gentiles who, like Cornelius, feared God, and worked righteousness, living up to what light they had, were kindly regarded by God, and their sincere service was accepted. (3SP 330.3)

But the faith and righteousness of Cornelius could not be perfect without a knowledge of Christ; therefore God sent that light and knowledge to him for the farther development of his righteous character. Many refuse to receive the light which the providence of God sends them, and, as an excuse for so doing, quote the words of Peter to Cornelius and his friends: "But in every nation he that feareth Him, and worketh righteousness, is accepted with him." They maintain that it is of no consequence what men believe, so long as their works are good. Such ones are wrong; faith must unite with their works. They should advance with the light that is given them. If God brings them in connection with his servants who have received new truth, substantiated by the Word of God, they should accept it with joy. Truth is onward. Truth is upward. On the other hand, those who claim that their faith alone will save them, are trusting to a rope of sand; for faith is strengthened and made perfect by works only. (3SP 331.1)

Peter preached Jesus to that company of

Chapter 25 - The Ministry of Peter (**3SP 331.2**)

attentive hearers; his life, ministry, miracles, betrayal, crucifixion, resurrection, and ascension, and his work in Heaven, as man's Representative and Advocate, to plead in the sinner's behalf. As the apostle spoke, his heart glowed with the Spirit of God's truth which he was presenting to the people. His hearers were charmed by the doctrine they heard, for their hearts had been prepared to receive the truth. The apostle was interrupted by the descent of the Holy Ghost, as was manifested on the day of Pentecost. "And they of the circumcision which believed were astonished, as many as came with Peter, because that on the Gentiles also was poured out the gift of the Holy Ghost. For they heard them speak with tongues, and magnify God. Then answered Peter, Can any man forbid water, that these should not be baptized, which have received the Holy Ghost as well as we? And he commanded them to be baptized in the name of the Lord. Then prayed they him to tarry certain days." (**3SP 331.2**)

The descent of the Holy Ghost upon the Gentiles was not an equivalent for baptism. The requisite steps in conversion, in all cases, are faith, repentance, and baptism. Thus the true Christian church are united in one Lord, one faith, one baptism. Diverse temperaments are modified by sanctifying grace, and the same distinguishing principles regulate the lives of all. Peter yielded to the entreaties of the believing Gentiles, and remained with them for a time, preaching Jesus to all the Gentiles thereabout. (**3SP 332.1**)

When the brethren in Judea heard that Peter had preached to the Gentiles, and had met with them, and eaten with them in their houses, they were surprised and offended by such strange movements on his part. They feared that such a course, which looked presumptuous to them, would tend to contradict his own teachings. As soon as Peter visited them, they met him with severe censure, saying, "Thou wentest in to men uncircumcised, and didst eat with them." (**3SP 332.2**)

Then Peter candidly laid the whole matter before them. He related his experience in regard to the vision, and pleaded that it admonished him no longer to keep up the ceremonial distinction of circumcision and uncircumcision, nor to look upon the Gentiles as unclean, for God was not a respecter of persons. He informed them of the command of God to go to the Gentiles, the coming of the messengers, his journey to Caesarea, and the meeting with Cornelius and the company collected at his house. His caution was made manifest to his brethren from the fact that, although commanded by God to go to the Gentile's house, he had taken with him six of the disciples then present, as witnesses of all he should say or do while there. He recounted the substance of his interview with Cornelius, in which the latter had told him of his vision, wherein he had been directed to send messengers to Joppa to bring Peter to him, who would tell him words whereby he, and all his house, might be saved. (**3SP 333.1**)

He recounted the events of this first meeting with the Gentiles, saying, "And as I began to speak, the Holy Ghost fell on them, as on us at the beginning. Then remembered I the word of the Lord, how that he said, John indeed baptized with water; but ye shall be baptized with the Holy Ghost. Forasmuch then as God gave them the like gift as he did unto us, who believed on the Lord Jesus Christ, what was I, that I could withstand God?" (**3SP 333.2**)

The disciples, upon hearing this account, were silenced, and convinced that Peter's course was in direct fulfillment of the plan of God, and that their old prejudices and exclusiveness were to be utterly destroyed by the gospel of Christ. "When they heard these things, they held their peace, and glorified God, saying, Then hath God also to the Gentiles granted repentance unto life." (**3SP 333.3**)

*****

Chapter 26
Deliverance of Peter

Herod was professedly a proselyte to the Jewish faith, and apparently very zealous in perpetuating the ceremonies of the law. The government of Judea was in his hands, subject to Claudius, the Roman emperor; he also held the position of tetrarch of Galilee. Herod was anxious to obtain the favor of the Jews, hoping thus to make secure his offices and honors. He therefore proceeded to carry out the desires of the Jews in persecuting the church of Christ. He began his work by spoiling the houses and goods of the believers; he then began to imprison the leading ones. He seized upon James and cast him into prison, and there sent an executioner to kill him with a sword, as another Herod had caused the prophet John to be beheaded. He then became bolder, seeing that the Jews were well pleased with his acts, and imprisoned Peter. These cruelties were performed during the sacred occasion of the passover. (3SP 334.1)

James was one of the three favored disciples who had been brought into the closest relationship with Christ. James, John, and Peter were his chief witnesses after his death. They saw the transfiguration of the Saviour, and beheld him glorified. They were in the garden with him during the night of his agony. James and John were the sons of Zebedee, the ones whom Jesus had asked, "Are ye able to drink of the cup that I shall drink of, and to be baptized with the baptism that I am baptized with?" When James was rudely thrust into prison, and unceremoniously summoned to execution, he understood more fully than ever before, the words of his Lord upon that occasion. (3SP 334.2)

There was great grief and consternation at the death of James. When Peter was also imprisoned, the entire church engaged in fasting and prayer. While the Jews were celebrating the memorial of their deliverance from Egypt, and pretending great zeal for the law, they were at the same time persecuting and murdering the believers in Christ, thus transgressing every principle of that law. At these great religious gatherings they stirred one another up against the Christians, till they were united in a bitter hatred of them. (3SP 335.1)

The people applauded the act of Herod in causing the death of James, though some of them complained of the private manner in which it was accomplished, maintaining that a public execution would have had the effect to more thoroughly intimidate all believers and sympathizers. Herod therefore held Peter in custody for the purpose of gratifying the Jews by the public spectacle of his death. But it was suggested to the ruler that it would not be safe to bring the veteran apostle out for execution before all the people who were assembled in Jerusalem for the passover. It was feared that his venerable appearance might excite their pity and respect; they also dreaded lest he should make one of those powerful appeals which had frequently roused the people to investigate the life and character of Jesus Christ, and which they, with all their artifice, were totally unable to controvert. In such a case, the Jews apprehended that his release would be demanded at the hands of the king. (3SP 335.2)

Peter's ardent zeal in vindicating himself, and in advocating the cause of Christ, had lost to the Jews many of their brethren, and they stood in great dread of his having an opportunity to lift up his voice in the presence of all the nations and people that had come to the city to worship. Therefore the apostle was placed under charge of sixteen soldiers, who alternated in guarding him day and night. But it was in vain that the puny arm of man was lifted against the Lord. He, by the putting forth of his might, was about to stay the precious blood which the Jews would have been emboldened to shed, had not divine power interposed. (3SP 336.1)

While the execution of Peter was being delayed, upon various pretexts, until after the passover, the church of Christ had time for deep searching of heart, and earnest prayer. Strong petitions, tears, and fasting were mingled

Chapter 26 - Deliverance of Peter (3SP 336.2)

together. They prayed without ceasing for Peter; they felt that he could not be spared from the Christian work; and they felt that they had arrived at a point, where, without the special help of God, the church of Christ would become extinct. (3SP 336.2)

Meanwhile worshipers of every nation sought the temple which had been dedicated to the service of God, and which remained, to all appearance, the same as when the shekinah had glorified it, with the exception of additional embellishment. But God was no longer to be found in that palace of loveliness, glittering with gold and precious stones, and presenting a spectacle of grandeur and beauty to all beholders. (3SP 337.1)

The day of Peter's execution was at last appointed; but still the prayers of the believers ascended to Heaven. And while all their energies and sympathies were called out in fervent appeals, angels of God were guarding the imprisoned apostle. Man's extremity is God's opportunity. Peter was placed between two soldiers, and was bound by two chains, each chain being fastened to the wrist of one of his guard. He was therefore unable to move without their knowledge. The prison doors were securely fastened, and a strong guard was placed before them. All chance of rescue or escape, by human means, was thus cut off. (3SP 337.2)

The apostle was not intimidated by his situation. Since his re-instatement after his denial of Christ, he had unflinchingly braved danger, and manifested a noble courage and boldness in preaching a crucified, risen, and ascended Saviour. He now called to mind the words of Jesus addressed to him: "Verily, verily, I say unto thee, When thou wast young, thou girdedst thyself, and walkedst whither thou wouldest; but when thou shalt be old, thou shalt stretch forth thy hands, and another shall gird thee, and carry thee whither thou wouldest not." He believed the time had now come when he was to yield up his life for Christ's sake. (3SP 337.3)

The night before his appointed execution, Peter, bound with chains, slept between the two soldiers, as usual. Herod, remembering the escape of Peter and John from prison, where they had been confined because of their faith, took double precautions on this occasion. The soldiers on guard, in order to secure their extra vigilance, were made answerable for the safe-keeping of the prisoner. He was bound, as has been described, in a cell of massive rock, the doors of which were bolted and barred. Sixteen men were detailed to guard this cell, relieving each other at regular intervals. Four comprised the watch at one time. But the bolts and bars, and Roman guard, which effectually cut off from the prisoner a possibility of human aid, were only to result in making the triumph of God more complete in Peter's deliverance from prison. Herod was lifting his hand against Omnipotence, and he was to be utterly humiliated and defeated in his attempt upon the life of the servant of God. (3SP 338.1)

On this last night before the execution, a mighty angel, commissioned from Heaven, descended to rescue him. The strong gates which shut in the saint of God, open without the aid of human hands; the angel of the Most High enters, and they close again noiselessly behind him. He enters the cell, hewn from the solid rock, and there lies Peter, sleeping the blessed, peaceful sleep of innocence and perfect trust in God, while chained to a powerful guard on either side of him. The light which enveloped the angel illuminated the prison, but did not waken the sleeping apostle. His was the sound repose that invigorates and renews, and that comes of a good conscience. (3SP 338.2)

Peter is not awakened until he feels the stroke of the angel's hand, and hears his voice saying, "Arise up quickly." He sees his cell, which had never been blessed by a ray of sunshine, illuminated by the light of Heaven, and an angel of great glory standing before him. He mechanically obeys the voice of the angel; and in rising lifts his hands, and finds that the chains have been broken from his wrists. Again the voice of the angel is heard: "Gird thyself, and bind on thy sandals." (3SP 339.1)

Again Peter mechanically obeys, keeping his wondering gaze riveted upon his heavenly visitant, and believing himself to be dreaming, or in a vision. The armed soldiers are passive as if chiseled from marble, as the angel again commands, "Cast thy garment about thee, and follow me." Thereupon the heavenly being moves toward the door, and the usually talkative Peter follows, dumb from amazement. They step over the motionless guard, and reach the heavily bolted and barred door, which swings open of its own accord, and closes again immediately; while the guard within and outside the door are motionless at their posts. (3SP 339.2)

The second gate, which is also guarded within and without, is reached; it opens as did the first, with no creaking of hinges, or rattling of

Chapter 26 - Deliverance of Peter (3SP 342.2)

iron bolts; they pass without, and it closes again as noiselessly. They pass through the third gateway in the same manner, and at last find themselves in the open street. No word is spoken; there is no sound of footstep; the angel glides on before, encircled by a light of dazzling brightness, and Peter follows his deliverer, bewildered, and believing himself to be in a dream. Street after street is threaded thus, and then, the mission of the angel being completed, he suddenly disappears. (3SP 339.3)

As the heavenly light faded away, Peter felt himself to be in profound darkness; but gradually the darkness seemed to decrease, as he became accustomed to it, and he found himself alone in the silent street, with the cool night air upon his brow. He now realized that it was no dream or vision that had visited him. He was free, in a familiar part of the city; he recognized the place as one which he had often frequented, and had expected to pass for the last time on the morrow, when upon the way to the scene of his prospective death. He tried to recall the events of the last few moments. He remembered falling asleep, bound between the two soldiers, with his sandals and outer garment removed. He examined his person, and found himself fully dressed, and girded. (3SP 340.1)

His wrists, swollen from wearing the cruel irons, were now free from the manacles, and he realized that his freedom was no delusion, but a blessed reality. On the morrow he was to have been led forth to die; but lo, an angel had delivered him from prison and from death. "And when Peter was come to himself, he said, Now I know of a surety that the Lord hath sent his angel, and hath delivered me out of the hand of Herod, and from all the expectation of the people of the Jews." (3SP 340.2)

The apostle made his way direct to the house where his brethren were assembled together for prayer; he found them engaged in earnest prayer for him at that moment. "And as Peter knocked at the door of the gate, a damsel came to hearken, named Rhoda. And when she knew Peter's voice, she opened not the gate for gladness, but ran in, and told how Peter stood before the gate. And they said unto her, Thou art mad. But she constantly affirmed that it was even so. Then said they, It is his angel. But Peter continued knocking; and when they had opened the door, and saw him, they were astonished. But he, beckoning unto them with the hand to hold their peace, declared unto them how the Lord had brought him out of the prison. And he said, Go show these things unto James, and to the brethren. And he departed, and went into another place." (3SP 340.3)

Joy and praise filled the hearts of the fasting, praying believers, that God had heard and answered their prayers, and delivered Peter from the hand of Herod. In the morning the people gathered together to witness the execution of the apostle. Herod sent officers to bring Peter from prison with great display of arms and guard, in order to insure against his escape, to intimidate all sympathizers, and to exhibit his own power. (3SP 341.1)

Meanwhile terror and mortification had seized the Roman guard at the prison, when they found that the prisoner was gone. It had been expressly stated to them that their lives would be answerable for the life of their charge, and for that reason they had been specially vigilant. But the God of Heaven had thwarted the purpose of wicked Herod. There was the guard at the door of the prison, the bolts and bars of the door still fast and strong, the guard inside, the chains attached to the wrists of the two soldiers; but the prisoner was gone. (3SP 341.2)

When the report of these things was brought to Herod, he was exasperated, and charged the keepers of the prison with unfaithfulness. They were accordingly put to death for the alleged crime of sleeping at their post. At the same time, Herod knew that no human power had rescued Peter. But he was determined not to acknowledge that a divine power had been at work to thwart his base designs. He would not humiliate himself thus, but set himself boldly in defiance of God. (3SP 342.1)

Herod, not long after Peter's deliverance from prison, went down from Judea to Caesarea, and there abode. He there made a grand festival, designed to excite the admiration and applause of the people. Pleasure-lovers from all quarters were assembled together, and there was much feasting and wine-drinking. Herod made a most gorgeous appearance before the people. He was clad in a robe, sparkling with silver and gold, that caught the rays of the sun in its glittering folds, and dazzled the eyes of the beholders. With great pomp and ceremony he stood before the multitude, and addressed them in an eloquent oration. (3SP 342.2)

The majesty of his appearance, and the

Chapter 26 - Deliverance of Peter (3SP 342.3)

power of his well-chosen language, swayed the assembly with a mighty influence. Their senses were already perverted by feasting and wine; they were dazzled by his glittering decorations, and charmed by his grand deportment and eloquent words; and, wild with enthusiasm, they showered upon him adulation, and proclaimed him a God, declaring that mortal man could not present such an appearance, or command such startling eloquence of language. They farther declared that they had ever respected him as a ruler, but from henceforth they should worship him as a god. (3SP 342.3)

These people had refused to acknowledge Christ, whose coarse and often travel-stained garments were worn over a heart of divine love, rich with that inward adorning, a meek and gentle spirit. Their eyes, blinded by sin, refused to see, beneath that humble exterior, the Lord of life and glory, though his mercy and divine power were revealed before them in works that no man could do. But they were ready to bow down and worship, as a God, the haughty king, whose splendid garments of silver and gold were worn over a corrupt and cruel heart. They did not attempt to penetrate his vain display, and read the depravity and deceit of his character, and the wickedness of his daily life. (3SP 343.1)

Herod knew that he deserved none of this praise and homage; yet he did not rebuke the idolatry of the people, but accepted it as his due. The glow of gratified pride was on his countenance as he heard the shout ascend: It is the voice of a God, and not of man! The same voices which now glorified a vile sinner, had, but a few years before, raised the frenzied cry of, Away with Jesus! Crucify him, crucify him! Herod received this flattery and homage with great pleasure, and his heart bounded with triumph; but suddenly a swift and terrible change came over him. His countenance became pallid as death, and distorted with agony; great drops of sweat started from his pores. He stood a moment as if transfixed with pain and terror, then, turning his blanched and livid face to his horror-stricken friends, he cried in hollow, despairing tones, He whom you have exalted as a God is struck with death! (3SP 343.2)

He was borne in a state of the most excruciating anguish from the scene of wicked revelry, the mirth, and pomp, and display of which he now loathed in his soul. A moment before, he had been the proud recipient of the praise and worship of that vast throng–now he felt himself in the hands of a Ruler mightier than himself. Remorse seized him; he remembered his cruel command to slay the innocent James; he remembered his relentless persecution of the followers of Christ, and his design to put to death the apostle Peter, whom God had delivered out of his hand; he remembered how, in his mortification and disappointed rage, he had wreaked his unreasoning revenge upon the keepers of the prisoner, and executed them without mercy. He felt that God, who had rescued the apostle from death, was now dealing with him, the relentless persecutor. He found no relief from pain of body or anguish of mind, and he expected none. Herod was acquainted with the law of God, which says, "Thou shalt have no other gods before me," and he knew that in accepting the worship of the people he had filled up the measure of his iniquity, and had brought upon him the just wrath of God. (3SP 344.1)

The same angel who had left the royal courts of Heaven to rescue Peter from the power of his persecutor, had been the messenger of wrath and judgment to Herod. The angel smote Peter to arouse him from slumber; but it was with a different stroke that he smote the wicked king, bringing mortal disease upon him. God poured contempt upon Herod's pride, and his person, which he had exhibited decked in shining apparel before the admiring gaze of the people, was eaten by worms, and putrefied while yet alive. Herod died in great agony of mind and body, under the retributive justice of God. (3SP 344.2)

This demonstration of divine judgment had a mighty influence upon the people. While the apostle of Christ had been miraculously delivered from prison and death, his persecutor had been stricken down by the curse of God. The news was borne to all lands, and was the means of bringing many to believe on Christ. (3SP 345.1)

*****

Chapter 27
Ordination of Paul and Barnabas

The apostles and disciples who left Jerusalem during the fierce persecution that raged there after the martyrdom of Stephen, preached Christ in the cities round about, confining their labors to the Hebrew and Greek Jews. "And the hand of the Lord was with them; and a great number believed, and turned unto the Lord." When the believers in Jerusalem heard the good tidings they rejoiced; and Barnabas, "a good man, and full of the Holy Ghost and of faith," was sent to Antioch, the metropolis of Syria, to help the church there. He labored there with great success. As the work increased, he solicited and obtained the help of Paul; and the two disciples labored together in that city for a year, teaching the people, and adding to the numbers of the church of Christ. (3SP 345.2)

Antioch had both a large Jewish and Gentile population; it was a great resort for lovers of ease and pleasure, because of the healthfulness of its situation, its beautiful scenery, and the wealth, culture, and refinement that centered there. Its extensive commerce made it a place of great importance, where people of all nationalities were found. It was therefore a city of luxury and vice. The retribution of God finally came upon Antioch, because of the wickedness of its inhabitants. (3SP 346.1)

It was here that the disciples were first called Christians. This name was given them because Christ was the main theme of their preaching, teaching, and conversation. They were continually recounting the incidents of his life, during the time in which his disciples were blessed with his personal company. They dwelt untiringly upon his teachings, his miracles of healing the sick, casting out devils, and raising the dead to life. With quivering lips and tearful eyes they spoke of his agony in the garden, his betrayal, trial, and execution, the forbearance and humility with which he endured the contumely and torture imposed upon him by his enemies, and the Godlike pity with which he prayed for those who persecuted him. His resurrection and ascension, and his work in Heaven as a Mediator for fallen man, were joyful topics with them. The heathen might well call them Christians, since they preached of Christ, and addressed their prayers to God through him. (3SP 346.2)

Paul found, in the populous city of Antioch, an excellent field of labor, where his great learning, wisdom, and zeal, combined, wielded a powerful influence over the inhabitants and frequenters of that city of culture. (3SP 346.3)

Meanwhile the work of the apostles was centered at Jerusalem, where Jews of all tongues and countries came to worship at the temple during the stated festivals. At such times the apostles preached Christ with unflinching courage, though they knew that in so doing their lives were in constant jeopardy. Many converts to the faith were made, and these, scattering to their homes in different parts of the country, dispersed the seeds of truth throughout all nations, and among all classes of society. (3SP 347.1)

Peter, James, and John felt confident that God had appointed them to preach Christ among their own countrymen at home. But Paul had received his commission from God, while praying in the temple, and his broad missionary field had been presented before him with remarkable distinctness. To prepare him for his extensive and important work, God had brought him into close connection with himself, and had opened before his enraptured vision a glimpse of the beauty and glory of Heaven. (3SP 347.2)

God communicated with the devout prophets and teachers in the church at Antioch. "As they ministered to the Lord, and fasted, the Holy Ghost said, Separate me Barnabas and Saul for the work whereunto I have called them." These apostles were therefore dedicated to God in a most solemn manner by fasting and prayer and the laying on of hands; and they were sent forth to their field of labor among the Gentiles. (3SP 347.3)

Both Paul and Barnabas had been laboring as ministers of Christ, and God had abundantly

Chapter 27 - Ordination of Paul and Barnabas (3SP 347.4)

blessed their efforts; but neither of them had previously been formally ordained to the gospel ministry by prayer and the laying on of hands. They were now authorized by the church, not only to teach the truth, but to baptize, and to organize churches, being invested with full ecclesiastical authority. This was an important era for the church. Though the middle wall of partition between Jew and Gentile had been broken down by the death of Christ, letting the Gentiles into the full privileges of the gospel, yet the vail had not yet been torn away from the eyes of many of the believing Jews, and they could not clearly discern to the end of that which was abolished by the Son of God. The work was now to be prosecuted with vigor among the Gentiles, and was to result in strengthening the church by a great ingathering of souls. (3SP 347.4)

The apostles, in this, their special work, were to be exposed to suspicion, prejudice, and jealousy. As a natural consequence of their departure from the exclusiveness of the Jews, their doctrine and views would be subject to the charge of heresy; and their credentials as ministers of the gospel would be questioned by many zealous, believing Jews. God foresaw all these difficulties which his servants would undergo, and, in his wise providence, caused them to be invested with unquestionable authority from the established church of God, that their work should be above challenge. (3SP 348.1)

The brethren in Jerusalem and in Antioch were made thoroughly acquainted with all the particulars of this divine appointment, and the specific work of teaching the Gentiles, which the Lord had given to these apostles. Their ordination was an open recognition of their divine mission, as messengers specially chosen by the Holy Ghost for a special work. Paul witnesses, in his Epistle to the Romans, that he considered this sacred appointment as a new and important epoch in his life; he names himself, "a servant of Jesus Christ, called to be an apostle, separated unto the gospel of God." (3SP 348.2)

The ordination by the laying on of hands, was, at a later date, greatly abused; unwarrantable importance was attached to the act, as though a power came at once upon those who received such ordination, which immediately qualified them for any and all ministerial work, as though virtue lay in the act of laying on of hands. We have, in the history of these two apostles, only a simple record of the laying on of hands, and its bearing upon their work. Both Paul and Barnabas had already received their commission from God himself; and the ceremony of the laying on of hands added no new grace or virtual qualification. It was merely setting the seal of the church upon the work of God–an acknowledged form of designation to an appointed office. (3SP 349.1)

This form was a significant one to the Jews. When a Jewish father blessed his children, he laid his hands reverently upon their heads. When an animal was devoted to sacrifice, the hand of the one invested with priestly authority was laid upon the head of the victim. Therefore, when the ministers of Antioch laid their hands upon the apostles, they, by that action, asked God to bestow his blessing upon them, in their devotion to the specific work which God had chosen them to do. (3SP 349.2)

The apostles started out upon their mission, taking with them Mark. They went into Seleucia, and from thence sailed to Cyprus. At Salamis they preached in the synagogues of the Jews. "And when they had gone through the isle unto Paphos, they found a certain sorcerer, a false prophet, a Jew, whose name was Barjesus; which was with the deputy of the country, Sergius Paulus, a prudent man; who called for Barnabas and Saul, and desired to hear the word of God. But Elymas the sorcerer (for so is his name by interpretation) withstood them, seeking to turn away the deputy from the faith." (3SP 349.3)

The deputy being a man of repute and influence, the sorcerer Elymas, who was under the control of Satan, sought by false reports, and various specious deceptions, to turn him against the apostles and destroy their influence over him. As the magicians in Pharaoh's court withstood Moses and Aaron, so did this sorcerer withstand the apostles. When the deputy sent for the apostles, that he might be instructed in the truth, Satan was on hand with his servant, seeking to thwart the purpose of God, and prevent this influential man from embracing the faith of Christ. This agent of Satan greatly hindered the work of the apostles. Thus does the fallen foe ever work in a special manner to prevent persons of influence, who could be of great service to the cause, from embracing the truth of God. (3SP 350.1)

But Paul, in the Spirit and power of the Holy Ghost, rebuked the wicked deceiver. He "set his eyes upon him, and said, O full of all subtilty and all mischief, thou child of the devil, thou enemy

Chapter 27 - Ordination of Paul and Barnabas (3SP 353.2)

of all righteousness, wilt thou not cease to pervert the right ways of the Lord? And now, behold, the hand of the Lord is upon thee, and thou shalt be blind, not seeing the sun for a season. And immediately there fell on him a mist and a darkness; and he went about seeking some to lead him by the hand. Then the deputy, when he saw what was done, believed, being astonished at the doctrine of the Lord." (3SP 350.2)

The sorcerer had closed his eyes to the evidences of truth, and the light of the gospel, therefore the Lord, in his righteous anger, caused his natural eyes to be closed, shutting out from him the light of day. This blindness was not permanent, but only for a season, to warn him to repent, and to seek pardon of God whom he had so offended. The confusion into which this man was brought, with all his boasted power, made all his subtle arts against the doctrine of Christ of none effect. The fact of his being obliged to grope about in blindness, proved to all beholders that the miracles which the apostles had performed, and which Elymas had denounced as being produced by sleight of hand, were in truth wrought by the power of God. The deputy was convinced of the truth of the doctrine taught by the apostles, and embraced the gospel of Christ. (3SP 351.1)

Elymas was not a man of education, yet he was peculiarly fitted to do the work of Satan. Those who preach the truth of God will be obliged to meet the wily foe in many different shapes. Sometimes it is in the person of learned, and often in the person of ignorant, men, whom Satan has educated to be his successful instruments in deceiving souls, and in working iniquity. It is the duty of the minister of Christ to stand faithfully at his post, in the fear of God, and in the power of his strength. Thus he may put to confusion the hosts of Satan, and triumph in the name of the Lord. (3SP 351.2)

Paul and his company now continued their journey, going into Perga, in Pamphylia. Their way was toilsome, they encountered hardships and privations, and were beset by dangers on every side, which intimidated Mark, who was unused to hardships. As still greater difficulties were apprehended, he became disheartened, and refused to go farther, just at the time when his services were most needed. He accordingly returned to Jerusalem, and to the peace and comfort of his home. (3SP 352.1)

Mark did not apostatize from the faith of Christianity; but, like many young ministers, he shrank from hardships, and preferred the comfort and safety of home to the travels, labors, and dangers of the missionary field. This desertion caused Paul to judge him unfavorably and severely for a long time. He distrusted his steadiness of character, and his devotion to the cause of Christ. The mother of Mark was a convert to the Christian religion; and her home was an asylum for the disciples. There they were always sure of a welcome, and a season of rest, in which they could rally from the effect of the fierce persecutions that everywhere assailed them in their labors. (3SP 352.2)

It was during one of these visits of the apostles to his mother's that Mark proposed to Paul and Barnabas that he should accompany them on their missionary tour. He had witnessed the wonderful power attending their ministry; he had felt the favor of God in his own heart; he had seen the faith of his mother tested and tried without wavering; he had witnessed the miracles performed by the apostles, and which set the seal of God upon their work; he had himself preached the Christian faith, and had longed to enter more fully into the work, and entirely devote himself to it. He had, as the companion of the apostles, rejoiced in the success of their mission; but fear and discouragement overwhelmed him in the face of privation, persecution, and danger; and he sought the attractions of home at a time when his services were most needful to the apostles. (3SP 352.3)

At a future period there was a sharp contention between Paul and Barnabas concerning Mark, who was still anxious to devote himself to the work of the ministry. Paul could not, at that time, excuse in any degree the weakness of Mark in deserting them and the work upon which they had entered, for the ease and quiet of home; and he urged that one with so little stamina was unfit for the gospel ministry, which required patience, self-denial, bravery, and faith, with a willingness to sacrifice even life if need be. (3SP 353.1)

Barnabas, on the other hand, was inclined to excuse Mark, who was his nephew, because of his inexperience. He felt anxious that he should not abandon the ministry, for he saw in him qualifications for a useful laborer in the field of Christ. This contention caused Paul and Barnabas to separate, the latter following out his convictions, and taking Mark with him in his work. (3SP 353.2)

Mark, therefore, accompanied Barnabas to

Chapter 27 - Ordination of Paul and Barnabas (3SP 353.3)

Cyprus, and assisted him there. Paul was afterward reconciled to Mark, and received him as a fellow-laborer. He also recommended him to the Colossians as one who was a "fellow-worker unto the kingdom of God," and a personal comfort to him, Paul. Again, not long prior to his death, he spoke of him as profitable to him in the ministry. (3SP 353.3)

Paul and Barnabas next visited Antioch in Pisidia, and on the Sabbath went into the synagogue, and sat down; "and after the reading of the law and the prophets, the rulers of the synagogue sent unto them, saying, Ye men and brethren, if ye have any word of exhortation for the people, say on." Being thus invited to speak, "Paul stood up, and beckoning with his hand said, Men of Israel, and ye that fear God, give audience." He then proceeded to give a history of the manner in which the Lord had dealt with the Jews from the time of their deliverance from Egyptian bondage, and how a Saviour had been promised of the seed of David. He then preached Jesus as the Saviour of men, the Messiah of prophecy. (3SP 354.1)

When he had finished, and the Jews had left the synagogue, the Gentiles still lingered, and entreated that the same words might be spoken unto them the next Sabbath day. The apostles created a great interest in the place, among both Jews and Gentiles. They encouraged the believers and converts to stand fast in their faith, and to continue in the grace of God. The interest to hear the words of the apostles was so great that the whole city came together on the next Sabbath day. But now, as in the days of Christ, when the Jewish priests and rulers saw the multitudes that had assembled to hear the new doctrine, they were moved by envy and jealousy, and contradicted the words of the apostles with blasphemy. Their old bigotry and prejudice were also aroused, when they perceived great numbers of Gentiles mingling with the Jews in the congregation. They could not endure that the Gentiles should enjoy religious privileges on an equality with themselves, but clung tenaciously to the idea that the blessing of God was reserved exclusively for them. This had ever been the great sin of the Jews, which Christ, on several occasions, had rebuked. (3SP 354.2)

They listened, on one Sabbath day, with intense interest to the teachings of Paul and Barnabas, who preached Jesus as the promised Messiah; and upon the next Sabbath day, because of the multitude of Gentiles who assembled also to hear them, they were excited to a frenzy of indignation, the words of the apostles were distorted in their minds, and they were unfitted to weigh the evidence presented by them. When they learned that the Messiah preached by the apostles was to be a light to the Gentiles, as well as the glory of his people Israel, they were beside themselves with rage, and used the most insulting language to the apostles. (3SP 355.1)

The Gentiles, on the other hand, rejoiced exceedingly that Christ recognized them as the children of God, and with grateful hearts they listened to the word preached. The apostles now clearly discerned their duty, and the work which God would have them do. They turned without hesitation to the Gentiles, preaching Christ to them, and leaving the Jews to their bigotry, blindness of mind, and hardness of heart. The mind of Paul had been well prepared to make this decision, by the circumstances attending his conversion, his vision in the temple at Jerusalem, his appointment by God to preach to the Gentiles, and the success which had already crowned his efforts among them. (3SP 355.2)

When Paul and Barnabas turned from the Jews who derided them, they addressed them boldly, saying, "It was necessary that the Word of God should first have been spoken to you; but seeing ye put it from you, and judge yourselves unworthy of everlasting life, lo, we turn to the Gentiles. For so hath the Lord commanded us, saying, I have set thee to be a light of the Gentiles, that thou shouldest be for salvation unto the ends of the earth." (3SP 356.1)

This gathering in of the Gentiles to the church of God had been traced by the pen of inspiration, but had been but faintly understood. Hosea had said, "Yet the number of the children of Israel shall be as the sand of the sea, which cannot be measured nor numbered; and it shall come to pass that in the place where it was said unto them, Ye are not my people, there it shall be said unto them, Ye are the sons of the living God." And again, "I will sow her unto me in the earth; and I will have mercy upon her that had not obtained mercy; and I will say to them which were not my people, Thou art my people; and they shall say, Thou art my God." (3SP 356.2)

During the life of Christ on earth he had sought to lead the Jews out of their exclusiveness. The conversion of the centurion, and that of the Syrophenician woman, were instances of his direct work outside of the acknowledged people of Israel. The time had now come for active and continued work among the Gentiles, of whom whole communities received the gospel gladly, and glorified God for the light of an intelligent faith. The unbelief and malice of the Jews did not turn aside the purpose of God; for a new Israel was being grafted into the old olive-tree. The synagogues were closed against the apostles; but private houses were thrown open for their use, and public buildings of the Gentiles were also used in which to preach the Word of God. (3SP 356.3)

The Jews, however, were not satisfied with closing their synagogues against the apostles, but desired to banish them from that region. To effect this purpose they sought to prejudice certain devout and honorable women, who had great influence with the government, and also men of influence. This they accomplished by subtle arts, and false reports. These persons of good repute complained to the authorities against the apostles, and they were accordingly expelled from those coasts. (3SP 357.1)

On this occasion the apostles followed the instruction of Christ: "Whosoever shall not receive you, nor hear you, when ye depart thence, shake off the dust under your feet for a testimony against them. Verily, I say unto you, it shall be more tolerable for Sodom and Gomorrah in the day of Judgment than for that city." The apostles were not discouraged by this expulsion; they remembered the words of their Master: "Blessed are ye when men shall revile you, and persecute you, and shall say all manner of evil against you falsely, for my sake. Rejoice, and be exceeding glad; for great is your reward in Heaven; for so persecuted they the prophets which were before you." (3SP 357.2)

Chapter 28
Preaching Among the Heathen

The apostles next visited Iconium. This place was a great resort for pleasure-seekers, and persons who had no particular object in life. The population was composed of Romans, Greeks, and Jews. The apostles here, as at Antioch, first commenced their labors in the synagogues for their own people, the Jews. They met with marked success; numbers of both Jews and Greeks accepted the gospel of Christ. But here, as in former places where the apostles had labored, the unbelieving Jews commenced an unreasonable opposition of those who accepted the true faith, and, as far as lay in their power, influenced the Gentiles against them. (3SP 358.1)

The apostles, however, were not easily turned from their work, for many were daily embracing the doctrine of Christ. They went on faithfully in the face of opposition, envy, and prejudice. Miracles were daily wrought by the disciples through the power of God; and all whose minds were open to evidence were affected by the convincing power of these things. (3SP 358.2)

This increasing popularity of the doctrine of Christ stirred the unbelieving Jews to fresh opposition. They were filled with envy and hatred, and determined to stop the labors of the apostles at once. They went to the authorities, and represented their work in the most false and exaggerated light, leading the officers to fear that the entire city was in danger of being incited to insurrection. They stated that great numbers were attaching themselves to the apostles, and suggested that it was for secret and dangerous designs. (3SP 358.3)

In consequence of these charges, the disciples were repeatedly brought before the authorities; but in every case they so ably defended themselves before the people, that, although the magistrates were prejudiced against them by the false statements they had heard, they dared not condemn them. They could but acknowledge that the teachings of the apostles were calculated to make men virtuous, law-abiding citizens. (3SP 359.1)

The unprejudiced Jews and Greeks took the position that the morals and good order of the city would be improved, if the apostles were allowed to remain and work there. Upon the occasions when the apostles were brought before the authorities, their defense was so clear and sensible, and the statement which they gave of their doctrine was so calm and comprehensive, that a considerable influence was raised in their favor. The doctrine they preached gained great publicity, and was brought before a much larger number of unprejudiced hearers than ever before in that place. (3SP 359.2)

The Jews perceived that their efforts to thwart the work of the apostles were unavailing, and only resulted in adding greater numbers to the new faith. The rage of the Jews was worked up to such a pitch on this account that they determined to compass their ends in some manner. They stirred up the worst passions of the ignorant, noisy mob, creating a tumult which they attributed to the efforts of the apostles. They then prepared to make a false charge of telling force, and to gain the help of the magistrates in carrying out their purpose. They determined that the apostles should have no opportunity to vindicate themselves; but that mob power should interfere, and put a stop to their labors by stoning them to death. (3SP 359.3)

Friends of the apostles, although unbelievers, warned them of the designs of the malicious Jews, and urged them not uselessly to expose themselves to their fury, but to escape for their lives. They accordingly departed from Iconium in secret, and left the faithful and opposing parties to battle for themselves, trusting God to give victory to the doctrine of Christ. But they by no means took a final leave of Iconium; they purposed to return, after the excitement then raging had abated, and complete the work they had begun. (3SP 360.1)

Those who observe and teach the binding claims of God's law frequently receive, in a

Chapter 28 - Preaching Among the Heathen (3SP 362.3)

degree, similar treatment to that of the apostles at Iconium. They often meet a bitter opposition from ministers and people who persistently refuse the light of God, and, by misrepresentation and falsehood, close every door by which the messenger of truth might have access to the people. (3SP 360.2)

The apostles next went to Lystra and Derbe, cities of Lycaonia. These were populated by a heathen, superstitious people; but among them were souls that would hear and accept the doctrine of Christ. The apostles chose to labor in those cities because they would not there meet Jewish prejudice and persecution. They now came in contact with an entirely new element,–heathen superstition and idolatry. (3SP 360.3)

The apostles, in their work, met all grades of people, and all kinds of faith and religions. They were brought in opposition with Jewish bigotry and intolerance, sorcery, blasphemy, unjust magistrates who loved to exercise their power, false shepherds, superstition, and idolatry. While persecution and opposition met them on every hand, victory still crowned their efforts, and converts were daily added to the faith. (3SP 360.4)

In Lystra there was no Jewish synagogue, though there were a few Jews in the place. The temple of Jupiter occupied a conspicuous position there. Paul and Barnabas appeared in the city together, teaching the doctrine of Christ with great power and eloquence. The credulous people believed them to be gods come down from Heaven. As the apostles gathered the people about them, and explained their strange belief, the worshipers of Jupiter sought to connect these doctrines, as far as they were able, with their own superstitious faith. (3SP 361.1)

Paul addressed them in the Greek language, presenting for their consideration such subjects as would lead them to a correct knowledge of Him who should be the object of their adoration. He directed their attention to the firmament of the heavens–the sun, moon, and stars–the beautiful order of the recurring seasons, the mighty mountains whose peaks were capped with snow, the lofty trees, and the varied wonders of nature, which showed a skill and exactitude almost beyond finite comprehension. Through these visible works of the Almighty, the apostle led the minds of the heathen to the contemplation of the great Mind of the universe. (3SP 361.2)

He then told them of the Son of God, who came from Heaven to our world because he loved the children of men. His life and ministry were presented before them; his rejection by those whom he came to save; his trial and crucifixion by wicked men; his resurrection from the dead to finish his work on earth; and his ascension to Heaven to be man's Advocate in the presence of the Maker of the world. With the Spirit and power of God, Paul and Barnabas declared the gospel of Christ. (3SP 361.3)

As Paul recounted the works of Christ in healing the afflicted, he perceived a cripple whose eyes were fastened upon him, and who received and believed his words. Paul's heart went out in sympathy toward the afflicted man, whose faith he discerned; and he eagerly grasped the hope that he might be healed by that Saviour, who, although he had ascended to Heaven, was still man's Friend and Physician, having more power even than when he was upon earth. (3SP 362.1)

In the presence of that idolatrous assembly, Paul commanded the cripple to stand upright upon his feet. Hitherto he had only been able to take a sitting posture; but he now grasped with faith the words of Paul, and instantly obeyed his command, and stood on his feet for the first time in his life. Strength came with this effort of faith; and he who had been a cripple walked and leaped as though he had never experienced an infirmity. (3SP 362.2)

This work performed on the cripple was a marvel to all beholders. The subject was so well known, and the cure was so complete, that there was no room for skepticism on their part. The Lycaonians were all convinced that supernatural power attended the labors of the apostles, and cried out with great enthusiasm that the gods had come down to them from Heaven in the likeness of men. This belief was in harmony with their traditions that gods visited the earth. They conceived the idea that the great heathen deities, Jupiter and Mercury, were in their midst in the persons of Paul and Barnabas. The former they believed to be Mercury; for Paul was active, earnest, quick, and eloquent with words of warning and exhortation. Barnabas was believed to be Jupiter, the father of gods, because of his venerable appearance, his dignified bearing, and the mildness and benevolence which was expressed in his countenance. (3SP 362.3)

The news of the miraculous cure of the cripple was soon noised throughout all that

Chapter 28 - Preaching Among the Heathen (3SP 363.1)

region, until a general excitement was aroused, and priests from the temple of the gods prepared to do the apostles honor, as visitants from the courts of Heaven, to sacrifice beasts to them, and to bring offerings of garlands and precious things. The apostles had sought retirement and rest in a private dwelling, when their attention was attracted by the sound of music, and the enthusiastic shouting of a vast assembly, who had come to the gate of the house where they were abiding. (3SP 363.1)

When these ministers of God ascertained the cause of this visit and its attendant excitement, they were filled with indignation and horror. They rent their clothing, and rushed in among the multitude to prevent farther proceedings. Paul, in a loud, ringing voice that rose above the noise of the multitude, demanded their attention; and, as the tumult was suddenly quelled, he inquired,– (3SP 363.2)

"Sirs, why do ye these things? We also are men of like passions with you, and preach unto you that ye should turn from these vanities unto the living God, which made heaven, and earth, and the sea, and all things that are therein; who in times past suffered all nations to walk in their own ways. Nevertheless he left not himself without witness, in that he did good, and gave us rain from heaven, and fruitful seasons, filling our hearts with food and gladness." (3SP 363.3)

The people listened to the words of Paul with manifest impatience. Their superstition and enthusiasm had been so great in regard to the apostles that they were loth to acknowledge their error, and have their expectations and purposes thwarted. Notwithstanding the apostles positively denied the divinity attributed to them by the heathen, and Paul made a masterly effort to direct their minds to the true God as the only object worthy of worship, it was still most difficult to turn them from their purpose. (3SP 364.1)

They reasoned that they had with their own eyes beheld the miraculous power exercised by the apostles; that they had seen a cripple who had never before used his limbs, made to leap and rejoice in perfect health and strength through the exercise of the marvelous power possessed by these strangers. But, after much persuasion on the part of Paul, and explanation as to the true mission of the apostles, the people were reluctantly led to give up their purpose. They were not satisfied, however, and led the sacrificial beasts away in great disappointment, that their traditions of divine beings visiting the earth could not be strengthened by this example of their favor in coming to confer special blessings upon them, which would exalt them and their religion in the estimation of the world. (3SP 364.2)

And now a strange change came upon the fickle, excitable people, because their faith was not anchored in the true God. The opposing Jews of Antioch, through whose influence the apostles were driven from that coast, united with certain Jews of Iconium, and followed upon the track of the apostles. The miracle wrought upon the cripple, and its effect upon those who witnessed it, stirred up their envy and led them to go to the scene of the apostles' labor, and put their false version upon the work. They denied that God had any part in it, and claimed that it was accomplished through the demons whom these men served. (3SP 364.3)

The same class had formerly accused the Saviour of casting out devils through the power of the prince of devils; they had denounced him as a deceiver; and they now visited the same unreasoning wrath upon his apostles. By means of falsehoods they inspired the people of Lystra with the bitterness of spirit by which they were themselves actuated. They claimed to be thoroughly acquainted with the history and faith of Paul and Barnabas, and so misrepresented their characters and work that the heathen idolaters, who had been ready to worship the apostles as divine beings, now considered them as worse than murderers, and that whoever should put them out of the world would do God and mankind good service. (3SP 365.1)

Those who believe and teach the truths of God's Word in these days meet with similar opposition from unprincipled persons who will not accept the truth, and who do not hesitate to prevaricate, and even to circulate the most glaring falsehoods in order to destroy the influence and hedge up the way of those whom God has sent with a message of warning to the world. While one class make the falsehoods and circulate them, another class are so blinded by the delusions of Satan as to receive them as the words of truth. They are in the toils of the arch-enemy, while they flatter themselves that they are the children of God. "For this cause, God shall send them strong delusion, that they should believe a lie; that they all might be damned who believed not the truth, but had pleasure in unrighteousness." (3SP 365.2)

The disappointment experienced by the idolaters in being refused the privilege of offering sacrifices to the apostles, prepared them to turn against these ministers of God with a zeal which approached that of the enthusiasm with which they had hailed them as gods. The malicious Jews did not hesitate to take full advantage of the superstition and credulity of this heathen people to carry out their cruel designs. They incited them to attack the apostles by force; and they charged them not to allow Paul an opportunity to speak, alleging that if they did so he would bewitch the people. (3SP 366.1)

The Lystrians rushed upon the apostles with great rage and fury. They hurled stones violently; and Paul, bruised, battered, and fainting, felt that his end had come. The martyrdom of Stephen was brought vividly to his mind, and the cruel part he had acted on that occasion. He fell to the ground apparently dead, and the infuriated mob dragged his insensible body through the gates of the city, and threw it beneath the walls. The apostle mentions this occurrence in the subsequent enumeration of his sufferings for the truth's sake: "Thrice was I beaten with rods; once was I stoned; thrice I suffered shipwreck; a night and a day I have been in the deep; in journeyings often; in perils of waters; in perils of robbers; in perils by mine own countrymen; in perils by the heathen; in perils in the city; in perils in the wilderness; in perils in the sea; in perils among false brethren." (3SP 366.2)

The disciples stood around the body of Paul, lamenting over him whom they supposed was dead, when he suddenly lifted his head, and arose to his feet with the praise of God upon his lips. To the disciples this seemed like a resurrection from the dead, a miracle of God to preserve the life of his faithful servant. They rejoiced with inexpressible gladness over his restoration, and praised God with renewed faith in the doctrine preached by the apostles. (3SP 367.1)

These disciples had been newly converted to the faith through the teachings of Paul, and had stood steadfast notwithstanding the misrepresentation and malignant persecution of the Jews. In fact, the unreasoning opposition of those wicked men had only confirmed these devoted brethren in the faith of Christ; and the restoration to life of Paul seemed to set the signet of God upon their belief. (3SP 367.2)

Timothy had been converted through the ministration of Paul, and was an eye-witness of the sufferings of the apostle upon this occasion. He stood by his apparently dead body, and saw him arise, bruised and covered with blood, not with groans nor murmurings upon his lips, but with praises to Jesus Christ, that he was permitted to suffer for his name. In one of the epistles of Paul to Timothy he refers to his personal knowledge of this occurrence. Timothy became the most important help to Paul and to the church. He was the faithful companion of the apostle in his trials and in his joys. The father of Timothy was a Greek; but his mother was a Jewess, and he had been thoroughly educated in the Jewish religion. (3SP 367.3)

*****

Chapter 29
Jew and Gentile

The next day after the stoning of Paul, the apostles left the city, according to the direction of Christ: "When they persecute you in this city, flee ye into another." They departed for Derbe, where their labors were blessed by leading many souls to embrace the truth. But both Paul and Barnabas returned again to visit Antioch, Iconium, and Lystra, the fields of labor where they had met such opposition and persecution. In all those places were many souls that believed the truth; and the apostles felt it their duty to strengthen and encourage their brethren who were exposed to reproach and bitter opposition. They were determined to securely bind off the work which they had done, that it might not ravel out. (3SP 368.1)

Churches were duly organized in the places before mentioned, elders appointed in each church, and the proper order and system established there. Paul and Barnabas labored in Antioch some time; and many Gentiles there embraced the doctrine of Christ. But certain Jews from Judea raised a general consternation among the believing Gentiles by agitating the question of circumcision. They asserted, with great assurance, that none could be saved without being circumcised, and keeping the entire ceremonial law. (3SP 368.2)

This was an important question, and one which affected the church in a very great degree. Paul and Barnabas met it with promptness, and opposed introducing the subject to the Gentiles. They were opposed in this by the believing Jews of Antioch, who favored the position of those from Judea. The matter resulted in much discussion and want of harmony in the church, until finally the church at Antioch, apprehending that a division among them would occur from any further discussion of the question, decided to send Paul and Barnabas, together with some responsible men of Antioch, to Jerusalem, and lay the matter before the apostles and elders. There they were to meet delegates from the different churches, and those who had come to attend the approaching annual festivals. Meanwhile all controversy was to cease, until a final decision should be made by the responsible men of the church. This decision was then to be universally accepted by the various churches throughout the country. (3SP 369.1)

The apostles, in making their way to Jerusalem, called upon the brethren of the cities through which they passed, and encouraged them by relating their experience in the work of God, and the conversion of the Gentiles to the faith. Upon arriving at Jerusalem, the delegates from Antioch related before the assembly of the churches the success that had attended the ministry with them, and the confusion that had resulted from the fact that certain converted Pharisees declared that the Gentile converts must be circumcised and keep the law of Moses in order to be saved. (3SP 369.2)

The Jews were not generally prepared to move as fast as the providence of God opened the way. It was evident to them from the result of the apostles' labors among the Gentiles that the converts among the latter people would far exceed the Jewish converts; and that if the restrictions and ceremonies of the Jewish law were not made obligatory upon their accepting the faith of Christ, the national peculiarities of the Jews, which kept them distinct from all other people, would finally disappear from among those who embraced the gospel truths. (3SP 370.1)

The Jews had prided themselves upon their divinely appointed services; and they concluded that as God once specified the Hebrew manner of worship, it was impossible that he should ever authorize a change in any of its specifications. They decided that Christianity must connect itself with the Jewish laws and ceremonies. They were slow to discern to the end of that which had been abolished by the death of Christ, and to perceive that all their sacrificial offerings had but prefigured the death of the Son of God, in which type had met its antitype, rendering valueless the divinely appointed ceremonies and sacrifices of

Chapter 29 - Jew and Gentile (3SP 373.1)

the Jewish religion. (3SP 370.2)

Paul had prided himself upon his Pharisaical strictness; but after the revelation of Christ to him on the road to Damascus, the mission of the Saviour, and his own work in the conversion of the Gentiles, were plain to his mind; and he fully comprehended the difference between a living faith and a dead formalism. Paul still claimed to be one of the children of Abraham, and kept the ten commandments in letter and in spirit as faithfully as he had ever done before his conversion to Christianity. But he knew that the typical ceremonies must soon altogether cease, since that which they had shadowed forth had come to pass, and the light of the gospel was shedding its glory upon the Jewish religion, giving a new significance to its ancient rites. (3SP 370.3)

The question of circumcision was warmly discussed in the assembly. The Gentile converts lived in a community of idolaters. Sacrifices and offerings were made to senseless idols by these ignorant and superstitious people. The priests of these gods carried on an extensive merchandise with the offerings brought to them; and the Jews feared that the Gentile converts would bring Christianity into disrepute by purchasing those things which had been offered to idols, and thereby sanctioning, in some measure, an idolatrous worship. (3SP 371.1)

Also the Gentiles were accustomed to eat the flesh of animals that had been strangled; while the Jews had been divinely instructed with regard to the food they should use. They were particular, in killing beasts, that the blood should flow from the body, else it was not regarded as healthful meat. God had given these injunctions to the Jews for the purpose of preserving their health and strength. The Jews considered it sinful to use blood as an article of diet. They considered that the blood was the life; that the shedding of blood was in consequence of sin, and was a sacred emblem of the Son of God. (3SP 371.2)

The Gentiles, on the contrary, practiced catching the blood which flowed from the victim of sacrifice, and drinking it, or using it in the preparation of their food. The Jews could not change the customs which they had so long observed, and which they had adopted under the special direction of God. Therefore, as things then stood, if Jew and Gentile came to eat at the same table, the former would be shocked and outraged by the habits and manners of the latter. (3SP 371.3)

The Gentiles, and especially the Greeks, were extremely licentious; and many, in accepting Christianity, had united the truth to their unsanctified natures, and continued to practice fornication. The Jewish Christians could not tolerate such immorality, which was not even regarded as criminal by the Greeks. The Jews, therefore, held it highly proper that circumcision, and the observance of the ceremonial law, should be brought to the Gentile converts as a test of their sincerity and devotion. This they believed would prevent the accession to the church of those who were carried away by mere feeling, or who adopted the faith without a true conversion of heart, and who might afterward disgrace the cause by immorality and excesses. (3SP 372.1)

The questions thus brought under the consideration of the council seemed to present insurmountable difficulties, viewed in whatever light. But the Holy Ghost had, in reality, already settled this problem, upon the decision of which depended the prosperity, and even the existence, of the Christian church. Grace, wisdom, and sanctified judgment were given to the apostles to decide the vexed question. (3SP 372.2)

Peter reasoned that the Holy Ghost had decided the matter by descending with equal power upon the uncircumcised Gentiles and the circumcised Jews. He recounted his vision, in which God had presented before him a sheet filled with all manner of four-footed beasts, and had bidden him kill and eat; that when he had refused, affirming that he had never eaten that which was common or unclean, God had said, "What God hath cleansed, that call not thou common." (3SP 372.3)

He related the plain interpretation of these words, which was given to him almost immediately in his summons to go to the Gentile centurion, and instruct him in the faith of Christ. This message showed that God was not respecter of persons, but accepted and acknowledged those who feared him, and worked righteousness. Peter told of his astonishment, when, in speaking the words of truth to the Gentiles, he witnessed the Holy Spirit take possession of his hearers, both Jews and Gentiles. The same light and glory that was reflected upon the circumcised Jews, shone also upon the countenances of the uncircumcised Gentiles. This was the warning of God that he should not regard the one as inferior to the other; for the blood of Jesus Christ could cleanse from all uncleanness. (3SP 373.1)

Chapter 29 - Jew and Gentile (3SP 373.2)

Peter had reasoned once before, in like manner, with his brethren, concerning the conversion of Cornelius and his friends, and his fellowship with them. On that occasion he had related how the Holy Ghost fell on them, and had said, "Forasmuch then as God gave them the like gift as he did unto us, who believed on the Lord Jesus Christ, what was I that I could resist God?" Now, with equal fervor and force, he said, "God, which knoweth the hearts, bare them witness, giving them the Holy Ghost, even as he did unto us, and put no difference between us and them, purifying their hearts by faith. Now, therefore, why tempt ye God, to put a yoke upon the neck of the disciples, which neither our fathers nor we were able to bear?" (3SP 373.2)

This yoke was not the law of the ten commandments, as those who oppose the binding claim of the law assert; but Peter referred to the law of ceremonies, which was made null and void by the crucifixion of Christ. This address of Peter brought the assembly to a point where they could listen with reason to Paul and Barnabas, who related their experience in working among the Gentiles. "Then all the multitude kept silence, and gave audience to Barnabas and Paul, declaring what miracles and wonders God had wrought among the Gentiles by them." (3SP 374.1)

James bore his testimony with decision–that God designed to bring in the Gentiles to enjoy all the privileges of the Jews. The Holy Ghost saw good not to impose the ceremonial law on the Gentile converts; and the apostles and elders, after careful investigation of the subject, saw the matter in the same light, and their mind was as the mind of the Spirit of God. James presided at the council, and his final decision was, "Wherefore my sentence is that we trouble not them which from among the Gentiles are turned to God." (3SP 374.2)

This ended the discussion. In this instance we have a refutation of the doctrine held by the Roman Catholic Church–that Peter was the head of the church. Those who, as popes, have claimed to be his successors, have no foundation for their pretensions. Nothing in the life of Peter gives sanction to those pretended claims. If the professed successors of Peter had imitated his example, they would have taken no authoritative position, but one on an equality with that of their brethren. (3SP 374.3)

James, in this instance, seems to have been chosen to decide the matter which was brought before the council. It was his sentence that the ceremonial law, and especially the ordinance of circumcision, be not in any wise urged upon the Gentiles, or even recommended to them. James sought to impress the fact upon his brethren that the Gentiles, in turning to God from idolatry, made a great change in their faith; and that much caution should be used not to trouble their minds with perplexing and doubtful questions, lest they be discouraged in following Christ. (3SP 375.1)

The Gentiles, however, were to take no course which should materially conflict with the views of their Jewish brethren, or which would create prejudice in their minds against them. The apostles and elders therefore agreed to instruct the Gentiles by letter to abstain from meats offered to idols, from fornication, from things strangled, and from blood. They were required to keep the commandments, and to lead holy lives. The Gentiles were assured that the men who had urged circumcision upon them were not authorized to do so by the apostles. (3SP 375.2)

Paul and Barnabas were recommended to them as men who had hazarded their lives for the Lord. Judas and Silas were sent with these apostles to declare to the Gentiles, by word of mouth, the decision of the council: "For it seemed good to the Holy Ghost, and to us, to lay upon you no greater burdens than these necessary things: that ye abstain from meats offered to idols, and from blood, and from things strangled, and from fornication, from which if ye keep yourselves, ye shall do well." The four servants of God were sent to Antioch with the epistle and message, which put an end to all controversy; for it was the voice of the highest authority upon earth. (3SP 375.3)

The council which decided this case was composed of the founders of the Jewish and Gentile Christian churches. Elders from Jerusalem, and deputies from Antioch, were present; and the most influential churches were represented. The council did not claim infallibility in their deliberations, but moved from the dictates of enlightened judgment, and with the dignity of a church established by the divine will. They saw that God himself had decided this question by favoring the Gentiles with the Holy Ghost; and it was left for them to follow the guidance of the Spirit. (3SP 376.1)

The entire body of Christians were not called to vote upon the question. The apostles and elders–men of influence and judgment–framed and issued the decree, which was thereupon generally accepted by the Christian churches. All were not pleased, however, with this decision; there was a faction of false brethren who assumed to engage in a work on their own responsibility. They indulged in murmuring and fault-finding, proposing new plans, and seeking to pull down the work of the experienced men whom God had ordained to teach the doctrine of Christ. The church has had such obstacles to meet from the first, and will ever have them to the close of time. (3SP 376.2)

Jerusalem was the metropolis of the Jews, and there were found the greatest exclusiveness and bigotry. The Jewish Christians who lived in sight of the temple would naturally allow their minds to revert to the peculiar privileges of the Jews as a nation. As they saw Christianity departing from the ceremonies and traditions of Judaism, and perceived that the peculiar sacredness with which the Jewish customs had been invested would soon be lost sight of in the light of the new faith, many grew indignant against Paul, as one who had, in a great measure, caused this change. Even the disciples were not all prepared to willingly accept the decision of the council. Some were zealous for the ceremonial law, and regarded Paul with jealousy, because they thought his principles were lax in regard to the obligation of the Jewish law. (3SP 376.3)

When Peter, at a later date, visited Antioch, he acted in accordance with the light given him from Heaven, and the decision of the council. He overcame his natural prejudice so far as to sit at table with the Gentile converts. But when certain Jews who were most zealous for the ceremonial law came from Jerusalem, he changed his deportment toward the converts from paganism in so marked a degree that it left a most painful impression upon their minds. Quite a number followed Peter's example. Even Barnabas was influenced by the injudicious course of the apostle; and a division was threatened in the church. But Paul, who saw the wrong done the church through the double part acted by Peter, openly rebuked him for thus disguising his true sentiments. (3SP 377.1)

Peter saw the error into which he had fallen, and immediately set about repairing it as far as possible. God, who knoweth the end from the beginning, permitted Peter to exhibit this weakness of character, in order that he might see that there was nothing in himself whereof he might boast. God also saw that, in time to come, some would be so deluded as to claim for Peter and his pretended successors, exalted prerogatives which belong only to God; and this history of the apostle's weakness was to remain as a proof of his human fallibility, and of the fact that he stood in no way above the level of the other apostles. (3SP 377.2)

*****

Chapter 30
Imprisonment of Paul and Silas

After a time Paul again visited Lystra, where he had been greeted as a God by the heathen; where the opposing Jews had followed on his track, and by falsehood and misrepresentation had turned the reverence of the people into insult, abuse, and a determination to kill him. Yet we find him again on the scene of his former danger, looking after the fruit of his labors there. (3SP 378.1)

He found that the converts to Christ had not been intimidated by the violent persecution of the apostles; but, on the contrary, were confirmed in the faith, believing that through trial and suffering, the kingdom of Christ would be reached. (3SP 378.2)

Paul found that Timothy was closely bound to him by the ties of Christian union. This man had been instructed in the Holy Scriptures from his childhood, and educated for a strictly religious life. He had witnessed the sufferings of Paul upon his former visit to Lystra, and the bonds of Christian sympathy had knit his heart firmly to that of the apostle. Paul accordingly thought best to take Timothy with him to assist in his labors. (3SP 378.3)

The extreme caution of Paul is manifested in this act. He had refused the companionship of Mark, because he dared not trust him in an emergency. But in Timothy he saw one who fully appreciated the ministerial work, who respected his position, and was not appalled at the prospect of suffering and persecution. Yet he did not venture to accept Timothy, an untried youth, without diligent inquiry with regard to his life and character. After fully satisfying himself on those points, Paul received Timothy as his fellow-laborer and son in the gospel. (3SP 379.1)

Paul, with his usual good judgment, caused Timothy to be circumcised; not that God required it, but in order to remove from the minds of the Jews an obstacle to Timothy's ministration. Paul was to labor from place to place in the synagogues, and there to preach Christ. If his companion should be known as an uncircumcised heathen, the work of both would be greatly hindered by the prejudice and bigotry of the people. The apostle everywhere met a storm of persecution. He desired to bring the Jews to Christianity, and sought, as far as was consistent with the faith, to remove every pretext for opposition. Yet while he conceded this much to Jewish prejudice, his faith and teachings declared that circumcision or uncircumcision was nothing, but the gospel of Christ was everything. (3SP 379.2)

At Philippi, Lydia, of the city of Thyatira, heard the apostles, and her heart was open to receive the truth. She and her household were converted and baptized, and she entreated the apostles to make her house their home. (3SP 379.3)

Day after day, as they went to their devotions, a woman with the spirit of divination followed them, crying, "These men are the servants of the most high God, which show unto us the way of salvation." This woman was a special agent of Satan; and, as the devils were troubled by the presence of Christ, so the evil spirit which possessed her was ill at ease in the presence of the apostles. Satan knew that his kingdom was invaded, and took this way of opposing the work of the ministers of God. The words of recommendation uttered by this woman were an injury to the cause, distracting the minds of the people from the truths presented to them, and throwing disrepute upon the work by causing people to believe that the men who spoke with the Spirit and power of God were actuated by the same spirit as this emissary of Satan. (3SP 379.4)

The apostles endured this opposition for several days; then Paul, under inspiration of the Spirit of God, commanded the evil spirit to leave the woman. Satan was thus met and rebuked. The immediate and continued silence of the woman testified that the apostles were the servants of God, and that the demon had acknowledged them to be such, and had obeyed their command. When the woman was dispossessed of the spirit of the devil, and restored to herself, her masters were alarmed for their craft. They saw that all hope of receiving money from her divinations and soothsayings was at an end, and perceived that, if the apostles were allowed to continue their work, their own source of income would soon be entirely cut off. (3SP 380.1)

A mighty cry was therefore raised against the servants of God, for many were interested in gaining money by Satanic delusions. They brought the apostles before the magistrates with the charge that "these men, being Jews, do exceedingly trouble our city, and teach customs which are not lawful for us to receive, being Romans." (3SP 380.2)

Satan stirred up a frenzy among the people. Mob spirit prevailed, and was sanctioned by the authorities, who, with their official hands, tore the clothes from the apostles, and commanded them to be scourged. "And when they had laid many stripes upon them, they cast them into prison, charging the jailer to keep them safely; who, having received such a charge, thrust them into the inner prison, and made their feet fast in the stocks." (3SP 381.1)

The apostles were left in a very painful condition. Their lacerated and bleeding backs were in contact with the rough stone floor, while their feet were elevated and bound fast in the stocks. In this unnatural position they suffered extreme torture; yet they did not groan nor complain, but conversed with and encouraged each other, and praised God with grateful hearts that they were found worthy to suffer shame for his dear name. Paul was reminded of the persecution he had been instrumental in heaping upon the disciples of Christ, and he was devoutly thankful that his eyes had been opened to see, and his heart to feel, the glorious truths of the gospel of the Son of God, and that he had been privileged to preach the doctrine which he had once despised. (3SP 381.2)

There, in the pitchy darkness and desolation of the dungeon, Paul and Silas prayed, and sung songs of praise to God. The other prisoners heard with astonishment the voice of prayer and praise issuing from the inner prison. They had been accustomed to hear shrieks and moans, cursing and swearing, breaking at night upon the silence of the prison; but they had never before heard the words of prayer and praise ascending from that gloomy cell. The guards and prisoners marveled who were these men, who, cold, hungry, and tortured, could still rejoice and converse cheerfully with each other. (3SP 381.3)

Meanwhile the magistrates had returned to their homes congratulating themselves upon having quelled a tumult, by their prompt and decisive measures. But upon their way home they heard more fully concerning the character and work of the men whom they had sentenced to scourging and imprisonment. They also saw the woman who had been freed from Satanic influence, and who had been a very troublesome subject to them. They were sensibly struck by the change in her countenance and demeanor. She had become quiet, peaceful, and possessed of her right mind. They were indignant with themselves when they discovered that, in all probability, they had visited upon two innocent men the rigorous penalty of the Roman law against the worst criminals. They decided that in the morning they would command them to be privately released, and escorted in safety from the city beyond the danger of violence from the mob. (3SP 382.1)

But while men were cruel and vindictive, or criminally negligent of the solemn responsibilities devolving upon them, God had not forgotten to be gracious to his suffering servants. An angel was sent from Heaven to release the apostles. As he neared the Roman prison, the earth trembled beneath his feet, the whole city was shaken by the earthquake, and the prison walls reeled like a reed in the wind. The heavily bolted doors flew open; the chains and fetters fell from the hands and feet of every prisoner. (3SP 382.2)

The keeper of the jail had heard with amazement the prayers and singing of the imprisoned apostles. When they were led in, he had seen their swollen and bleeding wounds, and he had himself caused their feet to be fastened in the instruments of torture. He had expected to hear bitter wailing, groans, and imprecations; but lo! his ears were greeted with joyful praise. He fell asleep with these sounds in his ears; but was awakened by the earthquake, and the shaking of the prison walls. (3SP 383.1)

Upon awakening he saw all the prison doors open, and his first thought was that the prisoners had escaped. He remembered with what an explicit charge the prisoners of the night before had been intrusted to his care, and he felt sure that death would be the penalty of his apparent unfaithfulness. He cried out in the bitterness of his spirit that it was better for him to die by his

Chapter 30 - Imprisonment of Paul and Silas (3SP 383.2)

own hand than to submit to a disgraceful execution. He was about to kill himself, when Paul cried out with a loud voice, "Do thyself no harm; for we are all here." (3SP 383.2)

The severity with which the jailer had treated the apostles had not roused their resentment, or they would have allowed him to commit suicide. But their hearts were filled with the love of Christ, and they held no malice against their persecutors. The jailer dropped his sword, and called for a light. He hastened into the inner dungeon, and fell down before Paul and Silas, begging their forgiveness. He then brought them up into the open court, and inquired of them, "Sirs, what must I do to be saved?" (3SP 383.3)

He had trembled because of the wrath of God expressed in the earthquake; he had been ready to die by his own hand for fear of the penalty of the Roman law, when he thought the prisoners had escaped; but now all these things were of little consequence to him compared with the new and strange dread that agitated his mind, and his desire to possess that tranquility and cheerfulness manifested by the apostles under their extreme suffering and abuse. He saw the light of Heaven mirrored in their countenances; he knew that God had interposed in a miraculous manner to save their lives; and the words of the woman possessed by the power of divination came to his mind with peculiar force: "These men are the servants of the most high God, which show unto us the way of salvation." (3SP 384.1)

He saw his own deplorable condition in contrast with that of the disciples, and with deep humility and reverence asked them to show him the way of life. "And they said, Believe on the Lord Jesus Christ, and thou shalt be saved, and thy house. And they spake unto him the word of the Lord, and to all that were in his house." The jailer then washed the wounds of the apostles, and ministered unto them; and was baptized by them. A sanctifying influence spread among the inmates of the prison, and the hearts of all were opened to receive the truths uttered by the apostles. They were convinced also that the living God, whom these men served, had miraculously released them from bondage. (3SP 384.2)

The citizens had been greatly terrified by the earthquake. When the officers informed the magistrates in the morning of what had occurred at the prison, they were alarmed, and sent the sergeants to liberate the apostles from prison.

"But Paul said unto them, They have beaten us openly, uncondemned, being Romans, and have cast us into prison; and now do they thrust us out privily? nay, verily; but let them come themselves and fetch us out." (3SP 384.3)

Paul and Silas felt that to maintain the dignity of Christ's church, they must not submit to the illegal course proposed by the Roman magistrates. The apostles were Roman citizens, and it was unlawful to scourge a Roman, save for the most flagrant crime, or to deprive him of his liberty without a fair trial and condemnation. They had been publicly thrust into prison, and now refused to be privately released, without proper acknowledgments on the part of the magistrates. (3SP 385.1)

When this word was brought to the authorities they were alarmed for fear the apostles would make complaint of their unlawful treatment to the emperor, and cause the magistrates to lose their positions. They accordingly visited the prison, apologized to the apostles for their injustice and cruelty, and themselves conducted them out of the prison, and entreated them to depart out of the city. Thus the Lord wrought for his servants in their extremity. (3SP 385.2)

The magistrates entreated them to depart, because they feared their influence over the people, and the power of Heaven that had interposed in behalf of those innocent men who had been unlawfully scourged and imprisoned. Acting upon the principles given them by Christ, the apostles would not urge their presence where it was not desired. They complied with the request of the magistrates, but did not hasten their departure precipitously. They went rejoicing from the prison to the house of Lydia, where they met the new converts to the faith of Christ, and related all the wonderful dealings of God with them. They related their night's experience, and the conversion of the keeper of the prison, and of the prisoners. (3SP 385.3)

The apostles viewed their labors in Philippi as not in vain. They there met much opposition and persecution; but the intervention of Providence in their behalf, and the conversion of the jailer and all his house, more than atoned for the disgrace and suffering they had endured. The Philippians saw represented in the deportment and presence of mind of the apostles the spirit of the religion of Jesus Christ. The apostles might have fled when the earthquake opened their prison doors, and loosened their fetters; but that would have been an acknowledgment that they were criminals, which would have been a disgrace to the gospel of Christ; the jailer would have been exposed to the penalty of death, and the general influence would have been bad. As it was, Paul controlled the liberated prisoners so perfectly that not one attempted to escape. (3SP 386.1)

The Philippians could but acknowledge the nobility and generosity of the apostles in their course of action, especially in forbearing to appeal to a higher power against the magistrates who had persecuted them. The news of their unjust imprisonment, and miraculous deliverance, was noised about through all that region, and brought the apostles and their ministry before the notice of a large number who would not otherwise have been reached. Christianity was placed upon a high plane, and the converts to the faith were greatly strengthened. (3SP 386.2)

Thus we have the establishment of the church at Philippi under peculiar circumstances, and its numbers steadily increased. Among them were men of wealth and influence, whose noble generosity and ready sympathy were ever on the side of right. They often came to the aid of the apostles in their affliction and pecuniary necessity. Paul said of these brethren, "Now ye Philippians, know also that in the beginning of the gospel, when I departed from Macedonia, no church communicated with me as concerning giving and receiving, but ye only. For even in Thessalonica ye sent once and again unto my necessity." (3SP 387.1)

He sends also salutations from the brethren to Caesar's household; for officers in the employment of the emperor had been converted under the labors of the apostles, and through the wonderful manifestation of God in their deliverance from prison. (3SP 387.2)

*****

Chapter 31
Opposition at Thessalonica

After leaving Philippi, Paul and Silas made their way to Thessalonica. They were there privileged to address a large concourse of people in the synagogue, with good effect. Their appearance bore evidence of their recent shameful treatment, and necessitated an explanation of what they had endured. This they made without exalting themselves, but magnified the grace of God, which had wrought their deliverance. The apostles, however, felt that they had no time to dwell upon their own afflictions. They were burdened with the message of Christ, and deeply in earnest in his work. (3SP 387.3)

Paul made the prophecies in the Old Testament relating to the Messiah, and the agreement of those prophecies with the life and teachings of Christ, clear in the minds of all among his hearers who would accept evidence upon the subject. Christ in his ministry had opened the minds of his disciples to the Old-Testament scriptures; "beginning with Moses and the prophets, he expounded unto them, in all the Scriptures, the things concerning himself." Peter, in preaching Christ, produced his evidence from the Old-Testament scriptures, beginning with Moses and the prophets. Stephen pursued the same course, and Paul followed these examples, giving inspired proof in regard to the mission, suffering, death, resurrection, and ascension of Christ. He clearly proved his identity with the Messiah, through the testimony of Moses and the prophets; and showed that it was the voice of Christ which spoke through the prophets and patriarchs from the days of Adam to that time. (3SP 388.1)

He showed how impossible it was for them to explain the passover without Christ, as revealed in the Old Testament; and that the brazen serpent lifted up in the wilderness symbolized Jesus Christ, who was lifted up upon the cross. He taught them that all their religious services and ceremonies would have been valueless if they should now reject the Saviour, who was revealed to them, and who was represented in those ceremonies. He showed them that Christ was the key which unlocked the Old Testament, and gave access to its rich treasures. (3SP 388.2)

Thus Paul preached to the Thessalonians three successive Sabbaths, reasoning with them from the Scriptures, upon the life, death, and resurrection of Christ. He showed them that the expectation of the Jews with regard to the Messiah was not according to prophecy, which had foretold a Saviour to come in humility and poverty, to be rejected, despised, and slain. (3SP 389.1)

He declared that Christ would come a second time in power and great glory, and establish his kingdom upon the earth, subduing all authority, and ruling over all nations. Paul was an Adventist; he presented the important event of the second coming of Christ with such power and reasoning that a deep impression, which never wore away, was made upon the minds of the Thessalonians. (3SP 389.2)

They had strong faith in the second coming of Christ, and greatly feared that they might not live to witness the event. Paul, however, did not leave them with the impression that Christ would come in their day. He referred them to coming events which must transpire before that time should arrive. He warned them that they should "be not shaken in mind, or be troubled, neither by spirit, nor by word, nor by letter as from us, as that the day of Christ is at hand. Let no man deceive you by any means; for that day shall not come, except there come a falling away first, and that man of sin be revealed, the son of perdition." (3SP 389.3)

Paul foresaw that there was danger of his words being misinterpreted, and that some would claim that he, by special revelation, warned the people of the immediate coming of Christ. This he knew would cause confusion of faith; for disappointment usually brings unbelief. He therefore cautioned the brethren to receive no such message as coming from him. (3SP 389.4)

In his Epistle to the Thessalonians, Paul

Chapter 31 - Opposition at Thessalonica (3SP 392.2)

reminds them of his manner of laboring among them. *1 Thessalonians 2:1-4.* He declares that he did not seek to win souls through flattery, deception, or guile. "But as we were allowed of God to be put in trust with the gospel, even so we speak; not as pleasing men, but God, which trieth our hearts." Paul rebuked and warned his converts with the faithfulness of a father to his children, while, at the same time, he cherished them as tenderly as a fond mother would her child. (3SP 390.1)

When the Jews saw that the apostles were successful in obtaining large congregations; that many were accepting their doctrines–among them the leading women of the city, and multitudes of Gentiles–they were filled with envy and jealousy. These Jews were not then in favor with the Roman power, because they had raised an insurrection in the metropolis not long previous to this time. They were regarded with suspicion, and their liberty was, in a measure, restricted. They now saw an opportunity to take advantage of circumstances to re-establish themselves in favor, and, at the same time, to throw reproach upon the apostles, and the converts to Christianity. (3SP 390.2)

This they set about doing by representing that the leaders in the new doctrine were raising a tumult among the people. They accordingly excited the passions of the worthless mob by cunningly devised falsehoods, and incited them to make an uproarious assault upon the house of Jason, the temporary home of the apostles. This they did with a fury more like that of wild beasts than of men. They had been instructed by the Jews to bring out Paul and Silas, and drag them to the authorities, accusing them of creating all this uproar, and of raising an insurrection. (3SP 390.3)

When they had broken into the house, however, they found that the apostles were not there. Friends who had apprehended what was about to occur, had hastened them out of the city, and they had departed for Berea. In their mad disappointment at not finding Paul and Silas, the mob seized Jason and his brother, and dragged them before the authorities with the complaint: "These that have turned the world upside down are come hither also; whom Jason hath received; and these all do contrary to the decrees of Caesar, saying that there is another king, one Jesus." (3SP 391.1)

The Jews interpreted the words of Paul to mean that Christ would come the second time in that generation, and reign upon the earth as king over all nations. The charge was brought against the apostles with so much determination that the magistrates credited it, and put Jason under bonds to keep the peace, as Paul and Silas were not to be found. The persecuting Jews flattered themselves that by their course toward the Christians they had regained the confidence of the magistrates, and had established their reputation as loyal citizens, while they had, at the same time, gratified their malice toward the apostles, and transferred the suspicion which had heretofore rested upon themselves to the converts to Christianity. (3SP 391.2)

In his first Epistle to the Thessalonians, Paul says, "For our gospel came not unto you in word only, but also in power, and in the Holy Ghost, and in much assurance; as ye know what manner of men we were among you for your sake. And ye became followers of us, and of the Lord, having received the word in much affliction, with joy of the Holy Ghost; so that ye were ensamples to all that believe in Macedonia and Achaia." (3SP 391.3)

Those who preach unpopular truth in our day meet with determined resistance, as did the apostles. They need expect no more favorable reception from a large majority of professed Christians than did Paul from his Jewish brethren. There will be a union of opposing elements against them; for however diverse from each other different organizations may be in their sentiments and religious faith, their forces are united in trampling under foot the fourth commandment in the law of God. (3SP 392.1)

Those who will not themselves accept the truth are most zealous that others shall not receive it; and those are not wanting who perseveringly manufacture falsehoods, and stir up the base passions of the people to make the truth of God of none effect. But the messengers of Christ must arm themselves with watchfulness and prayer, and move forward with faith, firmness, and courage, and, in the name of Jesus, keep at their work as did the apostles. They must sound the note of warning to the world, teaching the transgressors of the law what is sin, and pointing them to Jesus Christ as its great and only remedy. (3SP 392.2)

Chapter 32
Paul at Berea and Athens

At Berea Paul again commenced his work by going into the synagogue of the Jews to preach the gospel of Christ. He says of them, "These were more noble than those in Thessalonica, in that they received the word with all readiness of mind, and searched the Scriptures daily, whether those things were so. Therefore many of them believed; also of honorable women which were Greeks, and of men, not a few." (3SP 393.1)

In the presentation of the truth, those who honestly desire to be right will be awakened to a diligent searching of the Scriptures. This will produce results similar to those that attended the labors of the apostles in Berea. But those who preach the truth in these days meet many who are the opposite of the Bereans. They cannot controvert the doctrine presented to them, yet they manifest the utmost reluctance to investigate the evidence offered in its favor, and assume that even if it is the truth it is a matter of little consequence whether or not they accept it as such. They think that their old faith and customs are good enough for them. But the Lord, who sent out his ambassadors with a message to the world, will hold the people responsible for the manner in which they treat the words of his servants. God will judge all according to the light which has been presented to them, whether it is plain to them or not. It is their duty to investigate as did the Bereans. The Lord says through the prophet Hosea: "My people are destroyed for lack of knowledge; because thou hast rejected knowledge, I will also reject thee." (3SP 393.2)

The minds of the Bereans were not narrowed by prejudice, and they were willing to investigate and receive the truths preached by the apostles. If the people of our time would follow the example of the noble Bereans, in searching the Scriptures daily, and in comparing the messages brought to them with what is there recorded, there would be thousands loyal to God's law where there is one today. But many who profess to love God have no desire to change from error to truth, and they cling to the pleasing fables of the last days. Error blinds the mind and leads from God; but truth gives light to the mind, and life to the soul. (3SP 394.1)

The unbelieving Jews of Thessalonica, filled with jealousy and hatred of the apostles, and not content with having driven them from their labors among the Thessalonians, followed them to Berea, and again stirred up the excitable passions of the lower class to do them violence. The teachers of the truth were again driven from their field of labor. Persecution followed them from city to city. This hasty retreat from Berea deprived Paul of the opportunity he had anticipated of again visiting the brethren at Thessalonica. (3SP 394.2)

Although the opposers of the doctrine of Christ could not hinder its actual advancement, they still succeeded in making the work of the apostles exceedingly hard. God, in his providence, permitted Satan to hinder Paul from returning to the Thessalonians. Yet the faithful apostle steadily pressed on through opposition, conflict, and persecution, to carry out the purpose of God as revealed to him in the vision at Jerusalem: "I will send thee far hence unto the Gentiles." (3SP 394.3)

From Berea Paul went to Athens. He was accompanied on his journey by some of the Bereans who had been newly brought into the faith, and who were desirous of learning more from him of the way of life. When the apostle arrived at Athens, he sent these men back with a message to Silas and Timothy to join him immediately in that city. Timothy had come to Berea previously to Paul's departure, and with Silas had remained to carry on the work so well begun there, and to instruct the new converts in the principles of their holy faith. (3SP 395.1)

The city of Athens was the metropolis of heathendom. Paul did not here meet with an ignorant, credulous populace, as at Lystra; but he encountered a people famous for their intelligence and education. Statues of their gods and the deified heroes of history and poetry met the eye in every direction; while magnificent architecture and paintings also represented the national glory and the popular worship of heathen deities. (3SP 395.2)

The senses of the people were entranced by the beauty and glory of art. Sanctuaries and temples, involving untold expense, reared their lofty forms on every hand. Victories of arms, and deeds of celebrated men, were commemorated by sculptures, shrines, and tablets. All these things made this renowned city like a vast gallery of art. And as Paul looked upon the beauty and grandeur surrounding him, and saw the city crowded with idols, his spirit was stirred with jealousy for God, whom he saw dishonored on every side. (3SP 395.3)

His heart was drawn out in deep pity for the citizens of that grand metropolis, who, notwithstanding their intellectual greatness, were given to idolatry. Paul was not deceived by the grandeur and beauty of that which his eyes rested upon, nor by the material wisdom and philosophy which encountered him in this great center of learning. He perceived that human art had done its best to deify vice and make falsehood attractive by glorifying the memory of those whose whole lives had been devoted to leading men to deny God. (3SP 395.4)

The moral nature of the apostle was so alive to the attraction of heavenly things, that the joy and splendor of those riches that will never fade occupied his mind, and made valueless the earthly pomp and glory with which he was surrounded. As he saw the magnificence of the city, with its costly devices, he realized its seductive power over the minds of the lovers of art and science. His mind was deeply impressed with the importance of the work before him in Athens. His solitude in that great city where God was not worshiped was oppressive; and he longed for the sympathy and aid of his fellow-laborers. As far as human fellowship was concerned, he felt himself to be utterly isolated. In his Epistle to the Thessalonians he expresses his feelings in these words: "Left at Athens alone." (3SP 396.1)

Paul's work was to bear the tidings of salvation to a people who had no intelligent understanding of God and his plans. He was not traveling for the purpose of sight-seeing, nor to gratify a morbid desire for new and strange scenes. His dejection of mind was caused by the apparently insurmountable obstacles which presented themselves against his reaching the minds of the people of Athens. Grieved at the idolatry everywhere visible about him, he felt a holy zeal for his Master's cause. He sought out his Jewish brethren, and, in their synagogue at Athens, proclaimed the doctrine of Christ. But the principal work of Paul in that city was to deal with paganism. (3SP 396.2)

The religion of the Athenians, of which they made great boast, was of no value, for it was destitute of the knowledge of the true God. It consisted, in great part, of art worship, and a round of dissipating amusement and festivities. It wanted the virtue of true goodness. Genuine religion gives men the victory over themselves; but a religion of mere intellect and taste is wanting in the qualities essential to raise its possessor above the evils of his nature, and to connect him with God. On the very stones of the altar in Athens this great want was expressed by the inscription, "To the Unknown God." Yes; though boasting of their wisdom, wealth, and skill in art and science, the learned Athenians could but acknowledge that the great Ruler of the universe was unknown to them. (3SP 397.1)

The great men of the city seemed hungering for subjects of discussion, in which they would have opportunity to display their wisdom and oratory. While waiting for Silas and Timothy to meet him, Paul was not idle. "He disputed in the synagogue with the Jews, and with the devout persons, and in the market daily with them that met with him." The great men of Athens were not long in finding out this singular teacher, who presented to the people doctrines so new and strange. (3SP 397.2)

Some who prided themselves upon the extent of their intellectual culture entered into conversation with him. This soon drew a crowd of listeners about them. Some were prepared to ridicule the apostle as one far beneath them, socially and intellectually, and said jeeringly among themselves, "What will this babbler say？" Other some, He seemeth to be a setter forth of strange gods; because he preached unto them Jesus and the resurrection." (3SP 397.3)

The Stoics and the Epicureans encountered him; but they, and all others who came in contact with him, soon saw that he had a store of knowledge even greater than their own. His intellectual power commanded the respect and attention of the more intellectual and learned; while his earnest, logical reasoning, and his power of oratory, held the promiscuous audience. Thus the apostle stood undaunted, meeting his opposers on their own ground, matching logic with logic, and philosophy with

Chapter 32 - Paul at Berea and Athens (3SP 398.1)

philosophy. (3SP 398.1)

They reminded him of Socrates, a great philosopher, who was condemned to death because he was a setter forth of strange gods. Paul was counseled not to endanger his life in the same way. But the apostle's discourse riveted the attention of the people; and his unaffected wisdom commanded their respect and admiration. He was not silenced by the science or irony of the philosophers; and, after exchanging many words with him, and satisfying themselves that he was determined to accomplish his errand among them, and tell his story at all hazards, they decided to give him a fair opportunity to speak to the people. (3SP 398.2)

They accordingly conducted him to Mars' Hill. This was the most sacred spot in all Athens, and its recollections and associations were such as to cause it to be regarded with superstitious awe and reverence, that with some amounted to dread. Here, the most solemn court of justice had long been held to determine upon criminal cases, and to decide difficult religious questions. The judges sat in the open air, upon seats hewn out in the rock, on a platform which was ascended by a flight of stone steps from the valley below. At a little distance was a temple of the gods; and the sanctuaries, statues, and altars of the city were in full view. (3SP 398.3)

Here, away from the noise and bustle of crowded thoroughfares, and the tumult of promiscuous discussion, the apostle could be heard without interruption; for the frivolous, thoughtless class of society did not care to follow him to this place of highest reverence. Around him here were gathered poets, artists, and philosophers,–the scholars and sages of Athens,–who thus addressed him: "May we know what this new doctrine, whereof thou speakest, is? for thou bringest certain strange things to our ears; we would know, therefore, what these things mean." (3SP 399.1)

The apostle stood calm and self-possessed in that hour of solemn responsibility, relying upon the divine assurance, designed for such a time as this, "It shall be given you what ye ought to say." His heart was burdened with his important message, and the words that fell from his lips convinced his hearers that he was no idle babbler: "Ye men of Athens, I perceive that in all things ye are too superstitious. For as I passed by and beheld your devotions, I found an altar with this inscription, To the Unknown God. Whom therefore ye ignorantly worship, him declare I unto you." With all their intelligence and general knowledge, they were ignorant of the true God. The inscription upon their altar showed the strong cravings of the soul for greater light. They were reaching out for Infinity. (3SP 399.2)

With earnest and fervid eloquence, the apostle continued: "God that made the world and all things therein, seeing that he is Lord of Heaven and earth, dwelleth not in temples made with hands; neither is worshiped with men's hands, as though he needed anything, seeing he giveth to all life, and breath, and all things; and hath made of one blood all nations of men for to dwell on all the face of the earth, and hath determined the times before appointed, and the bounds of their habitation; that they should seek the Lord, if haply they might feel after him, and find him, though he be not far from every one of us." (3SP 400.1)

Thus, in the most impressive manner, with hand outstretched toward the temple crowded with idols, Paul poured out the burden of his soul, and ably exposed the fallacies of the religion of the Athenians. The wisest of his hearers were astonished as they listened to his reasoning. His words could not be controverted. He showed himself familiar with their works of art, their literature, and their religion. Pointing to their statuary and idols, he declared to them that God could not be likened to forms of man's device. The works of art could not, in the faintest sense, represent the glory of the infinite God. He reminded them that their images had no breath nor life. They were controlled by human power; they could move only as the hands of men moved them; and those who worshiped them were in every way superior to that which they worshiped. Pointing to noble specimens of manhood about him, he declared, "Forasmuch, then, as we are the offspring of God, we ought not to think that the Godhead is like unto gold, or silver, or stone, graven by art and man's device." (3SP 400.2)

Man was created in the image of this infinite God, blessed with intellectual power and a perfect and symmetrical body. The heavens are not large enough to contain God; how much less could those temples made with hands contain him. Paul, under the inspiration of his subject, soared above the comprehension of the idolatrous assembly, and sought to draw their minds beyond the limits of their false religion to correct views of the true Deity, whom they had styled the "Unknown God." This Being, whom he now declared unto them, was independent of man, needing nothing from human hands to add to his power and glory. (3SP 400.3)

The people were carried away with admiration of Paul's eloquence. The Epicureans began to breathe more freely, believing that he was strengthening their position, that everything had its origin in blind chance; and that certain ruling principles controlled the universe. But his next sentence brought a cloud to their brows. He asserted the creative power of God, and the existence of his overruling providence. He declared unto them the true God, who is the living center of government. (3SP 401.1)

This divine Ruler had, in the dark ages of the world, passed lightly over heathen idolatry; but now he had sent them the light of truth, through his Son; and he exacted from all men repentance unto salvation; not only from the poor and humble, but from the proud philosopher, and the princes of the earth. "Because He hath appointed a day, in the which he will judge the world in righteousness by that Man whom he hath ordained; whereof he hath given assurance unto all men, in that he hath raised him from the dead." (3SP 401.2)

As Paul thus spoke of the resurrection from the dead, his speech was interrupted. Some mocked; others put his words aside, saying, "We will hear thee again of this matter." Thus closed the labors of the apostle at Athens; for the Athenians persistently clung to their idolatry, and turned away from the light of a true and reasonable religion. When a people are wholly satisfied with their own attainments, little more need be expected of them. Highly educated, and boasting of their learning and refinement, the Athenians were constantly becoming more corrupt, and having less desire for anything better than the vague mysteries of idolatry. (3SP 401.3)

Many who listened to the words of Paul were convinced of the truths presented, but they would not humble themselves to acknowledge God, and to accept the plan of salvation. No eloquence of words, no force of argument, can convert the sinner. The Spirit and power of God can alone apply the truth to the heart of the impenitent. Of the Athenians it may be said, "The preaching of the the cross is to them that perish foolishness, but to them that are saved it is the power of God." (3SP 402.1)

In their pride of intellect and human wisdom may be found the reason why the gospel message met with so little success among that people. Our Saviour rejoiced that God had hid the things of eternal interest from the wise and prudent, and had revealed them unto babes in knowledge. All worldly wise men who come to Christ as poor, lost sinners, will become wise unto salvation; but those who come as distinguished men, extolling their own wisdom, will fail to receive the light and knowledge which he alone can give. (3SP 402.2)

The labors of Paul in Athens were not wholly in vain. Dionysius, one of the most prominent citizens, and some others, became converts to Christianity, and joined themselves to him. The words of the apostle, and the description of his attitude and surroundings, as traced by the pen of inspiration, were to be handed down through all coming generations, bearing witness of his unshaken confidence, his courage in loneliness and adversity, and the victory he gained for Christianity, even in the very heart of paganism. (3SP 402.3)

Inspiration has given us this glance at the life of the Athenians, with all their knowledge, refinement, and art, yet sunken in vice, that it might be seen how God, through his servant, rebuked idolatry, and the sins of a proud, self-sufficient people. The words of Paul become a memorial of the occasion, and give a treasure of knowledge to the church. He was in a position where he might easily have spoken that which would irritate his proud listeners, and bring himself into difficulty. Had his oration been a direct attack upon their gods, and the great men of the city who were before him, he would have been in danger of meeting the fate of Socrates. But he carefully drew their minds away from heathen deities, by revealing to them the true God, whom they were endeavoring to worship, but who was to them unknown, as they themselves confessed by a public inscription. (3SP 403.1)

Chapter 33
Paul at Corinth

Paul did not wait at Athens for his brethren, Silas and Timothy, but leaving word for them to follow him, went at once to Corinth. Here he entered upon a different field of labor from that which he had left. Instead of the curious and critical disciples of schools of philosophy, he came in contact with the busy, changing population of a great center of commerce. Greeks, Jews, and Romans, with travelers from every land, mingled in its crowded streets, eagerly intent on business and pleasure, and having little thought or care beyond the affairs of the present life. (3SP 404.1)

Corinth was one of the leading cities, not only of Greece, but of the world. Situated upon a narrow neck of land between two seas, it commanded the trade of both the east and the west. Its position was almost impregnable. A vast citadel of rock, rising abruptly and perpendicularly from the plain to the height of two thousand feet above the level of the sea, was a strong natural defense to the city and its two sea-ports. Corinth was now more prosperous than Athens, which had once taken the lead. Both had experienced severe vicissitudes; but the former had risen from her ruins, and was far in advance of her former prosperity, while the latter had not reached to her past magnificence. Athens was the acknowledged center of art and learning; Corinth, the seat of government and trade. (3SP 404.2)

This large mercantile city was in direct communication with Rome, while Thessalonica, Ephesus, Alexandria, and Antioch were all easy of access, either by land or water. An opportunity was thus presented for the spread of the gospel Once established at Corinth, it would be readily communicated to all parts of the world. (3SP 404.3)

Yet the apostle saw on every hand serious obstacles to the progress of his work. The city was almost wholly given up to idolatry. Venus was the favorite goddess; and a great number or dissolute women were employed in connection with the worship of this reigning deity, for the purpose of attracting the devotees of popular vice. The Corinthians had become conspicuous, even among the heathen, for their gross immorality. (3SP 405.1)

There was now a much larger number of Jews in Corinth than at any previous time. This people had been generally favored by the ruling powers. And treated with much consideration. But for some time they had been growing arrogant and insubordinate, and after they had rejected and crucified Christ, the light of the world, they followed their own darkened understanding, manifested more openly their envy and hatred of the powers that governed them, and proudly boasted of a king of the Jews who was to come with great power, overthrow their enemies, and establish a magnificent kingdom. It was in view of this vague belief that they had rejected the Saviour. The same malignant spirit that actuated them in their persecution of the Son of God led them to rebel against the Roman government. They were continually creating seditions and insurrections, until they were finally driven from Rome because of their turbulent spirit. Many of them found refuge in Corinth. (3SP 405.2)

Among the Jews who took up their residence here were many who were innocent of the wrongs that prevailed among them as a people. Of this class were Aquila and Priscilla, who afterward became distinguished as believers in Christ. Paul, becoming acquainted with the character of these excellent persons, abode with them; and having in his youth learned their trade of making tents, which were much used in that warm climate, he worked at this business for his own support. (3SP 405.3)

The Hebrews had been instructed of God, by his servant Moses, to train up their children to industrious habits. That people were thus led to look upon indolence as a great sin, and their children were all required to learn some trade by which, if necessary, they could gain a livelihood.

Chapter 33 - Paul at Corinth (3SP 408.2)

Those who neglected to do this were regarded as departing from the instruction of the Lord. Labor was considered elevating in its nature, and the children were taught to combine religion and business. In the time of Christ, the Jews, though wealthy, still followed their ancient custom. (3SP 406.1)

Paul was highly educated, and was admired for his genius and eloquence. He was chosen by his countrymen as a member of the Sanhedrim, and was a Rabbi of distinguished ability; yet his education had not been considered complete, until he had served an apprenticeship at some useful trade. He rejoiced that he was able to support himself by manual labor, and frequently declared that his own hands had ministered to his necessities. While in a city of strangers, he would not be chargeable to any one. When his means had been expended to advance the cause of Christ, he resorted to his trade in order to gain a livelihood. (3SP 406.2)

No man ever lived who was a more earnest, energetic, and self-sacrificing disciple of Christ than was Paul. He was one of the world's greatest teachers. He crossed the seas, and traveled far and near, until a large portion of the world had learned from his lips the story of the cross of Christ. He possessed a burning desire to bring perishing men to a knowledge of the truth through a Saviour's love. His whole soul was engaged in the work of the ministry; but he seated himself to the labor of his humble trade that he might not be burdensome to the churches that were pressed with poverty. Although he had planted many churches, he refused to be supported by them, fearing that his usefulness and success as a minister of Christ might be injured by suspicions that he was preaching the gospel for gain. He would remove from his enemies all occasion to misrepresent him, and thus to detract from the force of his message. (3SP 406.3)

As a laborer in the gospel, Paul might have claimed support, instead of sustaining himself; but this right he was willing to forego. Although feeble in health, he labored during the day in serving the cause of Christ, and then toiled a large share of the night, and frequently all night, that he might make provision for his own and others' necessities. The apostle would also give an example to the Christian ministry, dignifying and honoring industry. While thus preaching and working, he presented the highest type of Christianity. He combined teaching with his labor; and while toiling with those of his trade, he instructed them concerning the way of salvation. In pursuing this course, he had access to many whom he could not otherwise have reached. (3SP 407.1)

When ministers feel that they are suffering great hardships and privations in the cause of Christ, let them in imagination visit the workshop of the apostle Paul, bearing in mind that while this chosen man of God is fashioning the canvas, he is working for bread which he has justly earned by his labors as an apostle of Christ. At the call of duty, he would meet the most violent opponents, and silence their proud boasting, and then he would resume his humble employment. His zeal and industry should be a rebuke to indolence or selfish ease in the minister of Christ. Any labor that will benefit humanity or advance the cause of God, should be regarded as honorable. (3SP 407.2)

In preaching the gospel at Corinth, the apostle adopted a different course of action from that which had marked his labors at Athens. While in the latter place, he had adapted his style to the character of his audience; and much of his time had been devoted to the discussion of natural religion, matching logic with logic, and science with science. But when he reviewed the time and labor which he had there devoted to the exposition of Christianity, and realized that his style of teaching had not been productive of much fruit, he decided upon a different plan of labor in the future. He determined to avoid elaborate arguments and discussions of theories as much as possible, and to urge upon sinners the doctrine of salvation through Christ. In his epistle to his Corinthian brethren, he afterward described his manner of laboring among them:– (3SP 408.1)

"And I, brethren, when I came to you, came not with excellency of speech or of wisdom, declaring unto you the testimony of God. For I determined not to know anything among you, save Jesus Christ, and him crucified. And I was with you in weakness, and in fear, and in much trembling. And my speech and my preaching was not with enticing words of man's wisdom, but in demonstration of the Spirit and of power; that your faith should not stand in the wisdom of men, but in the power of God." (3SP 408.2)

Here the apostle has given the most successful manner of converting souls from ignorance and the darkness of error, to the light of truth. If ministers would follow more closely

Chapter 33 - Paul at Corinth (3SP 409.1)

the example of Paul in this particular, they would see greater success attending their efforts. If all who minister in word and doctrine would make it their first business to be pure in heart and life, and to connect themselves closely with Heaven, their teaching would have greater power to convict souls. (3SP 409.1)

When Christ was upon earth, the Jews all over the land were notified to watch his movements, for their religion was not safe where his influence was felt. He was continually followed by spies, who caught up every word and act which they could use against him. Paul had to meet the same spirit of opposition and blind prejudice. He preached first in the synagogue, reasoning from Moses and the prophets, showing what sins the Lord had most severely punished in olden times, and that murmuring and rebellion was the grievous crime that had brought God's displeasure upon the people of his choice. (3SP 409.2)

He brought his hearers down through the types and shadows of the ceremonial law to Christ,-to his crucifixion, his priesthood, and the sanctuary of his ministry,-the great object that had cast its shadow backward into the Jewish age. He, as the Messiah, was the Antitype of all the sacrificial offerings. The apostle showed that according to the prophecies and the universal expectation of the Jews, the Messiah would be of the lineage of Abraham and David. He then traced his descent from the great patriarch Abraham, through the royal psalmist. He proved from Scripture what were to have been the character and works of the promised Messiah, and also his reception and treatment on earth, as testified by the holy prophets. He then showed that these predictions also had been fulfilled in the life, ministry, and death of Jesus, and hence that he was indeed the world's Redeemer. (3SP 409.3)

The most convincing proof was given that the gospel was but the development of the Hebrew faith. Christ was to come for the special benefit of the nation that was looking for his coming as the consummation and glory of the Jewish system. The apostle then endeavored to bring home to their consciences the fact that repentance for their rejection of Christ could alone save the nation from impending ruin. He rebuked their ignorance concerning the meaning of those Scriptures which it was their chief boast and glory that they fully understood. He exposed their worldliness, their love of station, titles, and display, and their inordinate selfishness. (3SP 410.1)

But the Jews of Corinth closed their eyes to all the evidence so clearly presented by the apostle, and refused to listen to his appeals. The same spirit which had led them to reject Christ, filled them with wrath and fury against Paul. They would have put an end to his life, had not God guarded his servant, that he might do his work, and bear the gospel message to the Gentiles. (3SP 410.2)

"And when they opposed themselves, and blasphemed, he shook his raiment, and said unto them, Your blood be upon your own heads; I am clean; from henceforth I will go unto the Gentiles. And he departed thence, and entered into a certain man's house, named Justus, one that worshiped God, whose house joined hard to the synagogue." Silas and Timothy had joined Paul, and together they now labored for the Gentiles. (3SP 410.3)

Paul did not bind himself nor his converts to the ceremonies and customs of the Jews, with their varied forms, types, and sacrifices; for he recognized that the perfect and final offering had been made in the death of the Son of God. The age of clearer light and knowledge had now come. And although the early education of Paul had blinded his eyes to this light, and led him to bitterly oppose the work of God, yet the revelation of Christ to him while on his way to Damascus had changed the whole current of his life. His character and works had now become a remarkable illustration of those of his divine Lord. His teaching led the mind to a more active spiritual life, that carried the believer above mere ceremonies. "For thou desirest not sacrifice, else would I give it. Thou delightest not in burnt-offering. The sacrifices of God are a broken spirit. A broken and a contrite heart, O God, thou wilt not despise." (3SP 411.1)

The apostle did not labor to charm the ear with oratory, nor to engage the mind with philosophic discussions, which would leave the heart untouched. He preached the cross of Christ, not with labored eloquence of speech, but with the grace and power of God; and his words moved the people. "And Crispus, the chief ruler of the synagogue, believed on the Lord, with all his house; and many of the Corinthians, hearing, believed and were baptized." (3SP 411.2)

The feelings of hatred with which many of the Jews had regarded the apostle were now intensified. The conversion and baptism of Crispus had the effect to exasperate instead of to convince these stubborn opposers. They could not bring arguments to show that he was not preaching the truth, and for lack of such evidence, they resorted to deception and malignant attack. (3SP 411.3)

They blasphemed the truth and the name of Jesus of Nazareth. No words were too bitter, no device too low, for them to use in their blind anger and opposition. They could not deny that Christ had worked miracles; but they declared that he had performed them through the power of Satan; and they now boldly affirmed that the wonderful works of Paul were accomplished through the same agency. (3SP 412.1)

Those who preach unpopular truth in our day are often met by the professed Christian world with opposition similar to that which was brought against the apostle by the unbelieving Jews. Many who make the most exalted profession, and who should be light-bearers to the world, are the most bitter and unreasonable in opposing the work of the chosen servants of God. Not satisfied with choosing error and fables for themselves, they wrest the Scriptures from the true meaning, in order to deceive others and hinder them from accepting the truth. (3SP 412.2)

Though Paul had a measure of success, yet he became very weary of the sight of his eyes and the hearing of his ears in the corrupt city of Corinth, He doubted the wisdom of building up a church from the material he found there. He considered Corinth a very questionable field of labor, and determined to leave it. The depravity which he witnessed among the Gentiles, and the contempt and insult which he received from the Jews, caused him great anguish of spirit. (3SP 412.3)

As he was contemplating leaving the city for a more promising field, and feeling very anxious to understand his duty in the case, the Lord appeared to him in a vision of the night, and said, "Be not afraid, but speak, and hold not thy peace; for I am with thee, and no man shall set on thee to hurt thee; for I have much people in this city." Paul understood this to be a command to remain in Corinth, and a guarantee that the Lord would give increase to the seed sown. Strengthened and encouraged, he continued to labor there with great zeal and perseverance for one year and six months. A large church was enrolled under the banner of Jesus Christ. Some came from among the most dissipated of the Gentiles; and many of this class were true converts, and became monuments of God's mercy and the efficacy of the blood of Christ to cleanse from sin. (3SP 413.1)

The increased success of Paul in presenting Christ to the people, roused the unbelieving Jews to more determined opposition. They arose in a body with great tumult, and brought him before the judgment-seat of Gallio, who was then deputy of Achaia. They expected, as on former occasions of a similar character, to have the authorities on their side; and with loud and angry voices they preferred their complaints against the apostle, saying, "This fellow persuadeth men to worship God contrary to the law." (3SP 413.2)

The proconsul, disgusted with the bigotry and self-righteousness of the accusing Jews, refused to take notice of the charge. As Paul prepared to speak in self-defense, Gallio informed him that it was not necessary. Then, turning to the angry accusers, he said, "If it were a matter of wrong or wicked lewdness, O ye Jews, reason would that I should bear with you. But if it be a question of words and names, and of your law, look ye to it; for I will be no judge of such matters. And he drove them from the judgment-seat." (3SP 413.3)

The decided course of Gallio opened the eyes of the clamorous crowd who had been abetting the Jews. For the first time during Paul's labors in Europe, the mob turned on the side of the minister of truth; and, under the very eye of the proconsul, and without interference from him, the people violently beset the most prominent accusers of the apostle. "Then all the Greeks took Sosthenes, the chief ruler of the synagogue, and beat him before the judgment-seat. And Gallio cared for none of those things." (3SP 414.1)

Gallio was a man of integrity, and would not become the dupe of the jealous and intriguing Jews. Unlike Pilate, he refused to do injustice to one whom he knew to be an innocent man. The Jewish religion was under the protection of the Roman power; and the accusers of Paul thought that if they could fasten upon him the charge of violating the laws of their religion, he would probably be given into their hands for such punishment as they saw fit to inflict. They hoped thus to compass his death. (3SP 414.2)

Both Greeks and Jews had waited eagerly

Chapter 33 - Paul at Corinth (3SP 414.3)

for the decision of Gallio; and his immediate dismissal of the case, as one that had no bearing upon the public interest, was the signal for the Jews to retire, baffled and enraged, and for the mob to assail the ruler of the synagogue. Even the ignorant rabble could but perceive the unjust and vindictive spirit which the Jews displayed in their attack upon Paul. Thus Christianity obtained a signal victory. If the apostle had been driven from Corinth at this time because of the malice of the Jews, the whole community of converts to the faith of Christ would have been placed in great danger. The Jews would have endeavored to follow up the advantage gained, as was their custom, even to the extermination of Christianity in that region. (3SP 414.3)

It is recorded that Paul labored a year and six months in Corinth. His efforts, however, were not exclusively confined to that city, but he availed himself of the easy communication by land and water with adjacent cities, and labored among them both by letter and personal effort. He made Corinth his headquarters, and his long tarry and successful ministry there gave him influence abroad as well as at home. Several churches were thus raised up under the efforts of the apostle and his co-laborers. The absence of Paul from the churches of his care was partially supplied by communications weighty and powerful, which were received generally as the word of God to them through his obedient servant. These epistles were read in the churches. (3SP 415.1)

*****

Chapter 34
Paul at Ephesus

The city of Ephesus was the capital of the province of Asia, [As used in the New Testament, the word Asia does not apply to the continent of Asia, but to a Roman province which embraced the western part of Asia Minor, and of which Ephesus was the capital.] and the great commercial center of Asia Minor. Its harbor was crowded with shipping from all parts of the known world, and its streets thronged with the people of every country. It therefore presented, like Corinth, a favorable missionary field. (3SP 415.2)

The Jews, now widely dispersed in all civilized lands, were generally expecting the speedy advent of the Messiah. In their visits to Jerusalem at the annual feasts, many had gone out to the banks of the Jordan to listen to the preaching of John the Baptist. From him they had heard the proclamation of Christ as the Promised One, and on their return home they had carried the tidings to all parts of the world. Thus had Providence prepared the way for the apostle's labors. (3SP 416.1)

On his arrival at Ephesus, Paul found twelve brethren, who, like Apollos, had been disciples of John the Baptist, and like him had gained an imperfect knowledge of the life and mission of Christ. They had not the ability of Apollos, but with the same sincerity and faith they were seeking to spread the light which they had received. (3SP 416.2)

These disciples were ignorant of the mission of the Holy Spirit, that Jesus promised to his believing people, to be the life and power of the church. When asked by Paul if they had received the Holy Ghost, they answered, "We have not so much as heard whether there be any Holy Ghost." Paul inquired, "Unto what then were ye baptized?" and they said, "Unto John's baptism." The apostle then proceeded to set before them the great truths which are the foundation of the Christian's hope. (3SP 416.3)

He told them of the life of Christ on earth, and of his cruel and shameful death. He told them how the Lord of life had broken the barriers of the tomb, and risen triumphant over death. He repeated the Saviour's commission to his disciples: "All power is given unto me in Heaven and in earth. Go ye, therefore, and teach all nations, baptizing them in the name of the Father, and of the Son, and of the Holy Ghost." He told them also of Christ's promise to send the Comforter, through whose power mighty signs and wonders would be wrought, and described the glorious fulfillment of that promise on the day of Pentecost. (3SP 416.4)

With deep interest, and grateful, wondering joy, the disciples listened to the words of Paul. By faith they grasped the atoning sacrifice of Christ, and acknowledged him as their Redeemer. They were then baptized "in the name of Jesus;" and as Paul laid his hands upon them, they received also the baptism of the Holy Spirit, by which they were enabled to speak the languages of other nations and to prophesy. Thus these men were qualified to act as missionaries in the important field of Ephesus and its vicinity, and also from this center to spread the gospel of Christ in Asia Minor. (3SP 417.1)

It was by cherishing a humble and teachable spirit that these brethren gained their precious experience. Their example presents a lesson of great value to Christians of every age. There are many who make but little progress in the divine life, because they are too self-sufficient to occupy the position of learners. They are content to remain in ignorance of God's word; they do not wish to change their faith or their practice, and hence make no effort to obtain greater light. (3SP 417.2)

If the followers of Christ were but earnest seekers after divine wisdom, they would be led into rich fields of truth, as yet wholly unknown to them. Whoever will give himself to God as fully as did Moses, will be guided by the divine hand as verily as was the great leader of Israel. He may be lowly and apparently ungifted; yet if with a loving, trusting heart he obeys every intimation

Chapter 34 - Paul at Ephesus (3SP 417.3)

of God's will, his powers will be purified, ennobled, energized; his capabilities increased. As he treasures the lessons of divine wisdom, a sacred commission is intrusted to him; he is enabled to make his life an honor to God and a blessing to the world. "The entrance of Thy words giveth light; it giveth understanding unto the simple." (3SP 417.3)

A mere intellectual knowledge of religious truth is not enough. There are today many as ignorant as those men of Ephesus of the Holy Spirit's work upon the heart. Yet no truth is more clearly taught in the word of God. Prophets and apostles have dwelt upon this theme. Christ himself calls our attention to the growth of the vegetable world to illustrate the agency of his Spirit in sustaining religious life. (3SP 418.1)

The juices of the vine, ascending from the root, are diffused to the branches sustaining growth, and producing blossoms and fruit. So the life-giving power of the Holy Spirit, proceeding from Christ, and imparted to every disciple, pervades the soul, renews the motives and affections, and even the most secret thoughts, and brings forth the precious fruit of holy deeds. The life attests the union with the true and living Vine. (3SP 418.2)

The Author of this spiritual life is unseen, and the precise method by which it is imparted and sustained is beyond the power of human philosophy to explain. It is the mystery of godliness. Yet the operations of the Spirit are always in harmony with the written word. As in the natural, so in the spiritual world. Human life is preserved, moment by moment, by divine power; yet it is not sustained by a direct miracle, but through the use of blessings placed within our reach. So the life of the Christian is sustained by the use of those means which Providence has supplied. He must eat of the bread of life, and drink of the waters of salvation. He must watch, he must pray, he must work, in all things giving heed to the instructions of the word of God, if he would "grow up to the full measure of the stature of a man in Christ Jesus." (3SP 418.3)

There is still another lesson for us in the experience of those Jewish converts. When they received baptism at the hand of John, they were holding serious errors. But with clearer light they gladly accepted Christ as their Redeemer; and with this advance step came a change in their obligations. As they received a purer faith, there was a corresponding change in their life and character. In token of this change, and as an acknowledgment of their faith in Christ, they were rebaptized, in the name of Jesus. (3SP 419.1)

Many a sincere follower of Christ has had a similar experience. A clearer understanding of God's will, places man in a new relation to him. New duties are revealed. Much which before appeared innocent, or even praiseworthy, is now seen to be sinful. The apostle Paul states that though he had, as he supposed, rendered obedience to the law of God, yet when the commandment was urged upon his conscience by the Holy Spirit, "sin revived, and I died." He saw himself a sinner, and conscience concurred with the sentence of the law. (3SP 419.2)

There are many at the present day who have unwittingly violated one of the precepts of God's law. When the understanding is enlightened, and the claims of the fourth commandment are urged upon the conscience, they see themselves sinners in the sight of God. "Sin is the transgression of the law," and "he that shall offend in one point is guilty of all." (3SP 420.1)

The honest seeker after truth will not plead ignorance of the law as an excuse for transgression. Light was within his reach. God's word is plain, and Christ has bidden him search the Scriptures. He reveres God's law as holy, just, and good, and he repents of his transgression. By faith he pleads the atoning blood of Christ, and grasps the promise of pardon. His former baptism does not satisfy him now. He has seen himself a sinner, condemned by the law of God. He has experienced anew a death to sin, and he desires again to be buried with Christ by baptism, that he may rise to walk in newness of life. Such a course is in harmony with the example of Paul in baptizing the Jewish converts. That incident was recorded by the Holy Spirit as an instructive lesson for the church. (3SP 420.2)

As was his custom, Paul had begun his work at Ephesus by teaching in the synagogue of the Jews. He continued to labor there for three months, "disputing and persuading the things concerning the kingdom of God." He at first met with a favorable reception; but as in other fields of labor, he was soon violently opposed by the unbelieving Jews. As they persisted in their rejection of the gospel, the apostle ceased preaching in the synagogue. (3SP 420.3)

The Spirit of God had wrought with and through Paul in his labors for his countrymen. Sufficient evidence had been presented to

Chapter 34 - Paul at Ephesus (3SP 423.2)

convince all who honestly desired to know the truth. But many permitted themselves to be controlled by prejudice and unbelief, and refused to yield to the most conclusive evidence. Fearing that the faith of the believers would be endangered by continued association with these opposers of the truth, Paul separated the disciples as a distinct body, and himself continued his public instructions in the school of one Tyrannus, a teacher of some note. (3SP 421.1)

Paul saw that "a great door and effectual" was open before him, though there were "many adversaries." Ephesus was not only the most magnificent, but the most corrupt, of the cities of Asia. Superstition and sensual pleasure held sway over her teeming population. Under the shadow of her idol temples, criminals of every grade found shelter, and the most degrading vices flourished. (3SP 421.2)

The city was famed for the worship of the goddess Diana and the practice of magic. Here was the great temple of Diana, which was regarded by the ancients as one of the wonders of the world. Its vast extent and surpassing magnificence made it the pride, not only of the city, but of the nation. Kings and princes had enriched it by their donations. The Ephesians vied with one another in adding to its splendor, and it was made the treasure-house for a large share of the wealth of Western Asia. (3SP 421.3)

The idol enshrined in this sumptuous edifice was a rude, uncouth image, declared by tradition to have fallen from the sky. Upon it were inscribed mystic characters and symbols, which were believed to possess great power. When pronounced, they were said to accomplish wonders. When written, they were treasured as a potent charm to guard their possessor from robbers, from disease, and even from death. Numerous and costly books were written by the Ephesians to explain the meaning and use of these symbols. (3SP 421.4)

As Paul was brought in direct contact with the idolatrous inhabitants of Ephesus, the power of God was strikingly displayed through him. The apostles were not always able to work miracles at will. The Lord granted his servants this special power as the progress of his cause or the honor of his name required. Like Moses and Aaron at the court of Pharaoh, the apostle had now to maintain the truth against the lying wonders of the magicians; hence the miracles he wrought were of a different character from those which he had heretofore performed. As the hem of Christ's garment had communicated healing power to her who sought relief by the touch of faith, so on this occasion, garments were made the means of cure to all that believed; "diseases departed from them, and evil spirits went out of them." Yet these miracles gave no encouragement to blind superstition. When Jesus felt the touch of the suffering woman, he exclaimed, "Virtue is gone out of me. " So the scripture declares that the Lord wrought miracles by the hand of Paul, and that the name of the Lord Jesus was magnified, and not the name of Paul. (3SP 422.1)

The manifestations of supernatural power which accompanied the apostle's work, were calculated to make a deep impression upon a people given to sorcery, and priding themselves upon their intercourse with invisible beings. The miracles of Paul were far more potent than had ever before been witnessed in Ephesus, and were of such a character that they could not be imitated by the skill of the juggler or the enchantments of the sorcerer. Thus the Lord exalted his servant, even in the estimation of the idolaters themselves, immeasurably above the most favored and powerful of the magicians. (3SP 422.2)

But He to whom all the spirits of evil were subject, and who had given his servants authority over them, was about to bring still greater shame and defeat upon those who despised and profaned his holy name. Sorcery had been prohibited in the Mosaic law, on pain of death, yet from time to time it had been secretly practiced by apostate Jews. At the time of Paul's visit to Ephesus, there were in the city certain Jewish exorcists, who, seeing the wonders wrought by him, claimed to possess equal power. Believing that the name of Jesus acted as a charm, they determined to cast out evil spirits by the same means which the apostle had employed. (3SP 423.1)

An attempt was made by seven brothers, the sons of one Sceva, a Jewish priest. Finding a man possessed with a demon, they addressed him, "We adjure thee by Jesus, whom Paul preacheth." But the evil spirit answered with scorn, "Jesus I know, and Paul I know; but who are ye?" and the one possessed sprang on them with frantic violence, and beat and bruised them, so that they fled out of the house, naked and wounded. (3SP 423.2)

The discomfiture and humiliation of those who had profaned the name of Jesus, soon became known throughout Ephesus, by Jews and Gentiles. Unmistakable proof had been given of the sacredness of that name, and the peril which they incurred who should invoke it while they had no faith in Christ's divine mission. Terror seized the minds of many, and the work of the gospel was regarded by all with awe and reverence. (3SP 423.3)

Facts which had previously been concealed were now brought to light. In accepting Christianity, some of the brethren had not fully renounced their heathen superstitions. The practice of magic was still to some extent continued among them. Convinced of their error by the events which had recently occurred, they came and made a full confession to Paul, and publicly acknowledged their secret arts to be deceptive and Satanic. Many sorcerers also abjured the practice of magic, and received Christ as their Saviour. They brought together the costly books containing the mysterious "Ephesian letters," and the secrets of their art, and burned them in the presence of all the people. When the books had been consumed, they proceeded to reckon up the value of the sacrifice. It was estimated at fifty thousand pieces of silver, equal to about ten thousand dollars. (3SP 424.1)

The influence of these events was more widespread than even Paul then realized. The manifestation of the power of Christ was a grand victory for Christianity in the very stronghold of superstition. From Ephesus the news was widely circulated, and a strong impetus was given to the cause of Christ. These scenes in the ministry of Paul lived in the memory of men, and were the means of converting many to the gospel, long after the apostle himself had finished his course. (3SP 424.2)

When the Ephesian converts burned their books on magic, they showed that the things in which they had once most delighted were now the most abhorred. It was by and through magic that they had especially offended God and imperiled their souls, and it was against magic that they showed such indignation. Here was given the best evidence of true conversion. (3SP 425.1)

Those treatises on divination contained rules and forms of communication with evil spirits. They were the regulations of the worship of Satan,–directions for soliciting his help and obtaining information from him. By retaining these books, the disciples would have exposed themselves to temptation; by selling them they would have placed temptation in the way of others. They had renounced the kingdom of darkness, and they did not hesitate at any sacrifice to destroy its power. Thus the truth triumphed over men's prejudices, their favorite pursuits, and their love of money. (3SP 425.2)

It is fondly supposed that heathen superstitions have disappeared before the civilization of the nineteenth century. But the word of God and the stern testimony of facts declare that sorcery is practiced in this Christian age and Christian nation as verily as by the old-time magicians. The ancient system of magic is, in reality, the same as that which is now known as modern Spiritualism. Satan is finding access to thousands of minds by presenting himself under the guise of departed friends. The Scriptures of truth declare that "the dead know not anything." Their thoughts, their love, their hatred, have perished. The dead do not hold communion with the living. But true to his early cunning, when in the form of a serpent he deceived the mother of our race, Satan employs this device to gain control of the minds of men. (3SP 425.3)

The heathen oracles have their counterpart in the spiritualistic mediums, the clairvoyants, and fortune-tellers of today. The mystic voices that spoke at Endor and Ephesus, are still by their lying words misleading the children of men. The mysteries of heathen worship are replaced by the secret associations and seances, the obscurities and wonders, of the sorcerers of our time. Their disclosures are eagerly received by thousands who refuse to accept light from God's word or from his Spirit. While they speak with scorn of the magicians of old, the great deceiver laughs in triumph as they yield to his arts in a different form. (3SP 426.1)

His agents still claim to cure disease. They profess to employ electricity, magnetism, or the so-called "sympathetic remedies;" but in truth the magnetic power of which they boast is directly attributable to the sorcery of Satan. By this means he casts his spell over the bodies and souls of men. (3SP 426.2)

The sick, the bereaved, the curious, are communicating with evil spirits. All who venture here are on dangerous ground. The word of truth declares how God regards them. In ancient times he pronounced judgments upon one who sent for counsel to a heathen oracle: "Is it not because there is not a God in Israel that thou sendest to inquire of Baal-zebub, the god of Ekron? therefore thou shalt not come down from that bed on which thou art gone up, but shalt surely die." (3SP 426.3)

The visible and the invisible world are in close contact. Could the veil be lifted, we would see evil angels employing all their arts to deceive and destroy. Wherever an influence is exerted to cause men to forget God, there Satan is exercising his bewitching power. All who venture into scenes of dissipation or irreligious pleasure, or seek the society of the sensualist, the skeptic, or the blasphemer, by personal intercourse or through the medium of the press, are tampering with sorcery. Ere they are aware, the mind is bewildered and the soul polluted. The apostle's admonition to the Ephesian church should be heeded by the people of God today: "Have no fellowship with the unfruitful works of darkness, but rather reprove them." (3SP 427.1)

*****

Chapter 35
Trials and Victories of Paul

For upwards of three years, Ephesus was the center of Paul's work. A flourishing church was raised up here, and from this city the gospel spread throughout the province of Asia, among both Jews and Gentiles. (3SP 427.2)

The apostle had for some time contemplated another missionary journey. He desired again to visit the churches in Macedonia and Achaia, and after spending some time at Corinth, to go to Jerusalem, after which he hoped to preach the gospel at Rome. In pursuance of his plan, he sent Timothy and Erastus before him into Macedonia; but feeling that the cause in Ephesus still demanded his presence, he decided to remain till after Pentecost. An event soon occurred, however, which hastened his departure. (3SP 427.3)

The month of May was specially devoted to the worship of the goddess of Ephesus. The universal honor in which this deity was held, the magnificence of her temple and her worship, attracted an immense concourse of people from all parts of the province of Asia. Throughout the entire month the festivities were conducted with the utmost pomp and splendor. The gods were represented by persons chosen for the purpose, who were regarded as objects of worship, and were honored by processions, sacrifices, and libations. Musical contests, the feats of athletes, and the fierce combats of men and beasts, drew admiring crowds to the vast theaters. The officers chosen to conduct this grand celebration were the men of highest distinction in the chief cities of Asia. They were also persons of vast wealth, for in return for the honor of their position, they were expected to defray the entire expense of the occasion. The whole city was a scene of brilliant display and wild revelry. Imposing processions swept to the grand temple. The air rung with sounds of joy. The people gave themselves up to feasting, drunkenness, and the vilest debauchery. (3SP 428.1)

This gala season was a trying occasion to the disciples who had newly come to the faith. The company of believers who met in the school of Tyrannus were an inharmonious note in the festive chorus. Ridicule, reproach, and insult were freely heaped upon them. By the labors of Paul at Ephesus, the heathen worship had received a telling blow. There was a perceptible falling-off in attendance at the national festival, and in the enthusiasm of the worshipers. The influence of his teachings extended far beyond the actual converts to the faith. Many who had not openly accepted the new doctrines, became so far enlightened as to lose all confidence in heathen gods. The presence of Paul in the city called special attention to this fact, and curses loud and deep were uttered against him. (3SP 428.2)

Another cause of dissatisfaction existed. It had long been customary among heathen nations to make use of small images or shrines to represent their favorite objects of worship. Portable statues were modeled after the great image of Diana, and were widely circulated in the countries along the shores of the Mediterranean. Models of the temple which enshrined the idol were also eagerly sought. Both were regarded as objects of worship, and were carried at the head of processions, and on journeys and military expeditions. An extensive and profitable business had grown up at Ephesus from the manufacture and sale of these shrines and images. (3SP 429.1)

Those who were interested in this branch of industry found their gains diminishing. All united in attributing the unwelcome change to Paul's labors. Demetrius, a manufacturer of silver shrines, called together the workmen of his craft, and by a violent appeal endeavored to stir up their indignation against Paul. He represented that their traffic was endangered, and pointed out the great loss which they would sustain if the apostle were allowed to turn the people away from their ancient worship. He then appealed to their ruling superstition, saying: "Moreover ye see and hear, that not alone at Ephesus, but almost throughout all Asia, this Paul hath persuaded and turned away much people, saying that they be no gods which are made with hands; so that not only this our craft is in danger to be set at naught, but also that the temple of the great goddess Diana should be despised, and her magnificence should be destroyed, whom all Asia and the world worshippeth." This speech acted as fire to the stubble. The excited passions of the people were roused, and burst forth in the cry, "Great is Diana of the Ephesians!" (3SP 429.2)

A report of the speech of Demetrius was rapidly circulated. The uproar was terrific. The whole city seemed in commotion. An immense crowd soon collected, and a rush was made to the workshop of Aquila, in the Jewish quarters, with the object of securing Paul. In their insane rage they were ready to tear him in pieces. But the apostle was not to be found. His brethren, receiving an intimation of the danger, had hurried him from the place. Angels of God were sent to guard the faithful apostle. His time to die a martyr's death had not yet come. (3SP 430.1)

Failing to find the object of their wrath, the mob seized two of his companions, Gaius and Aristarchus, and with them hurried on to the theater. Paul's place of concealment was not far distant, and he soon learned of the peril of his beloved brethren. His courage was in keeping with the occasion. He was ever ready to press to the front in the battle for his Master. Forgetful of his own safety, he desired to go at once to the theater, to address the rioters. But his friends refused to permit him thus to sacrifice himself. Gaius and Aristarchus were not the prey that the people sought; no serious harm to them was apprehended. But should the apostle's pale, care-worn face be seen, it would arouse at once the worst passions of the mob, and there would not be the least human possibility of saving his life. (3SP 430.2)

Paul was still eager to defend the truth before the multitude; but he was at last deterred by a message of warning from the theater. Several of the most honorable and influential among the magistrates sent him an earnest request not to venture into a situation of so great peril. This proof of the regard in which Paul was held by the leading men of Asia was no mean tribute to the sterling integrity of his character. (3SP 431.1)

The tumult at the theater was continually increasing. "Some cried one thing, and some another; and the more part knew not wherefore they had come together." From the fact that Paul and some of his companions were of Hebrew extraction, the Jews felt that odium was cast upon them, and that their own safety might be endangered. Wishing it to be understood that they had no sympathy with the Christians, they thrust forward one of their own number to set the matter before the people. The speaker chosen was Alexander, one of the craftsmen, a coppersmith, to whom Paul afterward referred as having done him much evil. Alexander was a man of considerable ability, and he bent all his energies to direct the wrath of the people exclusively against Paul and his companions. But the crowd were in no mood to make nice distinctions. Seeing that Alexander was a Jew, they thrust him aside, the uproar continually increasing as all with one voice cried out, "Great is Diana of the Ephesians!" This cry continued for two hours. (3SP 431.2)

At last there came a momentary silence, from sheer exhaustion. Then the recorder of the city arrested the attention of the crowd, and by virtue of his office obtained a hearing. By his prudence and good judgment he soon succeeded in quieting the excitement. (3SP 432.1)

He met the people on their own ground, and showed that there was no cause for the present tumult. He appealed to their reason to decide whether the strangers who had come among them could change the opinions of the whole world regarding their ruling goddess. Said he: "Ye men of Ephesus, what man is there that knoweth not how that the city of Ephesus is a worshiper of the great goddess Diana, and of the image which fell down from Jupiter? Seeing then that these things cannot be spoken against, ye ought to be quiet, and to do nothing rashly." He bade them consider that Paul and his companions had not profaned the temple of Diana, nor outraged the feelings of any by reviling the goddess. (3SP 432.2)

He then skillfully turned the subject, and reproved the course of Demetrius: "Wherefore if Demetrius and the craftsmen which are with him have a matter against any man, the law is open, and there are deputies; let them implead one another. But if ye inquire anything concerning other matters, it shall be determined in a lawful assembly." He closed by warning them that such an uproar, raised without apparent cause, might subject the city of Ephesus to the censure of the Romans, thus causing a restriction of her present liberty, and intimating that there must not be a repetition of the scene. Having by this speech completely tranquilized the disturbed elements,

Chapter 35 - Trials and Victories of Paul (3SP 432.3)

the recorder dismissed the assembly. (3SP 432.3)

The words of Demetrius reveal the real cause of the tumult at Ephesus, and also the cause of much of the persecution which followed the apostles in their work of promulgating the truth. "This, our craft, is in danger." With Demetrius and his fellows, the profitable business of image-making was endangered by the teaching and spread of the gospel. The income of pagan priests and artisans was at stake; and for this reason they instituted the most bitter opposition to the apostle, and refused to receive or investigate the new religion, which would have made them wise unto salvation. (3SP 433.1)

Paul's labors in Ephesus were at length concluded. He felt that the excitement which prevailed was unfavorable to the preaching of the gospel. His heart was filled with gratitude to God that his life had been preserved, and that Christianity had not been brought into disrepute by the tumult at Ephesus. The decision of the recorder and of others holding honorable offices in the city, had set Paul before the people as one innocent of any unlawful act. This was another triumph of Christianity over error and superstition. God had raised up a great magistrate to vindicate his apostle, and hold the tumultuous mob in check. (3SP 433.2)

Paul parted from his children in the faith with an affectionate farewell. He set out on his journey to Macedonia, designing on the way thither to visit Troas. He was accompanied by Tychicus and Trophimus, both Ephesians, who remained his faithful companions and fellow-laborers to the close of his life. (3SP 433.3)

Paul's ministry in Ephesus had been a season of incessant labor, of many trials, and deep anguish. He taught the people in public and from house to house, instructing and warning them with many tears. He was continually opposed by the unbelieving Jews, who lost no opportunity to stir up the popular feeling against him. Again and again he was attacked by the mob, and subjected to insult and abuse. By every means which they could employ, the enemies of truth sought to destroy the effects of his labor for the salvation of men. (3SP 434.1)

And while thus battling against opposition, and with untiring zeal pushing forward the gospel work and guarding the interests of a church yet young in the faith, Paul was bearing upon his soul the burden of all the churches. Nor was he released even from the tax of physical labor. Here, as at Corinth, he worked with his own hands to supply his necessities. In weariness and painfulness from unceasing toil and constant danger, enfeebled by disease, and at times depressed in spirits, he steadfastly pursued his work. (3SP 434.2)

The news which he received, of apostasy in churches of his own planting, caused him deep anguish. He greatly feared that his efforts in their behalf would prove to have been in vain. Many a sleepless night was spent in prayer and earnest thought, as he learned of the new and varied methods employed to counteract his work. As he had opportunity, he wrote to the churches, giving reproof, counsel, admonition, and encouragement, as their state demanded. In his epistles the apostle does not dwell on his own trials, yet there are occasional glimpses of his labors and sufferings in the cause of Christ. Stripes and imprisonment, cold and hunger and thirst, perils by land and sea, in the city and in the wilderness, from his own countrymen, from the heathen, and from false brethren,--all these he endured for the truth's sake. He was defamed, reviled, "made the offscouring of all things," "perplexed, persecuted, troubled on every side," "in jeopardy every hour," "alway delivered unto death for Jesus' sake." (3SP 434.3)

Amid the constant storm of opposition, the clamor of enemies, and the desertion of friends, the intrepid apostle at times almost lost heart. But he looked back to Calvary, and with new ardor pressed on to spread the knowledge of the Crucified. He was but treading the blood-stained path which Christ had trodden before him. He sought no discharge from the warfare till he should lay off his armor at the feet of his Redeemer. (3SP 435.1)

Eighteen centuries have passed since the apostle rested from his labors; yet the history of his toils and sacrifices for Christ's sake are among the most precious treasures of the church. That history was recorded by the Holy Spirit, that the followers of Christ in every age might thereby be incited to greater zeal and faithfulness in the cause of their Master. (3SP 435.2)

How does this hero of faith tower above the self-indulgent, ease-loving men who are today crowding the ranks of the ministry. When subjected to the ordinary difficulties and trials of life, many feel that their lot is hard. But what have they done or suffered for the cause of Christ? How does their record appear when compared with that of this great apostle? What burden of soul have they felt for the salvation of sinners? They know little of self-denial or sacrifice. The same obligation rests upon them which impelled the apostle to his unwearied labors. Only those who emulate his fidelity, will share with him the crown of life. (3SP 435.3)

*****

Chapter 36
Martyrdom of Paul and Peter

The apostles Paul and Peter were for many years widely separated in their labors, it being the work of Paul to carry the gospel to the Gentiles, while Peter labored especially for the Jews. But in the providence of God, both were to bear witness for Christ in the world's metropolis, and upon its soil both were to shed their blood as the seed of a vast harvest of saints and martyrs. (3SP 436.1)

About the time of Paul's second arrest, Peter also was apprehended and thrust into prison. He had made himself especially obnoxious to the authorities by his zeal and success in exposing the deceptions and defeating the plots of Simon Magus the sorcerer, who had followed him to Rome to oppose and hinder the work of the gospel. Nero was a believer in magic, and had patronized Simon. He was therefore greatly incensed against the apostle, and was thus prompted to order his arrest. (3SP 436.2)

The emperor's malice against Paul was heightened by the fact that members of the imperial household, and also other persons of distinction, had been converted to Christianity during his first imprisonment. For this reason he made the second imprisonment much more severe than the first, granting him little opportunity to preach the gospel; and he determined to cut short his life as soon as a plausible pretext could be found for so doing. Nero's mind was so impressed with the force of the apostle's words at his last trial that he deferred the decision of the case, neither acquitting nor condemning him. But the sentence was only deferred. It was not long before the decision was pronounced which consigned Paul to a martyr's grave. Being a Roman citizen, he could not be subjected to torture, and was therefore sentenced to be beheaded. (3SP 436.3)

Peter, as a Jew and a foreigner, was condemned to be scourged and crucified. In prospect of this fearful death, the apostle remembered his great sin in denying Jesus in the hour of trial, and his only thought was, that he was unworthy of so great an honor as to die in the same manner as did his Master. Peter had sincerely repented of that sin, and had been forgiven by Christ, as is shown by the high commission given him to feed the sheep and lambs of the flock. But he could never forgive himself. Not even the thought of the agonies of the last terrible scene could lessen the bitterness of his sorrow and repentance. As a last favor he entreated his executioners that he might be nailed to the cross with his head downward. The request was granted, and in this manner died the great apostle Peter. (3SP 437.1)

Paul was led in a private manner to the place of execution. His persecutors, alarmed at the extent of his influence, feared that converts might be won to Christianity, even by the scenes of his death. Hence few spectators were allowed to be present. But the hardened soldiers appointed to attend him, listened to his words, and with amazement saw him cheerful and even joyous in prospect of such a death. His spirit of forgiveness toward his murderers, and his unwavering confidence in Christ to the very last, proved a savor of life unto life to some who witnessed his martyrdom. More than one erelong accepted the Saviour whom Paul preached, and fearlessly sealed their faith with their blood. (3SP 437.2)

The life of Paul, to its very latest hour, testified to the truth of his words in the second Epistle to the Corinthians: "For God, who commanded the light to shine out of darkness, hath shined in our hearts, to give the light of the knowledge of the glory of God in the face of Jesus Christ. But we have this treasure in earthen vessels, that the excellency of the power may be of God, and not of us. We are troubled on every side, yet not distressed; we are perplexed, but not in despair; persecuted, but not forsaken; cast down, but not destroyed; always bearing about in the body the dying of the Lord Jesus, that the life also of Jesus might be made manifest in our body." His sufficiency was not in himself, but in the presence and agency of the divine Spirit that filled his soul, and brought every thought into subjection to the will of Christ. The fact that his own life exemplified the truth he proclaimed, gave convincing power to both his preaching and his deportment. Says the prophet, "Thou wilt keep him in perfect peace, whose mind is stayed on Thee; because he trusteth in Thee." It was this Heaven-born peace, expressed upon the countenance, that won many a soul to the gospel. (3SP 438.1)

The apostle was looking into the great beyond, not with uncertainty or in dread, but with joyful hope and longing expectation. As he stood at the place of martyrdom, he saw not the gleaming sword of the executioner, or the green earth so soon to receive his blood; he looked up through the calm blue heaven of that summer's day to the throne of the Eternal. His language was, O Lord, thou art my comfort and my portion. When shall I embrace thee? when shall I behold thee for myself, without a dimming vail between? (3SP 438.2)

Paul carried with him through his life on earth the very atmosphere of Heaven. All who associated with him felt the influence of his connection with Christ and companionship with angels. Here lies the power of the truth. The unstudied, unconscious influence of a holy life is the most convincing sermon that can be given in favor of Christianity. Argument, even when unanswerable, may provoke only opposition; but a godly example has a power which it is impossible wholly to resist. (3SP 439.1)

While the apostle lost sight of his own near sufferings, he felt a deep solicitude for the disciples whom he was about to leave to cope with prejudice, hatred, and persecution. He endeavored to strengthen and encourage the few Christians who accompanied him to the place of execution, by repeating the exceeding precious promises given for those who are persecuted for righteousness' sake. He assures them that nothing shall fail of all that the Lord hath spoken concerning his tried and faithful ones. They shall arise and shine; for the light of the Lord shall arise upon them. They shall put on their beautiful garments when the glory of the Lord shall be revealed. For a little season they may be in heaviness through manifold temptations, they may be destitute of earthly comfort; but they must encourage their hearts by saying, I know in whom I have believed. He is able to keep that which I have committed to his trust. His rebuke will come to an end, and the glad morning of peace and perfect day will come. (3SP 439.2)

Paul declared to his brethren, It did not appear to our fathers what great and good things should be given to those who believe in Jesus. They desired to see the things which we see, and to hear the things which we hear, but they died without the sight or the knowledge. The greater light which we have received is shed upon us by the gospel of Christ. Holy men of old were acknowledged and honored of God because they were faithful over a few things; and it is only those that improve with the same fidelity their greater trust, who will with them be counted profitable servants, and be crowned with glory, honor, and immortality. (3SP 440.1)

This man of faith beholds the ladder presented in Jacob's vision,–the ladder which rested upon the earth and reached to the highest heavens, and upon which angels of God were ascending and descending. He knows that this ladder represents Christ, who has connected earth with Heaven, and finite man with the infinite God. He hears angels and archangels magnifying that glorious name. His faith is strengthened as he calls to mind that patriarchs and prophets relied upon the same Saviour who is his support and consolation, and for whom he is giving his life. Those holy men who from century to century sent down their testimony for the truth, and the apostles, who to preach the gospel of Christ went out to meet religious bigotry and heathen superstition, who counted not their lives dear unto themselves if they might bear aloft the light of the cross amid the dark mazes of infidelity,–all these he hears witnessing to Jesus as the Son of the Most High, the Saviour of the world. The martyr's shout of triumph, the fearless testimony for the faith, falls upon his ear from the rack, the stake, the dungeon, from the dens and caves of the earth, from steadfast souls who are destitute, afflicted, tormented, yet of whom the world is not worthy. With a continually strengthening assurance they declare, "I know whom I have believed." And as they yield up their lives as witnesses for the faith, they bear a solemn, condemning testimony to the world, declaring that He in whom they trusted has proved himself able to save to the uttermost. (3SP 440.2)

The Captain of our salvation has prepared his servant for the last great conflict. Ransomed by the sacrifice of Christ, washed from sin in his blood, and clothed in his righteousness, Paul has

Chapter 36 - Martyrdom of Paul and Peter (3SP 441.1)

the witness in himself that his soul is precious in the sight of his Redeemer. His life is hid with Christ in God, and he is persuaded that He who has conquered death is able to keep that which is committed to his trust. His mind grasps the Saviour's promise, "I will raise him up at the last day." His thoughts and hopes are centered in the second advent of his Lord. And as the sword of the executioner descends, and the shadows of death gather about the martyr's soul, his latest thought springs forward, as will his earliest thought in the great awakening, to meet the Lifegiver who shall welcome him to the joy of the blest. (3SP 441.1)

Well-nigh a score of centuries have passed since Paul the aged poured out his blood as a witness for the word of God and for the testimony of Christ. No faithful hand recorded for the generations to come, the last scenes in the life of this holy man; but inspiration has preserved for us his dying testimony. Like a trumpet peal has his voice rung out through all the ages, nerving with his own courage thousands of witnesses for Christ, and wakening in thousands of sorrow-stricken hearts the echo of his own triumphant joy: "I am now ready to be offered, and the time of my departure is at hand. I have fought a good fight, I have finished my course, I have kept the faith. Henceforth there is laid up for me a crown of righteousness, which the Lord, the righteous Judge, shall give me at that day; and not to me only, but unto all them also that love his appearing." (3SP 442.1)

Made in United States
Cleveland, OH
15 August 2025